Second Edition
GROUP WORK

SAGE SOURCEBOOKS FOR THE HUMAN SERVICES SERIES

Series Editors: ARMAND LAUFFER and CHARLES GARVIN

Recent Volumes in This Series

Second Edition

GROUP WORK

A Humanistic and Skills Building Approach

Urania Glassman
Yeshiva University

Sage Sourcebooks for

the Human Services

Los Angeles • London • New Delhi • Singapore • Washington DC

MT

For information:

SAGE Publications, Inc.
2455 Teller Road
Thousand Oaks,
  California 91320
E-mail: order@sagepub.com

SAGE Publications Ltd.
1 Oliver's Yard
55 City Road
London EC1Y 1SP
United Kingdom

SAGE Publications India Pvt. Ltd.
B 1/I 1 Mohan Cooperative
  Industrial Area
Mathura Road, New Delhi 110 044
India

SAGE Publications Asia-Pacific
  Pte. Ltd.
33 Pekin Street #02-01
Far East Square
Singapore 048763

Printed in the United States of America

Library of Congress Cataloging-in-Publication Data

Glassman, Urania.
Group work: a humanistic and skills building approach/Urania Glassman. —2nd ed.
    p. cm. — (Sage sourcebooks for the human services series ; 13)
Includes bibliographical references and index.
ISBN 978-1-4129-6662-7 (cloth)
ISBN 978-1-4129-6663-4 (pbk.)
  1. Social group work. I. Title.

HV45.G56 2009
361.4—dc22   2008026116

This book is printed on acid-free paper.

08   09   10   11   12   10   9   8   7   6   5   4   3   2   1

Acquisitions Editor:	Kassie Graves
Editorial Assistant:	Veronica Novak
Production Editor:	Carla Freeman
Copy Editor:	Trey Thoelcke
Typesetter:	C&M Digitals (P) Ltd.
Proofreader:	Theresa Kay
Indexer:	Kay Dusheck
Cover Designer:	Candice Harman
Marketing Manager:	Carmel Schrire

1/2/09

Contents

List of Practice Illustrations

Chapter 5

Chapter 6

Chapter 7

Chapter 8

Preface

The humanistic method of social work with groups embodies the values and practices of social group work's heritage and the social work profession. As a group approach, the humanistic method may be used to assist clients with their preventive, rehabilitative, treatment, and social action goals. The humanistic group work method may be employed by human service professionals—psychologists, psychiatrists, mental health workers, child welfare staff, activities and rehabilitation therapists, nurses, and special educators—who assist people in attaining effectiveness and change in their interpersonal relationships and circumstances.

This book has been written about values, norms, and practice techniques in humanistic group work to share those experiences and approaches with group practitioners who appreciate the potency of the professionally guided small group. These practitioners recognize the supportive effects that social responsibility, caring, mutual aid, and respect for individual uniqueness have on the member. This book supports the human spirit and the humanistic visions of the teachers, students, clients, and colleagues who champion personal and social change through the social work group.

This volume presents the special features and processes of humanistic group work method, which are used to develop a unique social form for assisting people in their change efforts (Lang, 1981). My experiences in a variety of types of groups strengthen my conviction about the value of the small, face-to-face group built on humanistic method. In this special productive milieu, members can feel belonging, acceptance, friendship, challenge, and support for developing abilities to achieve social goals and actions that enhance quality of life.

Forms of racism, classism, ethnocentrism, sexism, and stigmatizations, as well as the repression of humanistic mores, highlight the urgency to spotlight the role of social work in developing humanistic groups. The mass suicides in Jonestown were brought about by totalitarian group processes. It is clear that prior to committing a murderous act, the terrorist has been deeply involved in a secretive small group whose values were antithetical to those of social group work. Even to this day, in the face of the lessons of the Nazi debacle, people are damaged and repressed by political and professional demagogues who use power to distort people's humanity and connection to one another.

The leaders of authoritarian groups attempt to intimidate people into meeting narrowly and selfishly derived ideological or pseudoprofessional objectives by controlling interactional environments and debate. This volume continues the spirit of the first edition by Len Kates and me, and our wish to bear symbolic witness to the plights of victims of authoritarianism whose social interactions were defiled by intimidation and terror, and to the memory of those who have lost their lives as a consequence.

It is gratifying to picture the groups currently being run for victims of trauma or frail elderly persons, for persons with Alzheimer's disease and groups for their caretakers, school children's groups, substance abuse treatment groups, groups in mental health treatment and developmental disabilities, groups in oncology and HIV/AIDS. These groups thrive in hospitals, residential treatment settings, continuing day treatment programs, schools, settlement houses, and senior centers.

As in the first edition with Len, this book continues to describe an art and its technology of expression through techniques of group work practice that emanate from humanistic values and unique experiences of clinical and community groups. The book remains centered on the role of the social group work practitioner, or other like-minded facilitator, using the group work method to contribute to the personal growth and empowerment of members in their community and institutional contexts. It is my hope that practitioners will find it worthwhile.

—Urania Glassman

Acknowledgments

I first learned about membership from the huge New York Greek community I grew up in, my friends in the surrounding Jewish community I grew up with, and the high school and college student activities programs I was involved in—all of these abounding in belonging opportunities.

It was my privilege to have been mentored by Dr. Jerome Gold of New York's City College. As a young professional staff member and director of House Plan Association, a multiservice group work student activities program, I learned every facet of group work and T-groups from Jerry Gold, including the values and norms guiding group life. I cherished our relationship and my time there with students, some of whom became my colleagues and continue to be in my world.

My gratitude is infinite to *Social Work With Groups* and to the Association for the Advancement of Social Work with Groups founders—Catherine Papell, the late Beulah Rothman, and the late Ruth Middleman—to its members and everyone who ensured its survival. These institutions, now completing 30 years, provided the venue for Len Kates and myself to present this book's first edition.

This new volume builds on our earlier edition, developing humanistic group work and unique practice techniques, and draws on my role in field education and clinical practice. I am profoundly grateful to Lenny for that joint endeavor we took so much pride in.

Charles Garvin shepherded the first edition and has labored over the present volume, providing invaluable feedback. I owe him a huge debt of thanks for his three decades of generosity and belief in the importance of this work.

Marvin Parnes and Jane Hassinger have throughout our friendship encouraged this enterprise. Marvin's roots in House Plan, as well as mine, continue to define how we work now. I hope this volume validates everything that we experienced.

I am so thankful to Kassie Graves at SAGE for her encouragement from day one, patience, and aplomb in this process.

I am indebted to my dear friend and coauthor Ellen Sue Mesbur, who has been committed to the first edition and unrelenting in encouraging me to produce this volume.

Sincere thanks to my devoted friend Pat Strasberg, with whom I had the best group life in the playground, and without whose reflection and support my clinical work would not have flourished.

I am eternally grateful to Erika Kraemer Sanchez for over half a century of unfaltering friendship and camaraderie.

As dean, Dr. Joseph Vigilante cultivated Adelphi's creativity and group work productivity. Louise Skolnik, my loyal colleague there, and Richie Skolnik from the City College faculty have been wonderful friends throughout. The late Joanne Gumpert, a respected friend, was a patron of our book wherever she went. I continue to pay tribute to the memory of Helene Fishbein; she championed Len's and my vision for this book.

The enduring validation of my friends in field education, Bart Grossman—with me since City College—Dean Schneck, Ginger Robbins, and the New York Area Field Directors, continues to be a morale booster.

I'd also like to thank the following reviewers for offering comments and suggestions, which helped to improve the manuscript:

Rachel C. Freeman
University of Tennessee

Ken Norem
University of Northern Colorado

My gratitude goes to Carla Freeman, Veronica Novak, and Trey Thoelcke from SAGE, for their scrupulous review of the manuscript and immeasurable assistance in meeting the difficult schedule. Hats off to Candice Harman for the cover design.

I am proud to be a part of Wurzweiler School of Social Work of Yeshiva University (YU). The school remains committed to practice and the joy of joys is that it nurtures a group work concentration! I could not have asked more from colleagues. I thank Jay Sweifach for his insight in critiquing the first edition. Shantih Clemans, you will have a new volume for group work students. Many thanks for bugging me every day about it. Kudos to Susan Ciardiello for your vision and your group work dissertation.

To Nancy Beckerman, Michele Sarracco, Joan Beder, Susan Mason, Cathy Cassidy, Charlie Auerbach, and Heidi Heft LaPorte my heartfelt thanks for your friendship, incisiveness, and appreciation of group work.

I am particularly grateful to my trusted field department team, Raesa Kaiteris, Dolly Sacristan, and Gloria Marin, for being such an inspired, wonderful, and supportive staff. I could not have had better or smarter or more skillful people to be proud of every day.

To Dr. Sheldon Gelman, Wurzweiler's dean, I have my deepest appreciation and gratitude for bringing me to YU and profound respect for building a school sustained by scholarship and group work values. His generosity and largesse have fostered my focus on scholarly endeavors. This book recognizes that his commitment to group work reaches far back into his education at Pitt.

My husband, Ronny, is my utmost fan. We have had a great ride, and without his backing I could not have done this book, or any other for that matter. I do suspect that while he appears to have been sacrificing, he was happy to have me home working rather than out shoe shopping! My connection to "group woik" has been the brunt of many jokes by our children. Alex, now a master in social work who I carted around in the womb while in social work school, challenged me not to dumb down the book for the generation that prefers bullets to complex sentences. Danny, my other booster, who was introduced to City College groups in his first year, demonstrated his absolute belief in me with frequent reminders of how much more money I would be making working in finance. All of this is to say that central to what made "group woik" work for me is humor. I try to live that every day. I learned that through belonging to groups.

Introduction

Humanism and Democracy

The humanistic group developed through the humanistic group work method is similar to other small group forms that have been developed and studied. It exhibits the universal characteristics of small groups. It has norms, a culture, face-to-face interaction, affective bonds, and cohesion. It also reflects the various themes of group life that revolve around closeness (Garland, Jones, & Kolodny, 1973) and the dynamics of power and love (Bennis & Shepard, 1962).

The humanistic group aims to develop and sustain a particular kind of small, face-to-face group that is built on selected values that link its members to each other through a distinct set of affective bonds; these affects include trust, care, respect, acceptance, and anger. These values and feelings are used to develop and intensify members' individual interpersonal potentials and foster growth in the context of their needs and interests. Not all small group experiences have as an outcome people's growth, nor connect them with ways of developing their capabilities within their individual and collective capacities. Some group experiences, while providing affective bonds, inhibit members' growth. This occurs because the group's standards for behavior violate or do not support individuation or difference.

The humanistic group method is rooted in the history and traditions of humanism and democracy. Humanism is built on particular values that cast people in society as responsible for and to one another; democracy is defined by particular standards of interaction that yield equality in relation to power, position, and resources. The aim of the humanistic method is the development of effective behavior for the group and the members within the group's milieu and its external social environment. The method's objectives are designed to assist the members with their interactional and problem-solving processes. The unique process of this method is denoted by a culture of humanistic values and democratic norms that shape the interactions of the members and the practitioner.

Humanistic values shape people's stances and attitudes about themselves and others in the group. Humanistic values for social group work were stated by Gisela Konopka (1978, 1983). They have stood the test of time as fundamental means for the development of group experiences. This set of values takes the following positions: (1) Individuals are of inherent worth; (2) people are mutually responsible for each other; and (3) people have the fundamental right to experience mental health brought about by social and political conditions that support their fulfillment (Konopka, 1983).

Democratic norms are the specific standards that develop the patterns and qualities of the members' behaviors. Democratic norms chart pathways for cooperative interaction and fluid distribution of position, power, and resources; they motivate the change efforts of the members in the humanistic group (White & Lippitt, 1968).

These values and norms, through the leadership behaviors they sanction, celebrate each member and the practitioner as participants who actively create and sustain this experiment for social living characterized by trial and error, give and take, and considerable efforts to bring about change in their collective and individual experiences.

Members seek enhanced social interactions in the group, as well as in their formal and informal relationships outside of it. The latter include family, couple, peer, and work relationships; they also include the situations that come about through members' voluntary and involuntary participation in health, education, and social welfare programs. The group members have related needs for effectiveness and change in their social environments that provide the arena for achieving the group's purpose. The group members may or may not know one another. They may be single parents, prisoners, children in a child guidance clinic, clients in an outpatient mental health clinic, elderly people living alone, persons receiving economic and social welfare entitlements, adolescents in residential care, victims of domestic violence, homeless persons, persons dealing with chronic illness, relatives of dying loved ones, or participants in groups typically run at community centers or settlement houses.

Another important principle that defines the humanistic group is the principle of "externality" (Papell & Rothman, 1980a). In this frame of reference, the members develop experiences in relating that reach beyond the boundaries of the meeting time itself into their actual community. Members are encouraged to build social networks with each other by using the time between sessions to support and enhance one another's interpersonal and environmental goals. Members also are encouraged to include significant others from their external networks into the group's experiences to the extent that this involvement enhances the group as a viable organism. The group develops programs, experiential situations, and activities for all concerned to provide alternative avenues for socialization, experimentation, and exposure to circumstances that have the power to affect the well-being of the members (Ciardiello, 2003).

The humanistic group work method takes into account that people have different capacities to take care of themselves. Some can care for themselves because they have had family, cultural, socioeconomic, and life experiences that provide the means to live effectively and with satisfaction. Others might have difficulty because the necessary conditions of society and economics have prevented and continue to prevent their caring for themselves and others. Still others may have severe physical or emotional inabilities that prevent them from being fully able to care for themselves and others. The thesis of humanistic group work is antithetical to blaming the victim. While some physically or mentally disabled people have been born into circumstances that provide emotional and social sustenance for them to contribute to their peers, others have not been involved in these necessary conditions. Consequently, the latter are less skilled in expressing their abilities and contributing to others; they have been in conditions that barely meet their needs or respect their rights.

The practitioner in the humanistic group joins with or forms a small, face-to-face group in which members are assisted to participate and interact genuinely and undefensively. The practitioner consciously uses humanistic values and democratic norms, as well as derivative practice techniques, in a human and connected way. He or she has developed understanding, appreciation, and acceptance of the humanistic values and democratic standards of interaction. The practitioner can signify attitudes and actions that represent a democratic humanistic process. This process propels the group and provides perspective for members' evaluations of the values, norms, and processes that exist in the situations that have brought them together. The core worker's activities are ethically employed to assist the members in forming and using the group experience for effectiveness and change in their external situations.

Driven by its values, norms, and practitioner stances, the humanistic group work method is experiential, experimental, existential, and interactional.

It is experiential primarily because it creates a social organism that has the capacity for externality (Papell & Rothman, 1980a), which lives in and affects the social, political, and economic environments of the members. Members experience themselves and their caring abilities in situations with one another and significant others. They enact their desires, they reflect upon these actions, and they act again with one another as well as in important situations.

The method is experimental because the members are encouraged to try out different ways of interacting within the group's meeting environment and in the social milieu. Driven by its ethos, members are not encouraged to try out all behaviors, but rather those that are in keeping with values that respect human dignity and the worth of self and others. Emotionally and socially unethical behaviors, as well as those that are harmful, are not encouraged.

Humanistic group work is existential because in the process members develop their own values and assume personal responsibility for their own behavior and future actions as they integrate the values and norms provided by the practitioner in their intersubjective relationships with the members. It is existential because the group process is in a perpetual state of engagement and growth, providing opportunities for change and self-actualization for each member.

Because it is an interactional method, humanistic group work focuses on and supports efforts toward developing satisfying interpersonal situations. Self-expression is examined within the group's interpersonal relations and in other significant settings. The viewpoint of the humanistic method includes the intrapsychic as a unit of attention in the helping or belonging process. Through the group's experiences within its environment and in social situations, persons express themselves both as members and as individuals, simultaneously changing their interpersonal and inner selves. (In the group psychotherapy experience, persons express themselves as individuals changing their inner selves. Interpersonal change in group therapy is assumed to be a byproduct of the treatment of psychological and emotional difficulties within the self.) In sum, there are several essentials that comprise this book's thesis.

First, humanistic group work makes a philosophical, political, and experiential statement about the conditions that most helpfully govern human intersubjectivity. It affirms the dignity and worth of individuals; it affirms those values that foster striving for mutual fulfillment of people, while at the same time negating values based on elitism, dominance, and disrespect for human relations. It seeks to establish a milieu of caring and belonging that symbolizes an enlightened form of human interaction and social order. The values and norms it espouses have broad implications for the well-being not only of the group members themselves, but of society at large as well.

It places a positive value on the development of the goodness of people rather than their destructiveness; it affirms that the individual strives for positive growth, quality of life, and interpersonal connection, rather than destructiveness and isolation.

In this affirmation of values, humanistic group method may go against prevailing social values, and even certain prevailing practices in the helping professions. Nonetheless, humanistic group work espouses these values because it is built on a vision and conviction growing out of experiences; it is not built on a position of neutrality about the stance and attitude of the practitioner within the group.

Second, the humanistic method of group work is built on a set of behaviors the practitioner uses to operationalize its values and norms. Not all practitioner strategies in groups build humane social milieus. Within the context of humanistic values and democratic norms, the group work practitioner sees domination, submission, exclusion, isolation, scapegoating, and destructiveness as attitudes and acts carried out when people are fearful and anxious, often about their own survival. These interactions breed variations of disregard and repression that do harm.

Through these beliefs the group practitioner uses empathic relationships, group work techniques, and a range of derivative knowledge to help members deal with and overcome interpersonal obstacles. The group work techniques help members develop abilities, while at the same time affecting significant others as well. In fact, group work techniques may represent not only what the practitioner does in humanistic group work practice, but effective ways in which members can interact with one another toward self-development and role enhancement in and out of the group experience.

Third, humanist group work strives to empower persons who might have been victimized by dint of disability or lower status in the society at large. From this perspective the group practitioner engages the members in a process that focuses and assists them all in their entitlement to a range of social, economic, and political conditions that ensure survival and satisfaction.

The effort of this book is to make a statement about a particular value base on which social group work has been established in its history and traditions, as well as to delineate practice approaches and techniques for the group worker that are in direct consonance with these values. In addition, the effort of this treatise is to recognize and affirm that group life can be a powerful corrective experience for the member when the practitioner operates within a framework of humanistic values. It is also an effort that attests to the importance of democratic actions in the practitioner's use of self as a safeguard for the member against demagoguery in group life that will sow the seeds of destructiveness and do violence to the human spirit. And finally, it is the hope that not only the practitioner, but the member, too, of a humanistic group will use many of the behaviors that emanate from its values.

With love, to Ronny, Danny, and Alex

PART I

Dimensions of the Humanistic Approach

1

Humanistic Values and Democratic Norms

Equal Rights

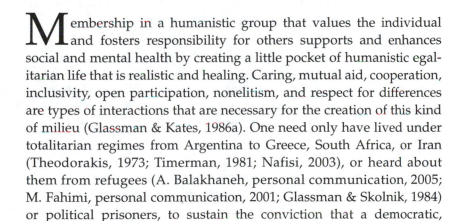

Membership in a humanistic group that values the individual and fosters responsibility for others supports and enhances social and mental health by creating a little pocket of humanistic egalitarian life that is realistic and healing. Caring, mutual aid, cooperation, inclusivity, open participation, nonelitism, and respect for differences are types of interactions that are necessary for the creation of this kind of milieu (Glassman & Kates, 1986a). One need only have lived under totalitarian regimes from Argentina to Greece, South Africa, or Iran (Theodorakis, 1973; Timerman, 1981; Nafisi, 2003), or heard about them from refugees (A. Balakhaneh, personal communication, 2005; M. Fahimi, personal communication, 2001; Glassman & Skolnik, 1984) or political prisoners, to sustain the conviction that a democratic, humanistic group is a fundamental means for achieving enhanced mental and social health.

The timeless nature of these ethics is well stated in the words of Neva Boyd (1971), originally written half a century ago:

> Social group work is the promotion and leadership . . . of mutual participation groups in which the members participate collectively in the feeling, thinking, and action involved in carrying out communal interests. The psychological essence of such experience for the participants is psychological intimacy. (p. 141)

> Mutual participant groups reveal a possible gradation from those characterized by individuation to those characterized by collectivism. . . . The group that is responsible for its own destiny is forced to solve its own problems; hence everything that concerns any aspect of it becomes a group responsibility. This is a type of democratic collectivism in which the rights of the individual are neither exercised at the sacrifice of those of the group, nor subordinated to them, but are preserved as an essential part of the whole. (p. 148)

Expression of humanistic values and democratic norms reveals the practitioner's basic convictions about the members' and other people's worth. These attitudes and actions are messages to the members about how they may connect to and challenge one another meaningfully and productively. The practitioner's ability to own and express humanistic values and democratic norms is essential for achieving caring interactions among members in the social work group. The ability to own and use these norms is as important as, if not more important than, the practitioner's ability to use a set of behavioral skills or group work techniques. The use of practice techniques without values and norms is dangerous when they are used prescriptively to control, dominate, or coerce without respect for members' rights to determine their own processes and goals.

Furthermore, practitioners' lack of appreciation of the qualities of humanistic values and democratic norms may give rise to elitist attitudes. Using knowledge of human behavior and development that is devoid of values may effect an aloof image that does not permit the members to hold the practitioner accountable for his or her attempts to influence the members. By contrast, the group practitioner who uses the humanistic form represents its democratic standards by example, as well as by engaging with the members fully as the group evolves its experiences. The practitioner explicitly invokes sanctions against acts of physical violence, emotional violation, character assassination, acts of stereotyping, stigmatizing, scapegoating, and other attacking behaviors. All else in the process—a full range of emotions and activities—is grist for the mill for interaction, learning, and change.

❖ HISTORICAL OVERVIEW OF DEMOCRATIC PRINCIPLES

Social group workers have contributed to the efforts to understand the helpful and dangerous aspects of small groups. They have played an important part in the development of democratic practices in group process. Writings in group work in the past century by Bernstein (1973), Coyle (1948/1978), Garvin (1997), Gitterman and Shulman (2005), Klein (1953), Konopka (1978, 1983), Schwartz (1961), and Trecker (1972) reflect a historical commitment to motivating and sustaining an ethical and humane social system. These practitioner-scholars have used the small face-to-face group to educate members for citizenship and to expand members' economic and educational opportunities. Group workers have traditionally used the small group to educate, remediate, and empower members to meet their needs in their communities, whether these are in their natural social situations or institutional ones. Groups are formed in child guidance clinics, senior centers, medical centers, and in-patient and out-patient mental health settings, as well as in HIV-AIDS clinics, in domestic violence shelters, with the homeless, in substance abuse treatment, and with at-risk parents, foster parents, and foster children. These group experiences represent efforts to maximize participation and empowerment for people who may be economically disadvantaged and socially ostracized.

Efforts to define what is uniquely social group work have been made by contemporary theoreticians and practitioners such as Baruch Levine (1991), Garland, Jones, and Kolodny (1973), Garvin (1997), Gitterman and Shulman (2005), Lang (1981), and Papell and Rothman (1980b) in North America and Masanek (2001) in Europe. These colleagues have presented models including practice principles and skills that embrace humanistic values and democratic standards for the group's milieu. These efforts underline the necessity of using practice skills that express the values of the group work method to develop the group as a democratic helping system.

❖ VALUES OF THE HUMANISTIC GROUP

The following are the values that comprise the nature of the humanistic approach to group work practice:

Humanistic Value 1: People have inherent worth and equal right to opportunity regardless of race, class, status, age, religion, gender, and sexual orientation, as well as physical and psychological condition.

Humanistic Value 2: People are responsible for and to one another because social interdependence is a natural and necessary human characteristic.

Humanistic Value 3: People have a right to belong to and be included in socially and emotionally supportive systems.

Humanistic Value 4: People, having emotional and intellectual voices, have a right to take part and to be heard.

Humanistic Value 5: People have the right to freedom of speech and freedom of expression.

Humanistic Value 6: People who are different enrich one another.

Humanistic Value 7: People have a right to freedom of choice to determine their own destinies.

Humanistic Value 8: People have the right to question and challenge those professionals who have an authority role in their lives.

These humanistic values are fundamental and indisputable in group work. Evolving and sustaining them requires effort and conviction. The professional group worker must be willing to struggle with the group in order to have these emotional, social, and philosophical frames of reference bring about processes that lead the members to hold these values as uppermost. Acceptance of these values is but the first step in the process. The members will have to express these values through their actions and in the quality of their interactions with one another.

❖ DEMOCRATIC NORMS AS VALUES IN ACTION

The roots of a democratic culture do not lie in its theories and conceptions, but rather in conduct and its satisfactions.
—Lindeman, 1980

Group norms are the implicit and explicit standards developed in the members' transactions that guide their behavior. Norms develop in groups in a variety of complex ways. They develop through the planned as well as unplanned efforts of the participants; they also develop through the power and influence of those, including the practitioner, who are exerting leadership. There are no guarantees that a group's norms will be humane and democratic. Group norms that are based on the domination by a powerful clique, or that foster exclusion, can develop all too easily. By contrast, democratic norms are those standards that operationalize humanistic values, the substance of the social group work process.

Having a set of humanistic values without the capacity to follow through in behavior can be an empty gesture. Humanistic values and democratic standards are too important to the evolving process of social group work to be left to develop by chance. Without a planned and concerted effort by the practitioner to express these, there are no assurances that the humanistic, democratic culture will come about. There are also no assurances that members will hear the person with unique characteristics, or that they will make decisions that respect the positions of the members in the minority. Furthermore, there are no guarantees that members will reach out to connect to others without aggression. The practitioner has a fundamental ethical obligation and all-important practice role to play in affecting how the members value and interact with one another. The practitioner must be the most active proponent of these values until the members demonstrate their abilities to sustain them.

❖ HUMANISTIC VALUES 1–4

This section examines Humanistic Values 1, 2, 3, and 4 as they are expressed by the practitioner. How each value is enacted through a set of democratic norms that set standards for humanistic relationships among members will be presented. The role of the practitioner will be delineated and demonstrated through practice illustrations. (See Table 1.1 at the end of this chapter for a summary of values, norms, and practitioner roles.) In Chapter 2, Humanistic Values 5, 6, 7, and 8 are similarly presented (see Table 2.1 in the next chapter for a further summary).

Humanistic Value 1: People Have Inherent Worth and Equal Right to Opportunity Regardless of Race, Class, Status, Age, Gender, and Sexual Orientation, as Well as Physical and Psychological Condition

This value underlies all others in the formation of the humanistic group. It places emphasis on the individual as possessing a unique spirit and energy. Incorporating this value in the group sets the stage for subsequent ways in which members perceive, help, and work with one another. It helps the members develop an egalitarian milieu, rather than an elitist one that would undermine the efforts and strivings of some of the members.

Democratic Norm 1: The Group Protects Each Member's
Right to Contribute to and Receive Resources From the Group

The values that accompany membership in an egalitarian group do not lead to the denigration of the positions, contributions, and potentials of people. Members possessing more knowledge, prior experience, higher social status, or economic class cannot use these as reasons for defaming or subjugating others. Members in the humanistic group are responsible for developing continual awareness of their elitist and prejudicial approaches toward others and to work toward changing these attitudes and actions.

Adherence to this norm does not result in homogenization of members and denial of their distinctive qualities. Group members are called on to develop ways of presenting and taking pride in their participation and contributions. Members are called on to acknowledge the significance and quality of the contributions of other members without comparison with their own or to others. Members must also recognize their own knowledge gaps in relation to others' special expertise and resources.

Practitioner Role. The practitioner stresses the value of each member to the life and process of the group. The practitioner explicitly states that each member's contribution sets a direction for the group's process and experience. The group worker indicates that each member and the practitioner have cultural and psychological differences. The practitioner questions attitudes, perceptions, and actions divisive to this norm by actively intervening in the group's process.

| *Illustration* | *Parents of Preschool Children's Program* |

The parents of children in a preschool Head Start program began meeting last month to discuss the effect of the program on their 2- to 5-year-old children. They also learn about the special aspects of parenting pre-school-age children. One mother, Denise, is quite upset because the children are not given alphabet recognition or reading-readiness skills, claiming this is one of the major problems for poor kids in the inner-city schools. Some parents respond by talking about the need to build social skills first.

Marta insists that her older child has done quite well in this program and will learn to read in the first grade where it is more appropriate. Tameka wonders if Doris, who took courses in child development in community college, could enlighten the group. Doris hesitates. One parent jumps in, saying she doesn't think book learning could provide the answer. A discussion ensues about the need for learning basic reading and math skills to give the children a real "head start" versus learning through experiences. One parent points out that the experiences themselves are teaching them letters and numbers. Doris still has not responded.

The practitioner, Yvonne, asks the group how it is going to allow for the unique skill and knowledge of each member to be part of their process, pointing out the importance of hearing many views before reaching decisions. More discussion follows, centering on how to integrate members' feelings and experiences regardless of whether these come from book learning or intuition. Derek (the only father in the group) turns his attention back to Doris asking her once again, "Come on, I want to know what you know about this age group. Do you think they should be taught to read now?" Other members chime in, encouraging Doris, and asking to hear from others too. Doris explains that she feels that social skills come first, and that children eventually will be more open and ready to read when they feel good with each other and are also read to by the teacher and their parents. Derek points out to Denise that the teacher does do a lot of reading to the kids and they seem totally absorbed in it; more talk ensues.

Discussion

A fundamental error made by group practitioners who are overly concerned about individuals' feelings, rather than with their roles as group members, is to probe the individual member's feelings and opinions. Instead, the practitioner should first encourage the members to look at how all of them can contribute to the group process.

The practitioner in this illustration responded to the group issue by noting the importance of varied views and contributions.

If Doris had initially answered the questions without the prior discussion of how expertise and knowledge would be used by the group, differences concerning book learning in relation to experience would have gone underground. Fixed subgroups could have emerged, creating a tug-of-war between Doris's views and Denise's. If the member (Doris) had immediately answered the question, the practitioner should have encouraged discussion about how to respond to special expertise, as well as other types of contributions to the group's feelings and interactions.

Humanistic Value 2: People Are Responsible for and to One Another Because Social Interdependence Is a Natural and Necessary Human Characteristic

People can take responsibility for caring for and supporting each other in a cooperative environment. They also can compete, exploit, and ignore one another, thereby developing utilitarian relationships based on convenience rather than caring. Fulfilling needs at the expense of others precludes taking responsibility and being responsible for oneself and others.

Democratic Norm 1: Members Interact Through
Caring and Mutual Aid Rather Than Exploitive Relations

Members' attempts to control others, or turn away from them with selfish attitudes such as "You do your thing and I'll do mine" signify an avoidance of social responsibility. Membership requires developing and sustaining a caring environment of mutual aid (Schwartz, 1961).

Caring for others occurs when members respond to each others' hurts, discomforts, satisfactions, concerns, and fears. Caring means that members do not use what they learn about one another to exploit each other. This norm is demonstrated through sharing of emotional and practical abilities with the whole group, rather than withholding or hoarding for oneself or a select subgroup. The group that closes one member out from an impromptu group trip to the coffee shop after a meeting subverts the whole group's capacity to give and receive assistance and guidance.

Practitioner Role. The practitioner offers perspective to help the group to establish positive relationships. The group worker explicitly presents views about sharing, helping, and learning from each other. The members are encouraged in their development of mutuality to explore their visions of how they would like to participate in the group. The practitioner encourages caring and connecting, and affirms the unique importance of each member's contributions and interdependence while fostering the members' collective interdependence and mutual responsibility.

Illustration	***Maintaining Sobriety Group***

Joe, a member in a substance abuse treatment program group for people maintaining their sobriety, missed a meeting without calling anyone to explain. This is a warning of an impending relapse. During the better part of the meeting there is no mention of why Joe might be absent, except when the practitioner asks the group if anyone has heard from him. Members say "no" and quickly go on to other topics.

Further into the meeting—since Joe has not been mentioned—the practitioner asks what the members are feeling and thinking about his absence. This opens up a discussion focusing on concern that he might be drinking, and whether to call him before the next meeting. Several members point to the need to support and confront others who might be in trouble, even if they become angry at being confronted. Sally feels that Joe might be ashamed if he is on a binge. Willy talks about how important it has been for him to call up fellow members between meetings just to let off steam; he feels this helps to keep him sober.

After more discussion, the group members decide that Willy should be the one to call Joe because he feels closest to Joe and is comfortable about calling others—including Joe—to offer support.

Discussion

There are a few probable reasons why members did not mention Joe on their own without the practitioner taking the initiative. One is that the norm for caring and mutual aid is too narrowly defined by an implicit or explicit rule that members should give help only when it is directly asked for. Another dynamic is "the emperor's new clothes"; members do not mention another's condition, unless that member or a designee mentions it first. Another probability is "taboo topics" (Shulman, 2006)—subjects that members will not talk about until taboos are challenged by the practitioner. In essence, the group members handle certain problems by avoiding them. Sometimes this comes about because members do not have the abilities to work on the issue. The practitioner is called on to bring taboos to the surface and air them in order to help members expand their collective abilities to handle all kinds of emotional and social issues.

Had Joe's absence not been called to their attention, the members would have felt that this type of situation—and their discomforts with it—were not grist for the mill. They would have believed that issues to be openly dealt with depend on getting one another's formal permission. This state would counter the very nature of mutuality in humanistic group life. In this group, members are learning that they will be cared about and responded to by the group, should they regress or get into other difficulties.

---

*Democratic Norm 2: The Norm Is for Building Cooperative
Rather Than Competitive Relations in the Group*

Classic studies on cooperation show that cooperative relations among members foster their creativity in task completion and heighten their sense of self-esteem (Deutsch, 1968; Sherif, 1965a). On the contrary, highly competitive group relations cause one-upmanship and attitudes of superiority, group dynamics that work against mutuality. In competitive situations, members withhold knowledge and abilities from one another for fear of being outdone. Competitiveness in group life shows up through behavior such as inattentiveness, preoccupation with one's own importance and power, interrupting, and ignoring others. Cooperative efforts are presented when members listen and include others' ideas to build on their own experiences, as well as to learn new and different ways of behaving.

Practitioner Role. The practitioner points out when and how members are being uncooperative, helping them work with rather than against each other. Members are helped to perceive when they are interrupting and more involved in talking rather than in listening, and helped to build listening skills. One-upmanship behavior is identified. Members are helped to share resources and capabilities. The group worker encourages members to learn from each other, rather than to covet each others' attributes. When the members are tense or defensive, they often form subgroups. The practitioner indicates that by cooperating everyone's needs can more readily be met.

Illustration	*Senior Center Newsletter Committee*

A new committee of the members of a senior center has been formed recently to take responsibility for composing and distributing a monthly newsletter. The past two meetings have been marked by repeated arguments among three of the nine members, arguments about the kinds of articles to include and about who will write them.

Mike wants to be sure there's something in there about the bowling tournament that several of the men are involved in. Tessie wants to write two articles—one on senior-citizen entitlements, especially prescription drugs, and another on hurricane relief efforts. She says, "No one is interested in bowling. It's just a few men who do that." Tessie feels many poor senior citizens are too embarrassed to ask for entitlements information. Faye feels that everyone on the committee should write whatever they want to write and that it wouldn't be a problem to have a longer newsletter. Mike insists that Tessie is stubborn.

While he is the only one to have said this about Tessie in the meeting, Mike has privately told the practitioner that other members see Tessie as a dictator. "She won't listen to anyone. If she isn't controlled, the others are going to quit the committee." Knowing this information, but not being able to share it directly in the group, the worker keeps this knowledge in her mind.

At this particular meeting, arguing has erupted after just 5 minutes. The practitioner had asked members to bring in articles. Before Irene can even read hers, Tessie interrupts her and says, "We all know about people who are sick. We don't need an article on that." The group worker asks the others, "Is that right, are articles on people's illnesses unnecessary?" Dora quietly says, "Even if we know about it, those people will feel the senior center really cares about them when they see something about themselves in the newsletter." Mike says to Tessie, "You see, I told you." Tessie sputters, whereupon the practitioner explains to Mike that for him to try to prove to Tessie he is right and she is wrong is not going to help the group cooperate in employing everyone's good ideas, "nor is Tessie's trying to prove that she's right and Mike is wrong going to help put together a good newsletter."

The practitioner then turns to the group and asks how they feel about people interrupting one another. Members indicate that it's hard to get points across when people cut in and don't cooperate. Conversation develops about the theme of interrupting, and there is agreement that they have to change these interactions. The members continue deliberations on how to implement some of the ideas people have for the paper, deciding to use Irene's article about several homebound seniors, and selecting two more topics for the future.

Quiet for a good part of the discussion, Tessie again begins to cut in abrasively. After stopping her several times with reassurance that she will have a chance to read her piece soon, the practitioner finally says, "Tessie, take your turn now and read us your article." Tessie reads a fine piece of work. Members like it and tell her so. With the practitioner's encouragement, the members reassure Tessie that her article will be included.

Discussion

The practitioner is in an uncomfortable situation, because a member has secretly told her that others might leave. (This is not atypical of what happens in community center groups where members have high access to each other through other programs.) Whether or not departure was imminent, it was a message to the practitioner that Tessie's interruptions and competitiveness were not being handled by the group's process; it was also a message that the practitioner had to be more direct and engaged in developing the group norm of fostering cooperation. Goals that are larger than the personal needs of individuals may serve to unite a group. These "superordinate goals" can foster group cohesion and harness cooperation (Sherif, 1965b). In this meeting, the practitioner elicited their cooperative spirit by focusing on writing a quality newsletter as the unifying theme that could motivate members to overcome their personal needs to dominate and compete for attention, affection, and acceptance.

The group is "practicing" cooperative interaction during the discussion of various ideas for the newsletter. The practitioner purposely subdues Tessie's interruptions in order to demonstrate that this can be done. Without this action, the group might have retaliated by rejecting Tessie and her work, perpetuating the competitive cycle. Instead the group accepts Tessie's contribution.

Humanistic Value 3: People Have the Right to Belong to and Be Included in Socially and Emotionally Supportive Systems

Belonging provides the most curative experience for group members (Yalom, 2005). It is a pivotal condition in the development of the humanistic milieu that will guide members' behaviors and attitudes. If not built upon humanistic values, some groups might have narrow membership criteria that exclude rather than include people who are perceived as different. They may also move to exclude people who act antisocially in the group, rather than work on how to change the situation. Working with the group's rejecting and aggressive reactions provides a special challenge to the practitioner and members of the humanistic group. They will strive for inclusion of a wide range of members who substantially identify with the group's raison d'etre, regardless of how helpful they are or their culturally or physically different characteristics.

Democratic Norm 1: In a Humanistic Group, the Norm Is for Inclusion Rather Than Exclusion

While all groups will establish boundaries that bind the members to one another, somewhat closing out others, boundaries in a humanistic group should be semipermeable. The practitioner early on establishes the value of and identifies the means for inclusion, thereby permitting inclusion to a wide spectrum of persons. This condition reflects an openness of spirit and a desire to be involved with a broad spectrum of different kinds of people and opinions. The practitioner encourages the group to be wary and to scrutinize carefully its attempts to be overtly and covertly exclusive. This is done to examine and challenge these attitudes and actions.

Practitioner Role. The practitioner recognizes that when the members feel insecure about themselves, they are more apt to establish narrow membership criteria. These criteria leave some members feeling that their membership is tenuous, and others feeling excluded from membership. People feel they are being labeled as "outsiders."

The practitioner sets a tone that inspires the members' confidence in their abilities to collaborate on their objectives and goals. The practitioner airs the members' fears of including people who they may not have easy affinity with by stating that there should be members with different personalities, perspectives, and experiences. The practitioner stresses that each member's contributions will become part of the group's experiences and outcomes. The practitioner provides perspective and confidence in the group's potential to include others in the group.

Illustration	*Senior Citizens Reminiscence Group*

A senior citizens reminiscence group is having its fourth meeting. All nine members are attending regularly. The members are talking about what it had been like to go out at night "in the old days" in the inner city—"how friendly everyone was, how unafraid people were, and how inexpensive things were." The practitioner notices that two members are not saying much, and turns to them, asking, "I notice, Sam and Florence, that you've been quiet during this discussion. Do you see things differently?" This opens up a discussion with Florence talking about how she thinks only of having lost her husband and how they used to do so many things together. She says, "I don't want to talk about it anymore because I don't want to be upset and to upset everybody." Sam says, "I was not yet in this country then. Europe was a difficult place to be before and after World War II." The members are silent.

The practitioner asks the other members how they are reacting to what Florence and Sam are bringing up. One member says that it's possible that when we look at aspects of the past we may find that it's not happy for everyone. Florence wonders, "Should I be in the group?" Elsa says, "Of course you should." There is a silence. The practitioner asks, "Are some of you saying that we should only talk about happy things?" Dora says, "I don't know if I can bear to hear about World War II." Sam reassures her that he isn't planning to say anything painful. The practitioner asks him, "But what if you change your mind and need to tell us your experiences?" Jerry (who is black) chimes in, "Don't worry, Sam. I've got stories about lynch mobs in Alabama that would make your hair stand on end." The practitioner notes, "So the feeling begins to develop that if members agree not to tell each other sad and uncomfortable stories, you would not have full relationships with each other." Conversation continues and intensifies about the members' different backgrounds and experiences, and they decide it is more important to know each other than to hold back in order to avoid causing pain.

Discussion

The practitioner easily could have let the discussion end by helping several members, besides Elsa, reassure Florence that she was needed and wanted. This action would have helped them experience acceptance. But Sam obliquely brings up being in Europe during the Second World War. His acceptance into the group, and whatever it brings with it—as well as Florence's or anyone else's—had to be dealt with. Furthermore, had the black man from Alabama been unable to refer spontaneously to his frightening life in a racist environment, the practitioner would have had to focus further on members' differences in the environments of their youth.

Racial and cultural differences need to be addressed in a timely manner, and the group practitioner is responsible for creating an atmosphere that allows all levels of difference to be raised. For instance, in this group we can assume that someone having come from Europe prior to World War II in some way witnessed or was a victim of persecution. If the practitioner had not responded to the cues in the moment, it is unlikely that the group would have easily given Jerry room for full membership. The practitioner must stress the essential need of members to accept and deal with their differences so the group may benefit from them.

Democratic Norm 2: A Humanistic Group Develops
Procedures for Considering Prospective Members

Criteria for forming new groups should not be based solely on ethnicity, race, class, or stereotype in order to exclude others. On the other hand, groups have been developed based on race, ethnicity, religion, and gender to address the issues of these populations. It is important for practitioners with these discreet groups to help members work on their own issues of inclusion or stereotyping of others outside of the group. In addition, possibilities exist for the creation of dialogue beyond the group that fosters improved intergroup relations.

Criteria governing the inclusion of new members into an existing group must be made explicit. These criteria must be based on interest, on abilities, and on the person's potential to work toward helping others to meet their needs and the group to meet its goals.

Criteria for inclusion are not to be based on ethnicity, race, class, or other forms of stereotyping and stigmatizing used to create barriers between people. Membership should be considered in genuinely open and nondefensive discussions. There should be no place for overt and covert rejections or hazing procedures. Approach-avoidance issues must be explicitly examined and resolved.

The group's screening criteria have to be readily available and explicitly presented to potential members. And criteria set up for new members that differ from those previously used tend to be exclusive unless these are made explicit and connected to the expansion of the group's horizons.

Practitioner Role. It is important to help members examine different opinions and feelings related to opening membership to others. The practitioner helps the members identify criteria, define procedures, and look at attitudes and feelings. Elitist and other negative criteria that would make the group appear to be sacred and mysterious (Bion, 1961) are pointed out. The practitioner gently and directly attends to prejudice and stigmatizing by suggesting when these attitudes are surfacing.

Focus is also drawn to members' needs to exclude some people because of prejudice, or feelings that the person is "too difficult" or won't "fit in." The practitioner, first and foremost, must look into these very same feelings and reactions in himself or herself before helping the members deal with these issues.

Illustration   *Teen Group in a High School*

A group of teens has been meeting for a year with Carla, a school social worker. They are talking about difficulties they are having in school and at home.

Recently the group has been trying to figure out if they want to add more members. One prospective member, Rick, is known to several of them. He wants to be part of the group. Unlike the rest of the members, Rick is into punk rock music and has a "goth" look, which includes a few prominent tattoos. Yolanda and Marcus know Rick; they feel he is okay, that he has problems at home, and that "he should be given a chance, even if he looks a little weird." Jocelyn says, "Eleven people are enough in the group." Cindy reminds the group that three members are graduating "and won't be around next year." Janet says she thinks that "maybe some of you are prejudiced because of the way Rick looks." Most deny this. The practitioner wonders, "What are your reasons for not including Rick, especially given that we will be losing a couple of members?" Jocelyn reluctantly says she doesn't want any group members who do drugs. A couple of others nod in agreement. Marcus says, "Even if Rick does drugs, he doesn't get all messed up. Besides, maybe that's what we can help him with. Just because he uses drugs doesn't mean he will get us to do what he does."

Several members wonder what it would be like for someone to join who hasn't been with them since the beginning. One asks, "Could we get close like this?" The practitioner reacts, saying, "It will take time to get close to a new person. When this group was formed, no one cared what kind of music each of you liked. It was just advertised for kids who wanted to talk about things." Janet joins in, indicating that Rick does have a lot to talk about and the group might really do him good. The members decide to ask Rick to join them. The practitioner says, "Now that you've agreed to ask Rick, you should deal with the fact that three of you are graduating and leaving the group. Will you want more new members? What criteria will you use? How will you get to others to see if they're interested?"

Discussion

The practitioner, Carla, wishes to help the members examine how they feel about the changes the group will undergo when some members leave. She does not directly pursue this. She is able to use the specific issue of the potential new member as a springboard to help them find flexibility so they can accept a new person with different characteristics. The practitioner points out that "in the past, music was not an issue for or against membership; why is it one now?" This helps the members focus on the prospective members' needs and how they might try to be helpful to him.

Airing concern that a new person with different values may seriously disturb their collective values and norms is an important step for the practitioner to take. In this illustration, note that members expressed these concerns in their own process. Had they not, the practitioner would have had to surface the issues. The turning point for this group is when they conclude that the new member cannot make them use drugs. Then they begin to experience their helping potential. As this peaks in the process, the practitioner wonders what they will experience when several members leave and the group considers new membership. The practitioner asks them to consider how new members might be helpful for the group and its meaning in the school and community.

Democratic Norm 3: A Humanistic Group Develops Ways of Permitting and Maintaining Membership to Members Who May Offend the Group

Acceptance of others' rights to belong is fundamental to the strength and fabric of a humanistic group. In it, members are not to attempt, hastily or judgmentally, to exclude the member who offends them, causes anxiety, or brings the group to the angry attention of others.

Members may find themselves challenged by a consistently difficult person or by a particular type of difficulty that evokes their discomfort. Under these circumstances, groups develop the position that the group would be a fine and good one if the difficult person was not a member. This is an exclusionary stance. The stance may represent a latent collusion with the difficult member and others to replicate earlier emotional and social exclusions from peer and family life.

Taking responsibility for including difficult members acknowledges that all members can derive benefits from dealing with meaningful although disturbing issues in group life. Struggling with a difficult member strengthens all of the members' abilities to deal with a range of interpersonal difficulties in their lives.

Practitioner Role. The practitioner stimulates and surfaces the members' desire to be helpful, pointing out that anger, fear, and frustration may be causing them to feel like excluding the member. The practitioner helps the group find different capabilities and means for interacting with a member who is having unusual difficulties.

In this process, the practitioner is on the line, having to consider his or her own desires to exclude the person. From this perspective, the practitioner has to carry out a major effort, helping both the difficult member and the rest of the group.

A precipitous exit of the "problem" member may bring about a guilt reaction that can harm the process. It may also engender relief at no longer having to deal with the member's difficult issues. Ambivalent feelings may exist hand in hand. Exclusion may fulfill a wish to be rejecting, in contradistinction to the wish to be omnipotently helpful. If ambivalent feelings are not worked on, they will hamper the group's future work.

Illustration	**Group for People With Chronic Mental Illness in Continuing Day Treatment**

A group of people with serious mental illness in a continuing day treatment program are aware that one of them, Hamid, is Muslim. This, however, has never been discussed. At the very end of the meeting, Hamid has an angry outburst toward the others. He tells them that he knows they do not want to be with him and don't like him because he is Muslim. The other members, stunned by the truth of the accusations, do not know what to say or how to respond. The practitioner responds. "You've been going through feeling extremely rejected and alone here. I'm sorry. Our quietness right now has to feel like more and more rejection." Hamid says, "I don't expect anything to change." He gets up and leaves. After several moments of sitting in silence, the other members begin to leave as well. The practitioner, intuiting and empathizing, remains silent and quietly leaves in the midst of everyone else.

At the following meeting, the members seem calm. During the week the incident has reverberated throughout the treatment center. Hamid announces, "I'm being discharged to a vocational program in one month." He thanks the group for the opportunity to "get things off my chest. I'm sorry for the outburst."

Members begin to tell Hamid and each other how they feel about Hamid's being Muslim. Stella says, "I know I am prejudiced around Hamid—since 9/11, I guess. This week I realized how unfair I am to you. I cannot think every Muslim I meet is bad, just because of what those people did." Similar talk continues for quite some time. Hamid talks a lot more explicitly about how he has been treated badly because he is Arab and Muslim, and it's still there. He tells the group how upset he was after 9/11 and ashamed to see that Muslims could behave that way. Sal says, "You can blow up anytime, man—get it out." Carlos asks Hamid if he can stay on as a member for the next three or four sessions.

Discussion

In this "critical incident" in the group, the practitioner contained any temptation to instantaneously repair the damage and hurt, and stayed empathetically connected to the members' processes. The practitioner was responsive to the intense affect without diluting it or trying to smooth it over, acting on the judgment that the strength of positive nonverbal communications after Hamid bolted was enough to sustain the group's process into the coming week.

Democratic Norm 4: The Norm for Guiding the Use of Exclusion From the Group as a Healing Tool

The threat of excluding a person from a group that is a helpful environment may be used to change a member's antisocial or dysfunctional behavior. A member who continues to deviate disruptively from group norms may be reasonably challenged with exclusion unless he or she changes his or her interactional style.

The principle of due process, however, should not be violated. Warning procedures should be set up and expressed. The member's behavior should be confronted in relationship to its effects on others. His or her behavior should be compared with the values and norms of the group. Should the person be unable to remain in the group, other helpful alternatives must be developed.

Practitioner Role. A group can move to exclude a member from meetings—or the group—if that person is not changing destructive ways of interaction. The practitioner has a great deal of power and the fundamental professional obligation to influence the development of this situation. The group worker has to exercise empathy, skill, and timing in helping all members use the promise of exclusion and the interactions that result.

The practitioner is obligated to protect the member's due process. This is done by the practitioner engaging all group members along with the difficult member in negotiation and exploration (by mediating directly), explaining needs and feelings, and pointing out the effects of different kinds of helpful and unhelpful interactions. This is an emotionally charged series of events with the practitioner maintaining an active and intense affective connection to all of the group members.

Illustration	Mothers of Children in Foster Care

Justine takes part in a group for abusing mothers whose children are not in their custody. The group is run out of the local community mental health clinic. Members are referred by the County Special Services for Children Department. All members know that participation is a prerequisite to having their children returned to them. Many members are struggling with their own historical issues concerning their childhood experiences with abusing and neglectful parents. Some admit having turned to drugs to deaden the painful memories that come up when their children make them nervous. Others find themselves in relationships with people who continue to hurt them. All, in varying degrees, have admitted they "took it out on our children."

Justine has missed the past three sessions. Marissa and Grace have tried to reach her, but Justine's home phone is disconnected and her cell phone as well. The word is that she has been beaten up by a man with whom she is involved. The group members have been trying to get Justine to leave him, reminding her that he is part of the reason she has lost custody of her daughter. She has been afraid to get an order of protection against him. The members have been quite angry and frustrated with Justine's inability to take this step. They have decided in her absence that if and when she returns, and if she has been beaten up, they will work with her to press charges of assault.

At this meeting, Justine looks bruised. After reluctantly admitting she has in fact been beaten up, Grace begins to get angry at her, saying, "You'd better press charges, girl." Justine hems and haws. Other members try to impress upon Justine how she is letting these bad things happen to her and that she is worth more. In general, Justine is told, "You've got to learn to help yourself. Each of us goes through bad stuff that's ruining us as parents. But it's never too late."

Justine, somewhat glibly, thanks the group for their concern. Grace senses her ambivalence and says, "If you don't press charges on this bum, then you shouldn't come back to the group, because you don't want to make your situation better. You don't want your kid back, either. You want to grovel to this pig who smashed up your face. You're just bullshitting us." Marissa says, "Damn, I'm tired of running around your neighborhood trying to see if you're okay and finding out that he beat you up." The practitioner asks the group, "How do the rest of you feel about what they've said to Justine?" Some agree that she is going around in circles, and they express similar frustrations.

Justine responds angrily. "I'll leave right now if that's how you want it." Marissa continues, "There's no point in you staying unless you make a bigger effort to change your circumstances." The practitioner says, "To my ear, they're saying that they have been trying to help you in good faith, and that they will continue to help you, but they want you to do your part in good faith, too." Justine says to the worker, "So you think I've gotta go, too. Okay fine, I'll go. That's it." The practitioner says, "I don't think you or anyone else should decide anything now, in the heat of the moment. You need to think about that for a while and let people know what you are trying to decide. Bring yourself into the group next week, that's the important thing to do."

Justine returns to the next meeting. She says, "No one has ever put things to me in that way, that straight, about my self-respect and given me so much support. I have decided to press charges." She begins to cry, saying she doesn't know where to begin to fix up her life. The members, emotional as well, express concern, advice, and hope. They tell her that "things are not easy," and that they will be there for her—in court and wherever they are needed—as long as she does her part and doesn't leave them shouldering the burden. The practitioner says, "Everyone has burdens they have to shoulder. It's good to get help in shouldering them. This is what the group is all about."

Discussion

It is unlikely that the road ahead for Justine will be smooth. However, this kind of confrontation presses members to own their goals and self-esteem, and to take personal responsibility for changing their individual patterns and actions. The practitioner's role combines mediation between the group and the member with direct confrontation of the member, his or her situation, and the group's circumstances. The practitioner does not smooth over the member's behavior or the group's reaction to it for fear of leaving the member in the lurch or losing her and the group. The practitioner helps the group temper its desire to exclude by centering on the mutual desire and effort of the members to pull together to achieve their goals.

The group worker does not protect the member; rather, the practitioner interprets the group's message. By leaving the door open, the practitioner has offered the member a way to reenter the group in the future sessions. In this way, the practitioner has provided an alternative—something that might have been difficult for others to do—while making the members aware of how they have to handle themselves when "she comes through the open door."

The member returns in a frame of mind that lets the other members know she is willing to work, thereby providing them with the willingness to support and be available to her.

Humanistic Value 4: People, Having Emotional and Intellectual Voices, Have the Right to Take Part and to Be Heard

The opportunity to be heard by others ensures the potential to use the group as a sounding board for experimentation and opportunities to contribute to others' growth. Without a chance to have a positive position and space for expression, members do not think that their ideas and feelings will be significant for others.

Democratic Norm 1: A Humanistic Group Develops
Procedures That Permit Everyone to Participate

Participation in group life cannot be quantitatively equal. The group's procedures need to include mechanisms that limit the input of members when they are overzealous, overanxious, or over-bearing. The group also needs to develop the means for including quiet members.

Ambiguous norms governing the nature and extent of participation cause questions and concerns about participation to remain unstated. This lack of clarity creates the risk of generating nonegalitarian norms, with highly talkative participants developing an inflated sense of their roles and contributions at the expense of others. Members need to learn to respond actively to cues that others wish to speak. They also need to recognize that the creation of opportunities for participation is a collective responsibility.

It is very important early in the group's life for the practitioner to assist in the development of a collective experience, one that emphasizes valuing the contributions of each member. Each individual problem should not become the dominant and exclusive focus of attention. Without efforts toward embracing all of the members' needs and interests, cohesion will be an illusion. Highly self-disclosing and assertive members will become grandiose, dominant, and prideful about their special contributions.

Practitioner Role. As members talk, the practitioner scans (Shulman, 2006), looking to see how quiet members are reacting. The practitioner addresses the obvious inequalities in participation. Those who have not been heard from recently are asked for comments. The practitioner is also sensitive to the need for the group to create opportunities for each member to participate. Picking up cues that a member has not made or been allowed space, the practitioner encourages the member by interrupting an ongoing interaction for the person. The practitioner notes that the person wishes to speak, modeling the creation of space, then asks the member what is on his or her mind. In this way, the practitioner helps the group take collective responsibility for creating opportunities for everyone. The practitioner asks the group to consider how it will involve those who feel unable to interrupt the process. Members all too often attribute their silence to the feeling that their opinions have already been expressed by others; they need to know that the group wants to hear from each member because each person is different and has helpful contributions.

The practitioner runs the risk of attending too often to one member's self-disclosures and encouraging only the most vocal participants. If a cohesive group is to emerge, everyone has to be engaged, and no one member's experience can be allowed to overwhelm the group's process. At such junctures the practitioner modulates the expression of an individual's self-disclosures, generalizing them into concerns common to all. This fosters group building and participation.

Without a concerted effort toward valuing all members' contributions, the group's cohesion becomes illusionary rather than actual. False cohesion stimulates the group to dissolve because members become distanced from the group and one another. The practitioner, often startled by this outcome, feels unsure of what went and is going wrong.

Illustration	*Placing Parents in a Nursing Home*

In a group where members are dealing with the many issues and complex feelings they have about placing their relatives in nursing homes, several people have been dominating the discussion process. One in particular, Nellie, is expressing a combination of guilt along with contrary beliefs that she has done the right thing by placing her mother. She says, "Mother is angry with me and doesn't talk to me when I visit." Without giving anyone else a chance to participate, Nellie goes right on to say, "I am terribly upset." The practitioner, Faith, looks around the group and sees that some people are starting to tune Nellie out and act uncomfortable with her. Bill and his wife, Sydelle, are throwing glances at each other; Marlene and Vanessa seem to be retreating.

The practitioner cuts into Nellie's now emotional monologue, saying, "I'm sorry to cut you off, Nellie, but you've been saying so many things that are relevant for you and everyone here." Turning to the rest of the group, Faith goes on, "I was wondering, since others of you have been quiet for a while, if you were feeling guilty like Nellie or had other feelings about placing your parents or relatives here?" Vanessa says, "I do feel guilty. Mom is so nice to me, but I also feel relief." More talk continues about guilt, with all speaking except for Bill.

Faith turns to Bill, saying, "And you, you've been quiet. I wonder how it's been for you and your father." Bill says, "Well, I agree with my wife. She said it all." Faith smiles and says, "Sydelle did say your father is giving you, but not your brother, a hard time. How do you react to that? Tell us." Bill says, somewhat reluctantly, "This is the way he has always been with my brother and me. I don't take it to heart too much." Several members ask Bill how his brother reacts. He says his brother is usually very helpful and that's why he doesn't take it to heart. The practitioner says, "And I guess your wife is, too?" Bill replies, "Oh, very much so."

The group goes on. Nellie, who has been comparatively quiet and inactive for the past half hour, listening to the others attentively, joins in and supports the couple. She adds, "I wish I had more support from my family." Marlene says, "Well, at least the group is here for us, Nellie." Nellie says, "Yes, I'm grateful for that. I would be feeling alone without this group."

Discussion

The practitioner interrupts Nellie's "long story," especially after scanning the group and noticing that several members are not listening. To leave a member in a social and emotional vacuum because he or she is talking into the air would sabotage the group's milieu. It would also interfere with the member's chance to become part of the group's mutual aid. The member with this presentation needs support. The overbearing member in this case has the experience of finding out that she can be comforted by attending to others' experiences and needs.

Interrupting the group is very difficult for a beginning practitioner. When a member does not stop to take a breath, the practitioner tends to experience "cutting in" as rude. Often the member tacitly appreciates being stopped. The group is grateful because it is rescued from its urge to distance itself from the member. The practitioner shows the member that she has been heard; she restates what the member has been saying, and by presenting it to the group, she creates a general connection between the member's circumstances and those of the other members.

❖ SUMMARY

In this chapter, the eight basic humanistic values that underlie the group method have been presented. These emphasize members' rights, along with their mutual responsibilities for one another. These rights revolve around inclusion, free speech, being heard, being different, self-determination, and the right to challenge the practitioner.

The humanistic values focusing on people's inherent worth, people's responsibility to and for one another, people's right to belong, and people's rights to be heard have been described. The democratic norms the group develops that operationalize these values have been discussed. Among them are the following norms: the norm for cooperation, rather than competition; the norms for caring and mutual aid, rather than exploitive relations; the norms governing and guiding inclusion, rather than the exclusion, of members; the norms guiding inclusion of difficult members; the norm guiding the use of exclusion as a therapeutic tool; and the norm for an open communication system.

The role of the practitioner as a guiding force in the development of each norm was delineated, specific skills were identified, and illustrative examples were described and discussed.

The next chapter describes norms governing freedom of choice, free speech, the right to be different, and the right to challenge the group practitioner.

Table 1.1   Values, Norms, and the Practitioner Role

Value 1: People Are Inherently Worthy

    1. The norm for protecting equal rights of each member

    Practitioner role
- Makes explicit that all contributions and members will have value, highlighting necessity for understanding
- Acknowledges difference, including worker's difference
- Slows down process to foster egalitarian sharing

Value 2: People Are Responsible for and to One Another

    1. The norm for caring and mutual aid rather than exploitive relations

    Practitioner role
- Models caring
- Reinforces importance of hearing from all
- Makes assessment regarding group's potential to reach out across differences

    2. The norm for cooperative rather than competitive relations

    Practitioner role
- Points out competition nonjudgmentally
- Enables resource sharing versus hoarding for self or clique
- Enables use of subgroup needs to establish broader goals

Value 3: People Have the Right to Belong and Be Included in Supportive Systems

1. **The norm for inclusion rather than exclusion**

   Practitioner role
   - Prevents establishing narrow criteria for membership
   - Challenges exclusions based on racial or ethnic biases
   - Models acceptance of difference
   - Models openness to difference and appropriate curiosity

2. **The norm for dealing openly and rationally with prospective members**

   Practitioner role
   - Directly points out implications of hazing and antidemocratic nature of two-tiered membership structure
   - Shows group that trial memberships are for both parties

3. **The norm for permitting membership to members who may offend the group**

   Practitioner role
   - Enables stretching of resources and capacities to sustain membership of dissident person
   - Examines own biases and needs to exclude member
   - Acknowledges mutual enrichment that may occur

4. **The norm for guiding the use of exclusion as a healing tool**

   Practitioner role
   - Protects member's due process if group moves to exclude
   - Helps group confront member
   - Maintains affective ties to all sides
   - Enables member to find ways to use group

Value 4: People Have the Right to Take Part and Be Heard

1. **The norm for developing procedures for the participation of all**

   Practitioner role
   - Scans group, creates space
   - Recognizes when cultural differences are creating social distance and tenuous participation
   - Reaches for silent members, models for group
   - Helps group take responsibility for inclusion of all
   - Directly enables fullest participation of all
   - Helps group deal directly with difference, bias, or stereotyping

2

Further Humanistic Values and Democratic Norms

Freedoms

This chapter continues to identify the democratic norms that are developed in the group to operationalize the humanistic values presented in Chapter 1. The norms specifically related to Value 5 (freedom of speech), Value 6 (the importance of accepting difference as enriching), Value 7 (freedom of choice), and Value 8 (the right of members to challenge the authority of the practitioner) will be discussed. The practitioner's role in the development of these norms will be presented, along with practice illustrations. (See Table 2.1 at the end of this chapter for a summary of further values, norms, and practitioner roles.)

❖ HUMANISTIC VALUES 5–8

Humanistic Value 5: People Have the Right to Freedom of Speech and Freedom of Expression

To function in a free environment, people have to feel that the expression of ideas and feelings is welcomed by all members. It is vital to feel free from intimidation and the possibility of destructive consequences. The milieu needs to be experienced as a testing ground for the members' feelings, ideas, and actions, rather than a place that supports only a narrow ideology and excludes those with different opinions and attitudes.

Democratic Norm 1: The Group Develops a Free and Open Communication System Without Reliance on a Narrow Ideology

A group where members speak freely and authentically, where they are listening to each other, and where each member has access to speak to and be heard by all members of the group is important for supporting and stimulating the human spirit. Positive sanctions are important that include recognition and praise for expressing new and developing ideas and feelings in an atmosphere that values experimentation. A group designed for the enhancement of one limited narrow ideology within a narrow set of opinions will not permit freedom of expression.

Practitioner Role. The practitioner encourages members to speak their minds directly to the other members of the group, thus weaving a broad and flexible network of participation and communication. The practitioner actively encourages the expression of different opinions and helps members test out unformulated ideas and feelings in a receptive atmosphere.

Illustration	High School Students' Community Service Group

A group of high school students has been working on developing and running a community service program for economically disadvantaged children. The adult leader of the group seeks to help the students to understand the effects of poverty on every aspect of life, and to understand the need for redistributive justice. Whenever the students get into developing a plan for taking the children to the zoo or to a movie downtown, the practitioner engages them in a discussion about underlying goals of the event being planned and the values they will be conveying to the youngsters. This essentially blocks and impedes their efforts. The students feel a mixture of frustration with their lack of movement and a sense of intellectual inferiority with regard to their understanding of broader social issues. This form of inferiority is a motivation that keeps them engaged in the group process with the practitioner, who often states, "You cannot design a program unless you understand your goals and values."

A minority of members caucus outside the meeting. They decide that they are less interested in goals and values and more interested in doing something productive with the children. They also express a sense that other members are discontented with the group, but that it is not possible for them to buck the leader's authority. With some trepidation, they decide to raise this in their next group meeting.

In the meeting, when they say that "we would rather run a program than talk about our values," the other members are quiet, looking with fear to their leader for approval. The leader interprets the silence as an indication that this subgroup is wrong and that the other members do not have clarity about their values. He goes on to imply that this confrontation is the reason why the group should continue to discuss its values.

Eventually, after weeks of efforts to convince other group members to change the direction of the group or to disband it altogether and run it without an adult, these four members leave the group.

Discussion

This leadership style represents totalitarianism in a small group. In this meeting, there are several serious problems. Caucusing in the subgroup represents an effort to gain control in a situation where members are feeling intimidated and ineffectual.

For the young people, the caucus provided an extra group setting where they could test out and clarify unformulated thoughts and feelings. Expression of these ideas in the group without prior caucus would most likely have been frightening and surely squelched by this leader. A practitioner committed to humanistic values would have accepted the feedback and opened up the discussion; this would have benefitted the group as well as his or her own leadership style. However, this leader persists in maintaining his prejudicial view of others' opinions and feelings. He does not help others speak their minds; in fact, he interprets the meaning of the silence as tacit agreement for the direction he has set for the group. The leader is more involved in meeting his own needs to have a forum that reflects his own beliefs than in helping the students develop ways of raising their social consciousness.

This type of leadership is dangerous for the members and the group. The young people who leave the group will experience guilt because they left their friends behind, even though they tried to influence them. They realize they cannot change the group from within, so by leaving they try to change the group from without.

*Democratic Norm 2: The Group Develops the Open Expression
of Feeling While Tempering Premature Self-Disclosure*

In new relationships, highly personal self-disclosures are usually dysfunctional for the member, and can result in the member and others leaving the group. Members need to feel free to express important feelings while at the same time recognizing that these expressions should be shaped by the group's nature at different points in its development. When strong cohesion and the capacity to work on difficult issues exists, highly personal self-disclosures are appropriate and necessary for fulfilling the group's purpose. At the juncture when relationships and the group's work deepen, members can experiment with increasingly sharing relevant personal information and feelings in nondefensive ways and seeking others' reactions to them.

Practitioner Role. The practitioner directly supports the expression of feelings. However, when highly personal self-disclosures occur too early in the process, the practitioner stops the story from unfolding in its fullest form, turning self-disclosures into general themes related to the group's purpose. The practitioner enables the group to examine feelings about the here and now of its experience. The practitioner does not let the group members focus attention solely on one person's self-disclosures.

| **Illustration** | **Bereavement Group** |

Members in a bereavement group in a mental health clinic are meeting for the second time. Several members are talking about how lonely they feel without their spouses. Maureen is talking about the shock she felt when her husband of 42 years died suddenly of a heart attack. He had been well, and the doctors had told him he was healthy. Vera tells how difficult it was for her during her husband's extended illness, his diabetes, the amputation of his feet, and his anger with all his circumstances. Frances begins to cry, saying how hard it is for her to have lost two husbands this way. Her husband of many years died 8 years ago, and she married her second husband 6 years ago. She does not understand how this happened again, with her second husband dying unexpectedly.

After a good deal of discussion about how some of them keep expecting their spouse to appear in the doorway when they return home and how quiet the house is, Vera says how she felt so guilty, but that she felt relief, too. The practitioner says to Vera, "When someone has been so ill for a long time, there can be a sense of relief when they die." She tells the group, "You might find yourselves feeling all kinds of ways you don't want to feel—like angry at the person for dying, or relieved, or even remembering that your relationships were not good. There will be plenty of time to talk about those very difficult things if and when you want to."

Discussion

In the open atmosphere of a bereavement group, a good deal of feeling is usually expressed quickly and spontaneously. However, while the practitioner validates the member's self-disclosure, it is with the awareness that precipitous and intense expression of negative feelings about the spouse may not be helpful to either the member or the group. Thus, the practitioner uses the opportunity to validate the feeling, universalizing it and suggesting that these and other feelings will continue to be topics further along the way.

Humanistic Value 6: People Who Are Different Enrich One Another

Difference provides rich opportunities for interaction and learning. The trepidation that people experience about facing differences may be connected to their anxiety about conflict, fear of exposing their prejudices, and their ulterior motives to control or subjugate others.

Differences in experiences, attitudes, culture, physical ability, religious beliefs, and appearances are the nature of the human condition, reminding everyone of the variations that exist and the various ways in which people are unique. In a humanistic group, the rights of different members are protected.

Democratic Norm 1: The Norm Is for Members to Foster
Each Other's Diversity Rather Than Push for Conformity

It is known that a person in authority can pressure others to conform to expectations despite their better judgments (Milgram, 1963). Peer pressure can also be applied to secure conformity. This may cause conformity in social situations even when the conformity is in direct conflict with their perceptions and feelings (Asch, 1965). For example, the mass suicide of the people in Jonestown was a result of totalitarian leadership and community conformity.

A group that is unable to accept or tolerate one person—or a small cohort that displays differences in ideas, feelings, beliefs, and cultural, racial, or religious backgrounds—is usually governed by rigidities and a set of narrow norms that do not allow new ideas or solutions to emerge or to be examined (Shulman, 2006). The ability to tolerate difference, protecting the rights and due processes of different members, and allowing membership to a person with perceived difference, comes from exposure to and experience with diversity and its value for people.

Practitioner Role. How the practitioner helps bring about the group's acceptance of difference is partly determined by how threatened he or she is by the differences. Unthreatened, a practitioner can ask directly about the difference(s) in culture, belief, ethnicity, or religion with an air of curiosity and excitement. This indicates his or her fundamental appreciation of diversity.

A practitioner who can accept a member's deviance is able to assist the group to reflect on its own reactions of acceptance and rejection. Protecting the rights of the different person is crucial. The practitioner indicates to the member when the group is asking the member to change, emphasizing that the member is free to think or do whatever he or she pleases as long as all are safe. The worker points out to the group its responsibility to accept the person's right to be different, even if the majority does not agree with the belief or action.

Learning to accept differences of all kinds is supported and expanded by a practitioner's unequivocal statements that show respect for one's fellows and do not sanction prejudice and discrimination. The boundaries defining membership are broadened when the practitioner stretches the perimeter, enabling inclusion of people who are most different in culture, race, ideas, and interactional styles.

Illustration   *Elementary School Teachers Group*

A group of elementary school teachers meets regularly with a school social worker to discuss some of the problems they are having in class with some of the children. Many of the children come from single-parent homes. Several of the mothers are involved in a welfare-to-work program. At this meeting, Jim, a 20-year veteran in the school system, expresses strong negative feelings about the upbringing of some of the children. He tells the group that he agrees with the welfare-to-work program and goes off on how some of these parents have been on welfare too long and did not provide the right family environment to help their children become successful in school. He states that he believes the parents should be made to work. Several other teachers cut in and react with comments such as "here he goes again, blaming the victim." A fight ensues, with Jim saying, "The children can't learn if they don't have a structured day when they go home, and structure has to do with seeing adults go to work." One teacher reminds him sarcastically, "Children can't learn if they don't have good teachers, too."

The social worker finds herself getting angry at Jim. However, she reacts to him by saying, "You seem to be expressing a lot of frustration in the situation. It's hard to teach kids who need so much from you." Jim tells her, "I like the children, but it's the parents I don't like. They have been allowed to continue the cycle. I like it that they are being forced to work for their welfare benefits." Others react angrily, "You are so punitive." The practitioner says to the group, "I think Jim has a right to his opinion. And you have a right to yours also." Members talk more about how they do not like teachers who are down on the kids. The practitioner points out that Jim was not "down on the kids, but on the parents." Others reluctantly agree, but call him "conservative" and "redneck." The practitioner asks Jim, "How do you feel when they react to you this way?" Jim says, "I feel they will only accept me if I believe the way they do." Nellie replies, "Come on Jim, you love to bait us, because you love your different opinion," and laughs. Sandra says, "We know he's a good teacher and he likes the children." The practitioner presses them, "So what bothers you about his unpopular opinion?" More dialogue develops about people with unpopular opinions and about how they have rights to take part without being harassed.

Discussion

In this situation, joining into closing off Jim's access to the group because of his beliefs is contrary to the values of the humanistic group and detrimental to all the members. Thus, the practitioner modeled a way for members to include Jim in the process while not asking him to change his beliefs. In this case, the deviant member's frustration with the children's circumstances and concern for their well-being was shared by the other group members. The practitioner makes use of a common feeling as a means to help the others link up with Jim and accept an unpopular minority opinion.

Humanistic Value 7: People Have the Right to Freedom of Choice to Determine Their Own Destinies

People's rights to make free choices must be safeguarded in an environment that is not coercive. The principle of self-determination upholds and sustains people's right to use their abilities in assertive ways to forge their destinies in the face of oppression. Members join a group to fulfill needs in a collaborative environment. In the humanistic group, power for decision making resides in the hands of the entire group—not the leader or a small cadre. For this power to be distributed, several norms must become operationalized.

Democratic Norm 1: The Norm Is for Fostering
the Equal Distribution of Power in the Group

At various times in the life of a group, especially early on, power surfaces as an essential issue. Some individuals' need for power is based on the desire to control or dominate others. Others may assert power when they have expertise in a particular area. Still others may attempt to control due to beliefs about their own entitlement. Examination of the range of members' needs for power over others' behavior establishes an open (rather than a closed) group structure. Scrutinizing power issues in the group can help members more appropriately assert influence as well as accept the influence of others. Implicit decision-making processes should be examined. Members learn to recognize that leadership based on expertise as well as the desire to take charge should be shared, fluid, and not fixed.

Practitioner Role. The practitioner encourages the group to examine its implicit decision-making processes in order to make them explicit. He or she asks the group to reflect on which members, including the practitioner, have various types of influence. The practitioner, by encouraging the taking of leadership and follower roles, helps the members recognize that leadership does not have to be fixed, but can vary with the resources needed in the situation.

Illustration	**Young Adult Community Center Programming Group**

A committee of young adults responsible for social programs for their age group in a community center has been meeting regularly for the past two months. Jake, Claire, and Matt have been trying to get the group to run a big dinner dance at the center. They want to invite lots of people and also use it as a fund-raiser for the Day Camp's scholarship fund. They have made plans for a disc jockey (DJ) and have spoken to several caterers. They come to this meeting and present their plans.

The meeting begins with Matt saying that he would like to talk to the members about the plans they've gone ahead with for setting up the dinner dance. The group is quiet. Matt talks about the DJ, the cost, and that he will play a variety of dance and pop music. Claire interjects that she and Jake went to two different caterers. They preferred a buffet because it is somewhat cheaper. Claire tells the group that one caterer is a friend: "I know this one will do a good job because I've been to another party they catered." The group is still quiet. Some members are passing darting glances to each other.

The practitioner, Beverly, says, "Wait, let's hold on a minute. I think we need to know how all the other members feel about this idea for a dinner dance." Susan says to the three, "I hope you made no promises to them, because we never talked about this." Other members begin to mutter and talk to each other. The practitioner asks, "What are you all saying? Let's talk one at a time to each other." Andrew says, "I don't really want to have a dinner dance. It's too much work. I'd rather spend time going to parties that other people are giving. Besides, who said we wanted to run this program?" Nick chimes in, "But how will you do any fund-raising by going to parties? We have to run something to raise funds. That's part of our mission, also." Claire says, "I resent that, after I went out to get all this information." The practitioner says, "I don't think the issue is related to you getting the information." Another member says, "I appreciate that you did all that work, but I think there's a different issue." The practitioner asks, "Yes, can you all try to consider what the issues are right now." Andrew says, "I want to be sure that people who do things speak for all of us, and we have not decided yet."

There is a pause. Ben says to Claire, "I don't even know whether or not we should do such an event. And even if we can raise money doing it. The point is, we never talked about it together and decided to do it. You, Matt, and Jake look like you're railroading it. I don't know if you mean to do that, but that is what's happening." Hank says, "Maybe it's our fault they did all the work, because we haven't been doing much in the way of running anything social lately." Members nod in agreement.

The practitioner asks, "How can we develop plans and ideas and be sure that things happen in a direction we all want? On the other hand, how do we make certain we don't interfere with people who like to do things?" Derek says, "I don't want to prevent people from taking initiative. It just has to be brought back here for approval." Latrice says, "I think it's a question of whether or not we talk about it. Then whoever goes to investigate something knows they have to bring it back to us. No strings; that has to be the ground rule."

The practitioner says, "It looks like some of you feel things have to come back to the group for discussion first." Sondra agrees, saying, "I have an uncle who is a caterer. But I didn't have a chance to put his name in. I didn't know we were planning to have this event." The practitioner says, "That's a good point, how did we decide to do this? Did we decide?" Latrice says to the three, "You took it upon yourselves." Matt says defensively, "But you people don't ever want to do anything. Every time I try to get you to do something you back away. So, yes, we're tired of that." Claire adds, "Look, we don't have to do anything. I'm not going to work on this." Fred says, "Come on, don't be a drag." "No, really," Claire says. "Sondra, you handle the catering." The practitioner says, "I don't think that's the point. The point is how people feel when some of us try to make decisions we're not all a part of. How do you feel?" Derek says, "Well, I feel like I have no chance to get my point across." "Even if they have a good idea?" interjects the practitioner. "Right, even when it is a good idea, like this one," Derek responds.

The practitioner asks the group, "What about others, how do you feel?" Members express similar reactions. Matt, Jake, and Claire concede that they were "overzealous in getting things done." Members act to support their initiative and enthusiasm, and mechanisms are established for deciding things in the group. The group makes a great effort to move away from centering their issues on the three members. They then go on to discuss if they should run an event and what it should be.

Discussion

The three members have gone off on their own in an effort to get the group to do something they want to see done. However, they have not used the group's process to air this plan. This can be due, for example, to impatience with the democratic process or a desire for power and control. Much dissension occurs in groups where a small clique—like this one—is permitted to dominate the group.

The practitioner in this illustration was careful to support the initiatives of these members. The group needs members who are willing to take initiative and risk advancing an idea. On the other hand, she helped the members express their feelings of powerlessness and feeling controlled that resulted when others attempted to "railroad" an idea through, bypassing the process. Members could express how they felt to the subgroup. With the practitioner's help, they offered support and affirmation to them for their initiatives. Had this not happened naturally, the practitioner would have been called upon to react directly and assertively to help the group recognize the usefulness of the initiators for the process, and their own fears about being controlled.

The subgroup got the point that they would not be permitted to control the process. The group established the ground rule that actions would come back to the group for discussion and approval, and they could not rest solely with any one member or subgroup.

Democratic Norm 2: The Group
Develops Transparent Decision-Making Processes

Humanistically framed groups work on mastering the decision-making skills needed for optimal democratic functioning. Members learn how to make decisions together. They develop skill in including the thinking and feeling of members who are in the minority (Lowy, 1973), thereby expanding their ability to empathize with minority views. This enables the members to appreciate the value of and move toward compromise and consensus. The group members need to seek interpersonal ways for decision making, rather than simply voting or yielding to aggression or to opinionated members (Lowy, 1973).

Practitioner Role. The practitioner helps members empathize with minority views, moving the group to acts of compromise, a vote, or consensus (Lowy, 1973). The practitioner models an empathic group member by actively checking out members' feelings as the group moves toward making a decision. Recognizing when a preemptive or implicit decision has been made, the practitioner slows down the process, pointing out the interaction and asking the group if everyone concurs with the decision. This helps the members distinguish rapid voting or consensus from intimidation. The members' views of one another's—and the worker's—authority are of special importance for the connection between decision making and the distribution of power. A group whose members have many fears will require a great deal of help in arriving at a decision. (See Chapter 5 for more on the technique of *decision making*.)

Illustration	*Social Programming Committee*

The young professionals' social programming committee is still faced with the possibility of running a dinner dance program as a fund-raiser for the Day Camp. The three members who have been proponents of this idea—Jake, Matt, and Claire—have looked into caterers and DJs. The group has not had a chance to discuss these suggestions or to consider whether they want to hold such an event. After resolving their difficulties around the attempt to railroad the decision past the group to hold a dinner dance, members begin talking about having this type of event. Several quickly agree, "Let's have it." Others follow suit. The practitioner says, "Wait a minute, if we're going to agree on this so fast, I think we have to be sure we know what has to be done for the event and the time involved." Derek says, "I like the idea of doing this dinner dance because if we do a nice job, not only are we raising money for a good cause, but we can eventually become a center for young professionals." "Yes," agrees Claire. "Maybe we can run small informal events every Friday night." "That's a good idea, but hold it for later," says Latrice, adding, "what would we have to do to prepare for this dance?"

Andrew, who has been quiet for a while, says, "I want to know how much work there is." "So do I," chimes in Matt, "because even though I want to do it, I know we need a lot of people to get involved—invitations, Web site announcements, e-mail invitations." The practitioner asks, "What about those of you who haven't said anything? Sondra, Nick, Lauren, what are your views?" Sondra agrees that she is willing to do the work. Matt asks Sondra for information about her uncle's catering business. Nick says, "I think it is a very good idea to have a big social event, because it can be used by the group to expand the singles' program in the center." Lauren expresses her willingness to work by saying, "I've had some experiences before in another organization. It is very hard work. We all have to pitch in, otherwise it won't go right. The last time, people said they would work and didn't." Andrew says, "I'm willing to do work, but we need to have some people to coordinate." The other members agree. Andrew suggests that Claire, Matt, and Jake chair the event. More agreement follows. Jake reminds the group, "But you can't get mad at us for doing things." "No, we won't—we'll be glad," says Latrice, laughing.

Discussion

This group has already gone through a process of establishing that power has to be distributed among the members. Now they have to deal with the decision itself about whether to hold an event. Members quickly agree that they want to undertake one. The practitioner is mindful when she asks them to be certain they want the event, that there is work to do, and that making a decision also involves delegating tasks and recognizing the responsibilities that the decision entails.

In doing this, the practitioner reaches for everyone's opinions and support for the decision. In asking for the participation of the quieter members, the practitioner further ensures that all opinions about the decision come to the surface. Several members talk about the jobs to be done, and there appears to be a consensus about the program.

As the group considers aspects of the event, it becomes apparent that several members have conceived of the event as the forerunner of an institutionalized young professionals program for the community center. These members' views provide innovative direction for the group's purpose. Finally, by inviting the quiet members to offer their opinions, the practitioner helps them to examine further options, including the issues of division of labor and leadership. The members' suggestion that the three originators of the plan chair the event is happily accepted by the group in a spirit of collaboration and mutuality.

Democratic Norm 3: The Norm Fostering Freedom to Choose How or When to Change Rather Than Being Coerced

Implicit in group life is the movement toward change. The process of change is difficult to discern. Trust in one another, risk, self-disclosure, and experimenting with new behavior in a context of support are part and parcel of the change process. Trust, risk, disclosure, and experimentation come about through the freedom to choose when and to what degree to express oneself in the group. While support is needed for a person to change dysfunctional behavior, coercion has no place. The group must protect its members' right to choose what, when, and how to change.

Members need to ask one another directly if they wish to go on with a topic or to stop, recognizing that confrontations can become overzealous and potentially coercive.

Practitioner Role. As members feel a desire to change their social interactions, they will require help from others. The practitioner informs the members that change involves risk and trust of others, as well as acting differently—all of which may be difficult. The practitioner also ensures the members that the what and how of change is up to each one of them. Support and help for the member will come from the group. The practitioner lets the group know that a member can stop the process if he or she is feeling pressured by its members. The practitioner must act directly to interrupt overzealous confrontations, indicating that coercion will not help others change.

Illustration	*Group for Girls Who Have Been Sexually Abused*

In a group for 12- to 14-year-old girls in a child guidance clinic who have been sexually abused, some youngsters have been taking time out to tell their stories of molestation to the others. While they do not relive the experience by embellishing the story with many details, leaving that to their individual therapy, they might recount some detail about their abuser. When this occurs, usually, members listen attentively. One member, Kathy for whom the abuse went on since she was 5 years old, has great difficulty sitting through any talk of the abuse experience. She wanders around the room. The practitioner has alternatively asked her to join the group and given her tacit and explicit permission to walk around as long as she is not disruptive to others.

In this meeting, Tanya begins by asking the practitioner, Anna, "When is Kathy going to tell us about her story?" The other girls echo the same desire. As this happens, Kathy starts to fidget and tap her marker on the table. The practitioner says, "Kathy will tell us her story when she wants to. That's how you all did that." Then she asks the group, "Kathy, Tanya, Meryl, girls, would you like snacks?" While the girls are agreeing, Anna is handing out snacks, making sure to get to Kathy and Tanya first. She then asks the group to tell Kathy how they feel after they can tell some of their story. They all say they feel better.

Anna continues, "Does everyone feel better?" Lisa says, "Yes, because you can tell your secret to everyone." Kathy—who has already finished her snack—gets up and sits on the floor playing with markers and materials, alternately fidgeting and coloring. The practitioner says, "But you don't know when you'll feel like it, or if you'll feel better, do you? Each person has a different time when you want to tell your story, isn't that right?" The girls agree. "And Kathy, I think the girls are interested in hearing more about her story." Kathy, who has stopped fidgeting now, quietly nods. Anna turns to the group and says, "But you know, it isn't fair to try to get someone to do something when they don't want to do it." "No," the girls agree to how unfair it is.

The practitioner goes on to talk about how people respect one another, "When we let each other do things at our own pace." Colleen says it is like her bad cousin who touched her, who "didn't care if I said no." "Right," Anna says, but "here we care about each other and we will try to do things that show that." Anna continues, "But I think what you're trying to say to Kathy is that you care and when she's ready to tell her story, you are all ready to hear it." "Yes, yes," was echoed. "Whenever you want, Kathy," Colleen said.

Kathy by now has stopped coloring and returned to be closer to the group. The topic changes as the girls go on to talk about making friends in school.

Discussion

The practitioner is keenly aware of how unproductive and even destructive it will be for members to pressure Kathy to tell her story before she is ready. She quickly lets the group know that Kathy will not be required to reveal more about her abuse unless she wants to.

The practitioner then intervenes with a snack to provide nurturance for the group and for Kathy, who at this moment is especially vulnerable. Kathy's fidgeting is an indication that she needs outlets for containment of feeling. Eating together while talking about this painful group process gives the girls a chance to sustain the supportive environment they have developed and to go on handling this issue.

Having the girls explain that each told her own story at her own pace is important for Kathy as well as for the others. The practitioner has, of course, noted that Kathy leaves the table when she finishes her snack. She makes an effort to let Kathy know how much the girls care about her, and that they will be receptive to her when she chooses. This reaffirmation of the group's caring for Kathy and their empathy toward her is heard by Kathy. She returns to the table as the group moves on to another topic.

Democratic Norm 4: The Group Should Provide
Opportunity for Members to Try Out Different Roles

To enable members to experiment and to take risks with new forms of behavior, they must be encouraged to develop options to assume a variety of roles. Members are to be enabled to play various roles in the group, rather than fixed or stereotypic ones. For example, members who play task roles need chances to assume maintenance roles. Initiators and organizers need to try out spontaneity and taking someone else's lead. The member who approaches interaction with bravado should try to be gentle; those that are timid should try assertive roles.

Practitioner Role. The practitioner brings role behavior to the members' conscious awareness. They are helped to examine their behavior and decide whether to modify patterns. The practitioner points out when members are viewing themselves and one another stereotypically. When the group suggests that a member change, but then fails to offer necessary support, the practitioner points out that more help for the change is needed. Role plays and other structured exercises are useful tools in helping members practice new forms of expression, and to hear various reactions to them.

Illustration	Group for Boys With Disruptive Classroom Behaviors

The boys in a group for children who have been disruptive in the classroom are talking about the ways in which their teachers are misjudging them even though they have already begun to behave better. Keith tells the group, "The other day two kids near me got into a fight in the lunchroom. My teacher immediately called 'Keith,' as if it was me who was fighting. But it wasn't!" Vincent says, "I thought it was you." Jamal says that he was told by children in the school that it was Keith and "I figured it was you." Keith starts to get angry, exhibiting his earlier behavior: "Hey, you're not fair! This group sucks!"

Paul, the practitioner, says, "Relax, Keith, we know you weren't in any fight." Paul turns to the others and asks, "Why did you think it was Keith?" Vincent says, "Because that's the kind of thing Keith does. He doesn't take anything from anybody." Keith mumbles, "I'm gonna getcha later." Paul says to Keith, "Keep cool," turns back and asks, "Come on, Jamal, why did you think it was him? Was there anything Keith has done lately that made you think that?" Jamal says, "Not lately, but that's what he's known for."

Paul says, "The group is supposed to help you guys not do things like get into fights." "Right!" says Keith, "And I didn't! But teachers and you guys think I did. You were a witness, Richie, did I hit that kid, did I?" "No, man, you didn't," says Richie. The practitioner says, "And when we expect that Keith is going to do what he always did to get in trouble, we don't give him a chance to change, and we don't even see when he did change." The group is quiet.

The practitioner goes on, asking, "How do you guys think Keith has been han-dling things lately?" After a pause, Jamal says, "Keith's been keeping out of trouble lately." "That's interesting," says Paul. "Does anyone remember Keith getting into any trouble or hitting anyone in school recently?" None of them can remember. The practitioner goes on, "Some of us did the same thing to Keith that his teacher did to him. We prejudged him. But he didn't get into the fight." Members agree.

Paul asks, "Has that happened to you recently?" Vincent says that his mother expected him not to have cleaned up his room, but he did. She yelled at him as if he hadn't, then she was surprised because when she went into the room, it was all neat. More talk ensues about how hard it is to try to be good when no one acknowledges the effort. The kids laugh and say, "Yeah, we're gonna become nerds!" The practitioner spends more time helping them think about how to deal with these inevitabilities.

Discussion

The practitioner uses the opportunity that Keith's situation presents to help members connect to how they feel when teachers and other adults expect them to misbehave when they have already incorporated a change. Keith's example is used to help the members understand the ways in which they prejudged Keith, almost forcing him to revert to earlier dysfunctional behavior. The practitioner supports Keith to prevent this from occurring.

The practitioner asks the members if they remember Keith getting into trou-ble recently. This motivates them to relate to reality, rather to imaginations and stereotypes. By doing this, the practitioner offers support to the boys and their efforts to change in spite of the conflicting messages they receive from others.

Democratic Norm 5: The Norm Providing Flexibility
in How Member Behavior Outside the Group Is Shaped
by the Standards That Guide Behavior in the Group

Norms governing behavior in the group can modify self-expression in other situations. This is especially true as the group matures, and the internal frame of reference (Garland, Jones, & Kolodny, 1973) devel-oped within the context of the group becomes part of the member's internalized interpersonal repertoire.

Members learn to trust that the newly developing milieu in the group will become a crucial vehicle that enhances autonomy and affects external interpersonal relationships in expansive ways. However, a word of caution is in order. Authoritarian member and practitioner attitudes expecting members to carry over the group's norms to their daily lives may become invasive to their lives. The group under this condition can no longer offer a chance for experimentation and risk taking. Group cohesion in this case is being used negatively to control and coerce members.

A group that becomes overly authoritarian may be afraid of behavioral relapses. They will require extra support in the meetings that will allow their new norms to carry over between meetings. Members' risk factors, group type, and group purpose also will contribute to the extent members are expected to adhere to the group's norms beyond the group meetings.

Practitioner Role. Much as helpers would like to effect change in members' behaviors, the use of group process and group cohesion to control and coerce is dangerous because it can turn into authoritarian reactions and controls. This is a practice dilemma for the practitioner and a membership dilemma for the participants. The practitioner must regularly ask the group whether the practitioner and the group are exerting authoritarian control within and outside of the group. The practitioner helps the group find ways to sustain adherence to group norms without resorting to aggressive authoritarianism for support. This sets the stage for subsequent work with the group in developing a strong support system so that members may use relationships from the group outside of meetings between sessions.

Illustration	*Teen Substance Abuse Prevention Group*

A group of teens takes part in a community center program, an important focus of which is drug and alcohol prevention. These young people are in a constant struggle with their environment; drugs are all around them. They tell of party after party, outside of the auspices of the center, where young people are using drugs and abusing alcohol.

In this meeting, Freddy comes in wound up but not easily willing to talk about what is bothering him; some members seem to know. The practitioner, Maricella, begins the effort toward doing work by asking the group as a whole, "What's been happening that you'd like to talk about today?" There is silence. People look around at each other. Ellen says she doesn't know what's going on, but that something is. Victor says, "That's for sure." The practitioner responds, "I think you'd better talk about it, because I don't think we're going to be able to get anything else done if you don't." "Go ahead, Freddy, tell her," says Bob, looking at the practitioner.

Freddy begins to tell Maricella that when he was at a party this past weekend, several of the group members were there; some were smoking pot, and several were drinking booze. He is upset: "We have a rule at the center—no drugs, no drinking—and you guys broke it." Victor says, "The rule applies to the center itself, not to what we do outside. We never come into the center smashed and you know it."

Maricella says to the group, "How do the rest of you feel about all this?" Ellen says that she's afraid of drugs and wishes they didn't use at parties. She would feel more comfortable if the kids didn't "go sneaking into the other room to smoke a joint. You all look so stupid." Freddy says, "That's why we need a rule that we don't do that stuff out of here." Victor points out that he doesn't want to be told what to do morning, noon, and night: "What I do when I leave here is my business. I won't agree to such a rule, and I'll break it anyway." "So leave the group," Freddy says. Gwen says, "Freddy, every time someone does something you don't like, you either want to make a rule or ask them to leave. You're worse than my father." Members are quiet.

The practitioner says, "I think the issue here is, how do we help one another without intruding on people's lives?" Ellen says, "I don't know because I agree with Gwen, but I'm mad at you, Victor, for smoking pot at that party." Maricella responds, "It's true, but I think we have various issues here. Freddy, you want to make rules. What bothers you about what Victor did besides that it broke your rule?" Freddy consider for a moment, and says, "He left the party, went to the other room, and hung out trying to act cool for the girls." Ellen says to Victor, "I never thought you looked cool, though."

The practitioner looks at Victor and asks, "Well, how are you reacting to this?" Victor says, "I know you're not going to like this, Maricella, but I only smoke a joint once in a while, and most likely I'm going to keep on doing that, but I will try not to do that at parties where I know my friends will be mad at me." Maricella asks, "How do others feel about what Victor said?" Sal says, "It's his right. I don't want to tell him what to do. I wouldn't want you people constantly telling me what to do." "I play by the rules in here, but out there it's a different world," Gloria chimes in. Freddy asks, "Come on, Maricella, are you mad at what Victor said?" Maricella replies, "I don't like it that you smoke anything, Victor, and I hope as we continue in this group you and everyone else who uses drugs and booze outside of the center will consider stopping. But I wouldn't want us to set up rules that won't be followed." Ellen asks, "Why not? What if we did have rules like that?" Maricella answers, "What does your imagination tell you will happen?" Ellen says that no one will follow them, and Sal adds, "We'll have enforcers who snitch." The practitioner says, "Rules provide guidelines for behavior, but they can't be used as a way of controlling people's behavior. Ultimately that's up to the individual to do what he or she thinks is best."

Discussion

In this meeting, one member was anxious about the behavior of another member who violated group rules outside of the group's auspices. To engage a group in deciding not to use drugs or alcohol ever is certainly a tempting trap for a practitioner who feels committed to young people. However, the policy of the community center regarding the use of substances on the premises, and in any agency-sponsored activities, provides the necessary guidelines and enough lee-way for the member who is learning to use the internal group norms as a frame of reference (Garland et al., 1973) outside of the group and the center. With care-ful discussion and planning, the internal frame of reference developed by the members' process of committing themselves to each other can also become applicable in the social environment.

The practitioner does not agree with Freddy's desire for rules. By letting the issue remain in the group's attention without permitting rigidity, the practitioner enabled all members, the users and the nonusers, to focus on the helping process. Victor is able to reveal in the group what he does outside of it, without worrying about disapproval leading to rigid rules.

When a group attempts to dictate the behavior of its members in all aspects of their lives, it runs the risk of losing the less rigid members; it also usually loses those members who are struggling to use the group as a frame of reference for societal behavior.

The work of this group is not complete; they are involved in a valuable process. Future efforts will have to focus on male-female relations, sexuality, and when and how the members use substances, so as to develop broader options for social interactions.

One note: If this had been a group for members dealing with addictions, the sanctions against using drugs and alcohol in and out of the group would have been quite strong, illustrating that risk factors for the members need to be considered when gauging the carry over of group norms outside of the group.

Democratic Norm 6: The Norm for Using
Collaborative Programming to Enhance Members' Needs

Unlike a traditional psychotherapy group that only meets at its appointed time, a crucial aspect of the humanistic group form is its *externality* (Papell & Rothman, 1980b), its meaningful process outside the designated time and space of the meeting room, and the potential for contacts to occur between sessions. Undertaking of a program in the group's social environment is useful to help members enhance self-determination and decision making. The many tasks and endeavors of a group's program develop members' self-determination, mastery, and new experiences. This maximizes the members' opportunities for experimentation and change. Members can work on change in the here and now of the group within external environments that are peopled by significant others.

Practitioner Role. The practitioner supports and encourages between-meeting contacts and participation in activities as a group beyond the meeting that meet members' needs for role enhancement and support. The practitioner helps the group in the development of programs through exploration and carrying out the tasks associated with the programming process (see Chapter 6 for a fuller discussion of programming).

Illustration	***Women's Breast Cancer Support Group***

A group of women who have recently been diagnosed with breast cancer has been meeting for 2 weeks. At the end of the previous meeting, the members expressed an interest in having each other's phone numbers and e-mail addresses. The practitioner asked if this was something all of them wanted, or if there was anyone who for some personal reason did not want her phone number or e-mail address on a list. One member says, "No phone calls, please." The practitioner asks, "What about e-mail?" The member notes that e-mail is fine. The practitioner says, "Don't write your phone number in at all. This way no one will make a mistake." Once agreement was received, the practitioner circulated a list, and asked if anyone could set it up, and e-mail the list with the e-mail addresses and phone numbers. Vivian quickly volunteered.

At the start of this meeting, members thanked Vivian for her e-mail with the addresses and phone number. In fact, several members have already contacted one member, Jean, during the past week. Jean was beginning chemotherapy, and Vivian and Deirdre had called her to find out how she was; the practitioner had called her, too. Jean was not present this night because she did not feel well, but said she planned to return the following week.

Sara asks Deirdre if they had been able to give Jean the name of a wig maker. Deirdre says "No, as a matter of fact, she asked me to get the name from you. I'll call her later and give it to her." Members seem pleased to have access to each other, some saying they would e-mail her, and others preferring to call. They remark how quickly they had come to feel close to each other. The practitioner comments on the utility of being able to connect outside of the meeting, and "how important it is to be able to use e-mail and phone when you want to make contact or need to talk."

As the meeting is drawing to a close, Deirdre asks the members, "Will you all come for coffee tonight? Several of us just kind of spontaneously went out last week after the group, and we'd like to go again with whomever can." The members nod that they would go tonight. Some say it's a good idea to do this all the time.

Vivian invites the practitioner who says, "Thanks so much—it's a good idea, but I have to get home. I am not necessary at all of your events beyond the meeting."

Discussion

The practitioner early on in this group's process supports the members in e-mailing and calling each other, and is careful to respect the privacy of those members who might not want their names on the list.

The practitioner asks someone to circulate the list so as to encourage the networking to occur through the group's channels and auspices rather than through hers. This encourages the group's ownership of its externality and network. The phone calls to the absent member who was in a crisis further strengthen the supportive external structures. The practitioner did not need to explicitly support the phone work; it was already happening in the process.

When the practitioner is invited to have coffee with the group, she declines. She supports the group's efforts on its own behalf by indicating that she is not a necessary part of events outside the meeting. A practitioner's participation should not and cannot be expected in all of the external events conducted by adult groups. How participation is handled is also guided by agency practice and professional judgment. The practitioner will have to be present in activities where his or her help is needed by the group.

Humanistic Value 8: People Have the Right to Question and Challenge Professionals Who Have an Authority Role in Their Lives

People who recognize the persuasive and symbolic power of the practitioner can take these factors into account and challenge his or her authority. The anxiety about violating a felt taboo (Shulman, 2006) against expressing feelings about the practitioner in the group must be overcome if members' rights are to be supported. Members are required to develop and maintain ways of directly expressing feelings, opinions, and challenges to the practitioner who should be viewed as an accountable participant with a specialized role in the group.

Democratic Norm 1: In a Humanistic Group, Members Develop Direct Ways of Expressing Reactions to the Practitioner

The direct expression of feelings toward the practitioner is necessary. It prevents the practitioner from developing, feeding, and maintaining an aura of mystique and unapproachability that keeps the members from holding the practitioner accountable. Furthermore, unexpressed concerns about the practitioner's intentions and actions go underground, coloring and masking the group's spontaneity and depth of intimate relations (Levine, 1979).

Practitioner Role. It is very important to know that the feelings members express about other helpers or authorities (Shulman, 2006) are likely to be indicative of the group's concern about the practitioner. Helping the members express reactions directly to the practitioner is important in the group's early life. It helps center the practitioner and lodges the ownership of the group with the members.

When members begin to make indirect comments about the practitioner's authority, he or she takes note of the comments and directly asks the members how they are feeling about the practitioner's behavior in the group. Members may also have reactions and concerns about the perceived power and influence of the practitioner. It is valuable to note that some look to the practitioner for approval when they speak, while others seem consistently to ignore the practitioner's input. Bringing these behaviors to awareness helps further the group's understanding of its reactions to the practitioner's power (Shulman, 2006).

The practitioner's encouraging members' negative reactions, nondefensively accepting them, and responding with honesty shows members that the practitioner is fallible and values their criticism. It is of considerable help to the group not to preempt the full expression of criticism of the goals set early on by the practitioner by hasty efforts to recontract with them. This supports further examination and discussion of the practitioner's role.

Establishing a norm that the group may engage in dialogue with the practitioner about the meaning of his or her actions solidifies the egalitarian distribution of power, demystifies the practitioner's role, and sets the condition for trusting the practitioner as a caring professional with a stake in the group.

| Illustration | Latency Age Children of Divorce Group |

The 9- to 11-year-old children in a group convened to help deal with their parents' divorce have been talking about seeing the parent they don't live with during their Christmas vacations. One child, Alex, excitedly talks about going to a football game with his father and uncle. Teddy is quiet, and looks like he is pouting. Bill, the practitioner, asks Teddy, "How come you look so glum? Is something wrong?" Teddy says that he is confused because he wanted to spend Christmas with his mother and cousins, not his father: "I want to see Daddy, but later on." Bill asks, "Did you tell your mom or your dad this?" He says that he didn't, that "they won't understand."

Bill asks the group, "Have you had this happen?" Gary says yes. Pamela tells Bill that when she told her father she wanted to see him Christmas Eve and then go back to her mother's house he got mad and hurt, but then he was okay, and she is going to see them both: "They can change their plans a little." Teddy asks, "Bill, do you think I should tell my dad?" Bill asks, "Why wouldn't you, Teddy?" "He'll get mad at me," Teddy answers. "But remember what we said about when someone is angry at you?" asks Bill. Teddy says, "It doesn't mean they don't love you." The practitioner continues, "So you can take a chance and know that if you tell your parents, they'll still love you." Teddy seems comforted by this. After more support and talk, he agrees that he will discuss this with his mom first. The practitioner asks, "Teddy, do you want me to help you tell your mom when she comes to pick you up?" "Would you do that?" Teddy asks. "I would, if that's what you wanted," is Bill's reply. Teddy thinks about it and says "yes."

Gary asks, "Is that what you do, do you tell our parents about us?" Bill says, "Remember, when we started the group I said I wouldn't tell something unless you wanted me to and knew about it, except if there was some special danger I had to tell about." The group goes on to talk about how they could get Bill to intervene with their teachers, too. Eleanor asks, "Like when they don't like what I do, or when I get in trouble, would you talk to my teachers?" Bill says "I would if you wanted me to." He then asks her if "something special happened with your teacher." "No, not lately," Eleanor replies and giggles. Bill responds, "You just want to be sure that if something does happen you'll have someone on your side?" Eleanor agrees. "We're lucky you're not a teacher, because we can get to call you Bill," she says, "and you will sit on the floor with us and let us say bad words, too!" The children laugh.

The practitioner asks, "How about when I get angry with you in our group?" The children talk about how he's not "mean", adding that "we know you do it for our own good." He says, "Okay, but just remember, you can tell me if I get mean. Getting angry is different than getting mean. So you can say, 'Bill, you're being mean,' okay?" The children agree. Bill asks again, "Or if I do something else that you don't like?" The children agree once more.

Discussion

This illustration demonstrates the practitioner's overall accountability to the members. The practitioner responds to the individual members' needs, then reminds them that he will not betray their confidence except when someone is in danger. This seems to assure them, and they focus on the various ways in which the practitioner can and does use himself. Some see him as an advocate, a person who is on their side when they get into trouble. Others experience him as a nurturer who lets them be familiar with him on a first-name basis and by allowing them to say things they cannot say elsewhere.

Recognizing that early in the meeting the issue was raised about parents' expressions of anger with the children as a sign of possible rejection, the practitioner wonders how the children experience him when he is angry with them. They discuss "meanness," a typical concern and reaction children have to people in authority who try to control them. The practitioner shows them respect by telling them he wants to know when they think he is acting mean toward them. Furthermore, he gives them permission to tell him if there are others things they don't like. This will have to be picked up further along in the group's life.

For the time being, however, the members have been given full opportunities to express negative and positive feelings. This has great importance both in their relationships with the practitioner and with their parents, with whom they are struggling to express pent-up and confusing feelings.

❖ SUMMARY

In this chapter, the norms that are particularly effective in operationalizing the values of freedom of speech, freedom of expression, differences as enriching, freedom of choice, and the practitioner's accountability to the group were presented.

The following norms were discussed: the norm maintaining an open communication system without reliance on a narrow ideology; the norm fostering the expression of feeling, and tempering premature self-disclosure; the norm fostering a broad spectrum of deviance rather than conformity; the norm for an open role system rather than one built on stereotypes; the norm supporting the equal distribution of power; the norm providing flexibility in how member behavior outside of the group is shaped by the standards that guide behavior in the group; the norm for collaborative programming; and the norm for direct expression of reactions to the authority of the practitioner. Specific skills the practitioner uses to effect these norms were discussed, and practice illustrations demonstrating the development of each norm in a group were presented.

Given the information offered in these first two chapters, it is safe to assert that the confluence of these values and norms creates a humanistic and egalitarian ethos that gives special form to interpersonal expression within the group milieu, as well as out of it. Participation in such a group can provide a corrective social and emotional experience. As members engage with one another, the practitioner, and significant others, their interactions combine the special features of difference along with cohesion.

The next chapter shows the evolution of group life as patterned and sequenced flows of feeling and work. It looks at the unique feelings the members and practitioner experience during the group's stages of development, highlighting effective practitioner stances and strategies for each stage. How humanistic values and democratic norms are reflected during the group's cycle of development are evidenced.

Table 2.1   Further Values, Norms, and the Practitioner Role

Value 5: People Have the Right to Freedom of Speech and Freedom of Expression

1. **The norm for maintaining an open communication system without reliance on narrow ideology**

   Practitioner role
   - Encourages members to speak directly to each other
   - Helps weave flexible communication network
   - Enables expression and acceptance of unformulated thoughts, feelings, and ideas
   - Helps members take risks

2. **The norm for guiding open expression of feeling while tempering premature self-disclosure**

   Practitioner role
   - Is cognizant of issues related to stage theory; may or may not encourage self-disclosure
   - Enables and models sharing about here and now
   - Helps members take risks

Value 6: People Who Are Different Enrich One Another

1. **The norm for members to foster each other's diversity rather than push for conformity**

   Practitioner role
   - Examines own feelings related to deviance and difference
   - Models openness to dissident and unpopular views and feelings
   - Protects individual's rights
   - Supports understanding of difference in feelings, ideas, and values

Value 7: People Have the Right to Freedom of Choice to Determine Their Own Destinies

1. **The norm for fostering distribution of power in the group**

   Practitioner role
   - Encourages group to examine decision-making process
   - Enables and teaches flexibility in leadership

2. **The norm for developing transparent decision-making processes**

   Practitioner role
   - Uses decision-making techniques to clarify issues
   - Reaches for feelings of intimidation

(Continued)

Table 2.1 (Continued)

3. **The norm for fostering freedom to choose how or when to change rather than being coerced**

Practitioner role
- Explores risks involved in change
- Interrupts overzealous confrontations
- Enables acceptance of change goals as member's choice
- Checks out members' feelings: "Do you want to go on?"

4. **The norm for providing opportunity for members to try out different roles**

Practitioner role
- Encourages and enables flexible role taking
- Helps group scrutinize its need to lock member(s) into self-fulfilling prophecies and stereotypic behaviors

5. **The norm for providing flexibility in how member behavior outside the group is shaped by the standards for behavior in the group**

Practitioner role
- Does not permit group process to be used coercively
- Helps group develop support outside meeting

6. **The norm for using cooperative programming to enhance members' needs**

Practitioner role
- Helps group develop programs that are culturally sensitive and heighten mutual understanding
- Helps group understand use of program to enable ownership and meet needs

Value 8: **People Have the Right to Challenge Professionals Who Have an Authority Role in Their Lives**

1. **The norm for directly expressing reactions to the practitioner**

Practitioner role
- Recognizes that sharing about difference will be shallow without focus on group's issues with worker's authority
- Enables direct sharing of feeling to worker
- Reaches for indirect cues relates to worker's authority/power
- Reflects group's dependency issues with worker
- Reflects group and worker's differences
- Shares stake in group

3

Stage Themes of Group Development

To gain a fuller understanding of group interactions as members move toward and away from humanistic and democratic forms of relationship and work, the practitioner views the changing process through the lens of stage theories of group development. Many classic and contemporary practice theories consider the members' reactions, behaviors, and concomitant themes in terms of stages in the group's development (Bennis & Shepard, 1962; Garland, Jones, & Kolodny, 1973; Sarri & Galinsky, 1985; Toseland & Rivas, 2004). The stage model of change proposes that particular reactions emerge among the group members in patterned and sequenced forms. Understanding these patterns offers the practitioner a framework for taking professional action in relation to the salient themes presented in the group's evolution.

❖ OVERVIEW OF STAGE THEORY

The T-Group Model and the Boston Model

The T-group model described by Bennis and Shepard (1962) is a classic phase theory for group development that presented a new discovery, the unique and systematic analysis by the members, and the practitioner-trainer of the group's here and now (Herrold, 1965). Designed to study the group's interpersonal workings and dynamics, the T-group model advanced understanding of how groups develop and how members resolve their relationships with authority and with each other within the confines of the meetings.

The Boston University model delineated by Garland and colleagues (1973) was an early social work model of group development that continues to provide an important anchor for our understanding of life in the social work group. This model was developed through observation of adolescent groups by examining interactions in and out of the meeting room, as members participated in varied programs, took on varied group and life roles, and engaged with social workers. The model was also used by their colleagues with other group populations (Garland & Frey, 1976).

In describing the T-group, Bennis and Shepard (1962) posit the two distinct themes of power and love as central themes for group life that run through the stages. They identify two phases in group development: Phase I—Dependence (Authority Relations), and Phase II—Interdependence (Personal Relations).

Phase I comes about from members' reactions to the power and authority of the trainer or practitioner. Phase I contains three subphases: In Subphase 1—Dependence-Flight, the members anxiously look to the trainer for approval and direction. In Subphase 2—Counterdependence-Fight, while overtly ignoring the trainer, the members are covertly paying attention and at the same time vying among themselves for power. In Subphase 3—Resolution-Catharsis, finally, "There is a sudden increase in alertness and tension" (Bennis, 1964, p. 258) as they gather the strength to challenge the actual and illusionary position of the trainer.

Phase II concentrates on the quality of relationship among the members. It contains three subphases: In Subphase 4—Enchantment-Flight, the group views itself as a romantic icon to be worshiped, not challenged, whereas in Subphase 5—Disenchantment-Fight, they become disillusioned and frustrated by the members' foibles and withdrawals. In Subphase 6—Consensual Validation, members accept the group as a realistic work group with the task of providing feedback to the members about their roles in the here and now of group life (Bennis, 1964).

The Boston model identifies five stages of growth or "problem levels through which members and the group as a whole pass in the course of development" (Garland et al., 1973, p. 29). Through this lens, the authors posit that a significant and fundamental theme in group life is closeness. Each of these stages has a salient frame of reference through which the members view the group, and the closeness and distance within it.

In Stage 1—Preaffiliation, where members show an approach-avoidance conflict related to closeness, the frame of reference is societal. In Stage 2—Power and Control, since norms are ambiguous and in flux, the frame of reference is transitional; here members vie for leadership positions with each other and the practitioner. In Stage 3—Intimacy, the frame of reference is familial, with members referring to each other with reminiscences of significant others in their lives. Stage 4—Differentiation highlights an internal frame of reference wherein members exhibit more clarity about and deeper connection to the group's goals. The frame of reference in Stage 5—Separation now becomes a newly developed societal one as the members use growth gained in the group to guide future action. It appears that Stages 1 and 2 center most on the development of democratic mutual aid processes, and Stages 3, 4, and 5 focus on the achievement of group purpose.

In the T-group model, the reaction of the group to authority is viewed as a basic emotional underpinning of small group life. In the Boston model, though power and control is clearly acknowledged and dealt with as a stage, it is viewed more as an obstacle to closeness than as a separate theoretical entity. Thus, power conflicts in the social work group may not be encouraged in full-blown forms to the extent the authority rebellion may be encouraged and analyzed in the T-group. This is an important observation to ponder and experiment with, because the substance of the humanistic group involves helping members and the group to develop empowerment abilities and processes.

Beginning, Middle, and Ending Phases

The change process in a group is intertwined with the beginning, middle, and ending phases of the helping process described in generic social work practice theories. The beginning phase has to do with initial trust, authority, responsibility, and leadership. The "normative crisis" represents the group's affect and often tumultuous behavior in the face of ambiguity regarding which rules and behavioral expectations will be required and agreed upon in the group, and how agreement will be reached. Identified as the turning point when members struggle to develop rules governing their behaviors in the group, the "normative crisis" (Bennis & Shepard, 1962; Garland et al., 1973) leads to a consideration of standards the group will use to guide their future interactions and work.

The middle phase is considered to be the time when the members recognize and use each other's talents and strengths to work on meeting their goals. These goals may be limited ones in a short-term group, and comprehensive in a long-term one. Members learn to accept and trust each other without harboring exaggerated views of the intimacy of the group's relationships and the power of some group members. They learn that they may not necessarily always agree with or like all of the members all of the time.

The ending phase of the group signifies separation and reflecting on accomplishments. Ending reactions should not become debilitating, even though episodes of fear, avoidance, and regression are noted (Garland et al., 1973) during this final step in meeting members' goals and moving on to other ones.

Group Process and Group Purpose

Process in a group refers to the changing relationships the members and practitioner have with one another (Garvin, 1997). *Purpose* represents the material reasons the members are together. Without a process rooted in humanistic values and democratic standards, the group's purpose cannot be achieved. Process and purpose are inextricably linked. In the group's beginning phase, while purpose develops, it is its process rather than its purpose that requires emphasis and development (Lang, 1981). During the middle phase, purpose is highlighted and worked on in greater depth within the context of the processes of democratic mutual aid. Thus, as members work on meeting their mutual objectives, the means they have developed for democratic interpersonal relationships are used.

Stage Theory and Member Differences

The change process in the group is also related to members' differing capabilities. During the stages of the group's growth, each member brings different interpersonal abilities to meetings. The members' abilities for interaction in the group are a function of their physical, political, emotional, familial, and group experiences. In the group, the person will have to develop relationships and find common ground with others such as similar life situations and shared emotions. He or she will delineate differences, work on personal issues and goals, and assist others and the group in working on their issues and goals. The effort expended on developing relationships rather than on working on objectives will vary in relation to the members' interpersonal skills, leadership efforts, and the extent to which domination, shyness, and stereotyping are overcome in the group.

The typical life-stage characteristics that go along with the maturational processes of childhood and adolescence, adulthood, and aging— along with physiological disorders—will affect members' capabilities in the group's life (Lang, 1972). Certain long-standing psychosocial factors may inhibit full forms of participation; some are the result of cultural and political stereotyping and stigmatization. These may limit some members' full capacities for interaction and participation because of anticipatory reactions and externally imposed inhibitions. Other limitations are internalized by-products of the members' experiences in primary family groupings that now affect self-esteem and expectations that relationships are ones of domination, victimization, or persecution. Yet, whatever course individual development has taken, members are capable of growth or modification of internal and external states through the group process, though timing and pace will vary (Chapter 9 delineates how to assess individual members' behaviors within the context of stage themes).

Membership involves sharing some commonalities and identification with certain of the values and goals of the belonging system, organization, or entity, and for the small group, membership must include having face-to-face interaction, common goals, and affective bonds (Homans, 1950; Olmstead, 1959). The practitioner is a member of the group, albeit with a unique professional role and ethical responsibility to guide and direct the process. He or she will be part of the group's affective relationships, and having a professional stake in the process and purpose, the practitioner will use that stake to instill similar regard for the group within the members.

Stage Themes and Practitioner Reactions to Members

Stage themes are the patterned and sequenced reactions of the members to the group and practitioner. Certain stage themes are salient at different points in the process. They have been defined to shed light on practitioner and member transactions as the group develops experiences to meet members' goals, and they are presented below. The social work stage theory (Garland et al., 1973) and T-group theory of group dynamics (Bennis & Shepard, 1962) have been used to identify these themes. As a response to the group's enactments within stage-related themes, the practitioner experiences several generalizable theme-centered reactions in and about the group. Stage themes help guide the practitioner by highlighting interpersonal issues and feelings the practitioner will experience while trying to engage with and assist the members. This knowledge should help the group worker examine feelings and other perceptions, learning to use them as a barometer for understanding the group's collective experience as well as his or her own.

The practitioner's personal-life situations can either become a useful part of group life or interfere in members' efforts. The practitioner must work with whatever emotions are stirred up by the different phases of group life. While personal in content, many of these reactions are not merely idiosyncratic countertransferences, but a direct response to stage-theme-related issues, a vital aspect of his or her membership in the group, and a necessary part of the group experience. For example, when a practitioner feels left out of the group that is not responding directly to intervention or direction, the hurt feelings are not necessarily related to a personal history of fearing exclusion but a result of the group's need to overtly ignore the worker's comments to minimize the worker's importance.

In the beginning phase, the practitioner is concerned with being accepted and heard as a capable worker with a professional stake in the group. The practitioner is part of and contributes to the resolution of the normative crisis by presenting values and norms that yield humanistic and democratic relationships. During the middle phase, the practitioner is concerned with how to be helpful while the members receive, react to, and use feedback, interpretation, and confrontation from the members and the practitioner. Attention also centers on how to react to the different ways in which the members use the practitioner's contributions.

Stage Themes: Humanism and Democracy

This sequence of stage themes also serves as a significant conceptual mechanism for distinguishing the difference between process in response to a humanistic group work method and process in a nonhumanistic one. All group approaches reflect upon the values and techniques of the method used, as well as those of the practitioner. It is the philosophical position of this book that humanistic values are more fully representative of the nature and interpersonal potential of people than other configurations of values. Thus, a humanistic approach is better able to achieve fuller forms of democratic and differentiated interaction among members. Approaches with authoritarian or ill-defined values stifle the potential of full group development and do not allow each member to make active use of the group, assume leadership, share power, follow others' leads, and identify with many different people. These groups evolve structures and dynamics that, at best, only partially realize their potential. At worst, groups that are developed along authoritarian lines of relationship may become destructive to members and significant others. A group with an authoritarian character cannot achieve a full form of interpersonal and emotional differentiation, because its cohesion centers on attitudes and acts of domination and submission.

As the practitioner employs the values, norms, and skills of the method, stage theme reactions occur among the members about the expectations of membership in such a group. The resolutions of the members' thematic issues are viewed as evolving in some significant ways from the practitioner's use of humanistic method. For example, the practitioner's work with the members' perceptions of his or her impact and control of group process is a central issue. By opening up and facilitating discussion of the practitioner's behavior and role, the practitioner chooses to demystify the role, enabling members to assume leadership and share power. While groups of many types— whatever the members' values and norms—go through stages and reaction states, what is distinctive in the humanistic method is that members focus on their abilities to evolve and monitor their own processes in a manner of respect and shared leadership. By comparison, utilitarian or authoritarian values stimulate different interactions and present a different picture of the practitioner to the members.

❖ STAGE THEMES OF GROUP DEVELOPMENT

Juxtaposing the stages defined in the Boston model against the phases and subphases of the T-group model yields several newer ways of viewing these. The Boston model does not focus on the ways in which the group deals with and resolves its authority crisis with the practitioner. The phenomena described in the Boston model's power and control stage are delineated into two subphases in the T-group model (Counterdependence-Fight and Resolution-Catharsis). The stage of Intimacy in the Boston model is similar to the Enchantment-Flight in the T-group model. While the Boston model clearly delineates separation processes at the group's end, these are absent completely in the T-group model (and may be one reason why participants in traditional T-groups had difficulty after the groups ended).

The stage themes developed and described below are an effort to integrate the Boston model and the T-group model, in order to highlight those important processes in the humanistic group that can be used to inform practice:

Stage Theme 1: "We're Not in Charge"

Stage Theme 2: "We Are in Charge"

Stage Theme 3: "We're Taking You On"

Stage Theme 4: Sanctuary

Stage Theme 5: "This Isn't Good Anymore"

Stage Theme 6: "We're Okay and Able"

Stage Theme 7: "Just a Little Longer"

Table 3.1 clarifies how these themes have emerged from the Boston model and the T-group model.

Table 3.1   Stage Themes: Boston Model and T-Group Model

Stage Themes	*Boston Model*	*T-Group Model*
Stage Theme 1: *"We're Not in Charge"*	Stage 1 Preaffiliation	Phase I Dependence (Authority Relations) Subphase 1 Dependence-Flight
Stage Theme 2: *"We Are in Charge"*	Stage 2 Power and Control	Subphase 2 Counterdependence-Fight
Stage Theme 3: *"We're Taking You On"*	Stage 2 Power and Control	Subphase 3 Resolution-Catharsis
Stage Theme 4: *Sanctuary*	Stage 3 Intimacy	Phase II Interdependence (Personal Relations) Subphase 4 Enchantment-Flight
Stage Theme 5: *"This Isn't Good Anymore"*	Stage 4 Differentiation	Subphase 5 Disenchantment-Flight
Stage Theme 6: *"We're Okay and Able"*	Stage 4 Differentiation	Subphase 6 Consensual Validation
Stage Theme 7: *"Just a Little Longer"*	Stage 5 Separation	Subphase 6 Consensual Validation

The following material is an explication of each theme (further details about how the models have been integrated can be found in Glassman & Kates, 1983). Humanistic values and democratic norms are identified for each stage theme. The practitioner's issues and key roles are highlighted, along with practice illustrations.

Stage Theme 1: "We're Not in Charge"

Boston Model Stage 1	T-Group Stage	Relevant Values and Norms
Preaffiliation	Dependence-Flight	Right to belong, to be heard

As members begin meeting, they approach one another with varying degrees of caution. The members look to the practitioner to provide them with clues and direction about how to respond (Bennis & Shepard, 1962). While there are approach and avoidance feelings and actions (Garland et al., 1973), members' comments are specifically designed to gain approval and direction from the practitioner "whose reactions to comments are surreptitiously watched" (Bennis, 1964, p. 257). The members look to the practitioner to understand the meaning of his or her interventions, interactions, feelings, attitudes, and nonverbal signs. Members wish to find out if they will receive approval from the practitioner, given group members' proclivities to imbue the person in the leadership role with power over them. This desire to gain approval from the practitioner symbolically represents the members' desire to gain approval from one another as well.

Practitioner Issues

A committed professional is dedicated to the success of the group as a productive environment and experience for each member. The practitioner tries to figure out a variety of approaches to members and the group that will help sustain investment in the group experience. The practitioner has most likely put in much social and emotional effort in forming the group. Thus, it should be no surprise that the practitioner becomes professionally and personally invested in the success of the group, measuring success by the members' willingness to return, to try it out, and to make tenuous commitments. The practitioner is at risk of interpreting members' inabilities to develop commitment as professional failure in working with the group rather than as a normal stage reaction.

The practitioner may avoid or resist the members' dependence on him or her and not give the help and support necessary for them to make their initial commitments to the group. In this way, the practitioner defends against experiencing the anxiety of responsibility for the group, replacing it with rationalizations disguised as professional jargon. Feeling the group to be a failure, the practitioner avoids responsibility with phrases like "This group is yours" and offers the members minimal visions of their future together. The values and norms of the humanistic group method lead the practitioner into interactions that recognize and empathize with the members' needs for attention, involvement, and direction with the practitioner as well as one another.

Practitioner Role

The practitioner helps to identify needs and interests that are held in common, linking individuals' reasons for being in the group to those of other members. The practitioner points out that whether or not needs dovetail, as members of the group they can help one another to be effective, and that mutually supportive efforts of this kind are ubiquitous in all kinds of situations. By inviting trust (Garland et al., 1973), and encouraging the expression of feelings toward and ideas about the practitioner and the group, the practitioner paves the way for members to achieve eventual autonomy from the perceived and actual authority of the practitioner, and a partnership in mutual aid that can include the practitioner.

The practitioner recognizes the feared "taboo" (Shulman, 2006) about addressing latent interactions (i.e., that can be "read between the lines") and sets the stage for future discussions about latent and manifest aspects of the group's process. This is done within a context of humanistic values and democratic norms, so as not to permit damage to the group, or to a member, that may result from anomic or authoritarian group situations. For example, saying that "I hear some of you have some concern about how much you will be asked to share here" helps members accept their cautious reactions as vital. Recognizing the members' caution and couched reactions to the practitioner's authority as a necessity for the group's development helps all to discern the value of caution for their autonomy, rather than suggesting that these are deviant affects. The practitioner participates in and listens to discussions about people such as those in teacher and parent roles or prior helpers (Bennis & Shepard, 1962; Shulman, 2006). By asking if the members are fearful that the practitioner will do something that will make them uncomfortable, and by not defending other professionals, the practitioner allows the group the opportunity to openly criticize his or her expression in the group.

Illustration	*Frail, Blind Elderly in a Nursing Home*

A group of blind, frail elderly persons is getting started in the nursing home. This is their second meeting. Rodney, the worker, went to every room along with one of the nurses and brought the members to the meeting. Sara and Louis put up a battle about coming, saying they were tired or not feeling well, but with some encouragement agreed to come. The practitioner says, "If you start to feel like you want to leave, I'll have one of the aides bring you back to your room, okay?" Ruth, Marion, Wilbur, and the others agreed to come willingly. Several of the people are wheelchair bound as well.

After going over introductions to remind everyone where the others are sitting and how they sound, the practitioner notes that last week they said they wanted to talk about how some of them would like to have readers and taped books to help them spend their leisure time. Wilbur raises the fact that some of the residents and the nursing staff are not so considerate of them as blind people: "We don't get included in activities because there isn't always someone to help us get there." The practitioner acknowledges Wilbur by name, wondering if this is a common problem. Some agree. Then there is a silence.

Sara says, "None of these groups work out. Last year we had a group for blind people, and they didn't always ask us if we needed help getting to the meeting. If they don't come up we just plain forget." Some laughter ensues. The practitioner says, "Thank you, Sara. Yes, we will come to get you, no matter what time or effort it takes, whether you need it or not. But are there other things you are afraid I might do that won't help you? What does everyone think?" Louis says that in the previous group, "We talked about leisure time and taped books, but it never came to anything." The practitioner asks, "Louis, do you want me to help you carry out your plans and wishes?" He agrees, and Ruth chimes in, "Yes, because we can't always do what we say we want to do." "I understand, Ruth, that it's hard when you have things you want and can't get without help, because you can't see," Rodney says. "Right," Wilbur agrees. "And if that wasn't bad enough, we're old too," Sara says with humor.

Discussion

The practitioner carefully arranged for the members to be transported to the meeting room. This represents a commitment to the group and a recognition that members will be more ambivalent than the practitioner and need to feel expected and welcomed in an atmosphere that considers their limitations and frailties. He also accepts their ambivalence by encouraging them to attend while at the same time promising to have them returned to their rooms if they do not feel well.

The practitioner takes ample time for the introductions, cognizant of the fact that these members are blind and have to develop voice recognition. This communicates respect and consideration for the unique situations of the members. This also permits the group to talk about feeling left out of activities conducted by other staff who, by implication, are not as considerate. The practitioner affirms this commitment to bring them to the group, "whatever it takes."

Rodney focuses the group's attention on the development of future strategies to meet their needs as blind elderly in this nursing facility, using their needs and interests to offer them a vision of the future of the group. Having heard their unhappiness with the previous worker and with the nursing home staff, he uses the opportunity to focus on how this group might feel about and deal with him. He asks them if they are afraid he will do something they do not like.

Stage Theme 2: "We Are in Charge"

Boston Model Stage 2	T-Group Stage	Values and Norms
Power and Control	Counterdependence-Flight	Open decision making
		Accept differences
		Open role system
		Open communication

Now members are attempting to talk to and connect more with each other and less with the practitioner. Within this, varying intensities of arguing among members and assertions of will to set directions and establish agendas will surface. Some may withdraw from the fight, being fearful of taking sides or apparently uninterested in having power. Some will admonish the practitioner to take sides or take control of some members of the group as a whole. Some members experience the open and permissive atmosphere of the humanistic and democratic group as a failure on the part of the practitioner to take charge. Having in their estimations found the practitioner unable to exercise skill or use power properly, some members will move to exclude the practitioner by ignoring his or her interventions or comments. It is through the ensuing normative crisis that the group will develop *norms* about how they will interact together in this group with the practitioner. The standards that ensue come about as the members and the practitioner relate to the practitioner's use of social group work method. In developing group norms, the members will move from relying on the frame of reference that is external to the group experience, with impersonal norms, to an internal frame of reference, with interpersonally oriented group norms (Garland et al., 1973). The ambiguity of norms—as the group attempts to develop new ones—creates degrees of anxiety for members, contributing to the struggle for stability and control. As the members struggle with leadership, attempting to examine some of the difficult behaviors and emerging norms, they gather strength and develop mutuality.

Practitioner Issues

Being ignored or not responded to when intervening or trying to engage the group may leave the practitioner feeling threatened, tense, and ineffectual. Also, the conflicts for power, control, and leadership can create anxiety when a practitioner has difficulty accepting power struggles, especially those that focus on the practitioner as part of the problem and the resolution. The normative crisis the members experience (and the concomitant anxiety that results, followed by skirmishes and more anxiety) challenges the practitioner's ability to handle and deal with the powerful and stark ambiguity of this portion of the members' experiences with one another. When he or she does not recognize the significance of these dynamics, the practitioner may overcontrol the fighting in the group by asserting authority, or he or she may abdicate too much responsibility in order to placate the group.

Practitioner Role

While not preempting the conflict, the practitioner finds ways to help the members examine the ensuing process. Herein, the practitioner is helped by the explicit values and norms of the humanistic group work model, which hold differences and give-and-take in high regard. Pointing out the frustrations inherent in this struggle for control, stability, and standards of behavior facilitates the group's forward movement. The practitioner responds to the members' testiness—brought about by the ambiguity of norms—by nondefensively pointing out to the group that they can work on developing norms about how they will work together along with the practitioner, rather than excluding the practitioner or expecting that the practitioner will regulate their process for them. The prototypic response to the practitioner at this juncture ("You will make the rules anyway") must be met with an invitation to the group to explore the meaning of these opinions. By clarifying observations and pointing out events in the process to the members, the practitioner helps them to move to a more direct challenge of the practitioner's role.

Illustration	*Boys Group New to Residential Program*

A group of young teenage boys, new to a residential program, are having difficult with their young adult female worker, Lois. In this, the fourth meeting, they are misbehaving all over the place, often getting up to go around the room to slap or poke each other; so far, none of it is dangerous.

The practitioner gets them to settle down. They begin to jokingly make sexual innuendos, while making sure not to look to Lois for her reaction. The practitioner notices that when she is looking in one direction a couple of boys on the other side try to steal a glance at her. Several boys—Jimmy, who tries to control people when he gets uptight, and Leon, who is more quiet—try to switch topics, saying that "we're not supposed to say dirty words here." The practitioner asks the group, "I wonder what all this sex talk is all about. Is it that you want to have a chance to talk about sex in this group?" The boys laugh and snort. A couple of them, Frank and Terry, get up and go over to Leon, poking at his backpack. Jimmy indignantly gets up and tells them to "sit down and shut the fuck up." Terry says, "Who the hell made you boss?" "No one," Jimmy says, "but you can't do that here." "Who says I can't?" asks Terry.

A verbal battle ensues for a couple of minutes, and then a fight breaks out among several of the boys. (Lois determines that the boys are not throwing hard punches; they are half making believe.) However, this causes Lois to have to get up and physically go over into the midst of three of them and quietly say to "stop fighting, and sit down."

After a few moments, they respond to her and sit down. Lois suggests that "there are other ways to express how you feel here besides fighting. What do you think? Maybe we can talk about things in here that are too scary to talk about outside, even though you're male and I'm female."

Discussion

The group of boys is dealing with the newness of the total residential environment and being away from their familiar surroundings, whatever their limitations. While an assortment of societal and familial rules have governed their lives, many of their circumstances have been dysfunctional for them, providing at best a confused frame of reference. In this new facility, the boys are testing and trying to make sense out of the rules for the sake of their own survival. They place the practitioner, a woman with all these boys, in the position of having to absorb their challenges and tests; they watch her responses carefully.

Lois appropriately says nothing about the curse words. This is a group whose rules are in flux; they want to know if and how she will tolerate their sense of "boyness." However, when the group begins to fight physically, the practitioner intervenes, using her adult authority to limit their behavior. Once they sit down, the boys are controlled. This allows her to approach them nonpunitively, bypassing discussion of their behavior and asking them to figure out if they can talk about "scary" things, even though she is a woman.

Stage Theme 3: "We're Taking You On"

Boston Model Stage 2	T-Group Stage	Values and Norms
Power and Control	Resolution-Catharsis	Worker's accountability to group
		Equalizing power

The task of relating to, challenging, and joining with the position of the practitioner represents the group's foremost collective enterprise to this point in the process. This effort entails gathering the momentum and strength the members have been developing to collectively react to and engage with the practitioner. The members must find out about the practitioner's intentions by posing direct questions such as, "What are you doing here? How much will you share here? In what ways are you like us?" They need to develop the emotional capabilities to hear the practitioner's initial reactions without being overwhelmed by the fears, projections, and screens that have dominated their perception of the practitioner's role up to now.

This type of interaction sets the stage for learning how to include the practitioner and his or her technical skill and expertise in working on the group's purpose. The intense focusing of the group's attention on dealing with the practitioner's authority—in an almost voyeuristic way—offers the fullest arena for the members to observe the group's latent themes and processes as they strengthen their bonds.

Practitioner Issues

The practitioner, in anticipation of the group's challenge to his or her authority, may develop fears of being controlled by the group. Underneath doubts about his or her competency and skill is the feeling that another, more skilled practitioner would not be found to be at fault. The practitioner might try to get the members to bypass the challenge by asking them to reconsider their goals, rather than to engage with the practitioner about his or her role. Or the practitioner might attempt to direct the members to redefine how they want the practitioner to behave, thereby indirectly causing the members to reconsider their own relationships while in actuality avoiding engagement with the practitioner. Such moves deflect the members from the emotional imperative and social necessity the challenge to authority holds: that of learning about their perceptions of and reactions to the authority role, as well as their own roles in furthering democratic group process and purpose.

Practitioner Role

When the challenge comes, it is helpful to assist members in exploring their feelings about the practitioner. This enables the group to develop its here-and-now awareness of the practitioner role. This process helps remove projections and screens that have presented two-way communication and begins to permit the members to use the practitioner's technical expertise, life experience, and feelings. The practitioner, while helping members to look at their reactions, also has to reveal his or her own reactions to the group as a member who takes part in the process—not as an outsider. Because the humanistic method is postulated on members' rights and responsibilities to question those in authority, the practitioner is helped in this process by his or her adherence to the method's values and norms of conduct. This involves talking openly about his or her purpose and feelings, as well as sanctioning the group's feedback to the practitioner.

| *Illustration* | ***Pregnant Women's Group in Prison*** |

A group of pregnant women in a prison cell block are in their fifth meeting with a male practitioner, Dan. The focus to date has been on developing means for social and emotional survival.

The women are involved in educating the practitioner about what goes on in prison and suggesting that he change the system. The practitioner responds, "I know how badly you feel about being here and how awful it can be for you, but I can't change the system for you. This leaves me feeling worried. But in this group, you all have work to do, with each other and me, to figure out how to support each other and air your emotions so you are not bottled up." The women blow up, yelling in angry voices, "Who are you? What do you know about this place, coming in once a week—social worker!"

Somewhat anxious and wavering, Dan takes a deep breath and responds, "I don't know all that you know about this place, for sure. But I do feel convinced I'm on the right track about you all needing to deal with what's going on, so that you can use each other in this session and on the cell block for support." He goes on, "You're questioning me, and I'll try to answer. But also let me know more about how you think I have been handling myself in these meetings—what helps, and what doesn't." They continue, at first talking at once: "You're like this . . . you're like that." One member says, "When we talk to each other you listen too hard and make us paranoid." The practitioner says, "I don't intend for you to get paranoid, but I just don't want to miss something that could be useful."

The process of arguing and give-and-take moves more and more toward becoming effective, rather than accusative. The members begin to talk more openly about how much they feel demeaned in the prison by everyone in authority, and how the practitioner shows them respect. More talk develops about the practitioner: "Come on, Dan, why are you here? What are you getting out of this?" The practitioner responds, "At first I came not really knowing, but wanting to help out of a desire to contribute. I know something about your situation. I've had friends and family who got into trouble. Now as I know you, I feel more of a desire to try to change things, to help you and your babies get a better chance."

Discussion

The expectation that a prisoner's group might become angry is one of a practitioner's worse fears. That these women have a great deal to complain about in their situations cannot be denied. The practitioner does not deny the validity of their complaints; to do so would damage the relationship. It would show that the practitioner is not truly connected to their current reality.

It is not accidental that at this time in the group's development the issue of authority in the prison becomes a central concern. However, the practitioner holds to his conviction that the members' needs will be met best by staying focused on their work within the group that centers on supporting each other through their pregnancies and on developing future plans upon their release. Issues revolving around their own stigmatizations and those of their children will have to be dealt with as well. The practitioner walks a fine line with these members; he validates their concern about the correctional system, but stays with the work of the group. By asking them to respond to his efforts, the practitioner offers them direction for moving ahead with his authority and his power to understand their issues. As the members react to the practitioner, weaving and developing a collective set of perceptions, they once again ask him what he is doing there. The practitioner responds openly, acknowledging their situation within society as people who need a chance and offering his desire to be of help in the context of his own history. Beginning to share authentically is essential in an environment so full of mistrust, authority, and control.

Stage Theme 4: Sanctuary

Boston Model Stage 3	T-Group Stage	Values and Norms
Intimacy	Enchantment-Flight	Right to belong

The feelings of accomplishment and inclusiveness gained from working on power and authority issues bring the members to new feelings of caring, effectiveness, and closeness. These include wishing for comfortable, relaxed, and uncomplicated relationships with one another and the practitioner. Along with the authentic desire to include the practitioner as part of them, the members may try to get the practitioner to lose his or her role and become one of them in their safe haven away from the pressures of their real-life relationships, as well as the pressures attendant upon changes they anticipate within themselves and their group relationships.

The members feel that the group and its members, even the ones they had intense differences with before, are wonderful. In this "love" reaction, the group is held up as an icon (Bion, 1961). While serving the purpose of providing a breathing spell and setting the stage for work to come by motivating strong affective bonds among the members, this state may also be used counterproductively to avoid further difficult tasks by pressuring conformity from those members who attempt to alter the comfort and uniformity it provides.

In this stage, there are many familial-type transferential issues (Garland et al., 1973). These paradoxically serve both to enhance cohesiveness and to resist moving on to a more inclusive and differentiated process.

Practitioner Issues

The practitioner is vulnerable to feeding the group's desire for closeness by overengaging and wishing to connect with it. On the other hand, the practitioner may feel threatened by the closeness and by the fear that his or her authority and the demand for work may be disregarded. This heightens the risk that the practitioner will withdraw emotionally from the group so as not to be seen as part of the closeness.

The practitioner may not understand the meaning of family talk as a symbol of the members' desire for closeness, thereby stopping it by interpreting it as an immature dependency reaction. This would deflect the members from their needs to strengthen their affective bonds so they may proceed to work on purpose with a concerted emotional effort.

Practitioner Role

It is important that the practitioner experience a feeling of membership, inclusion, and warmth in the group. This strengthens the ability to cue into and motivate nuances of affect that are necessary for the members if they are to function at deeper emotional and intellectual levels. At the same time, the practitioner tunes into members' strivings to assert their wants and differences and to get beyond the glow of the "happy family." The practitioner, recognizing and respecting the group's desire to maintain its sanctuary, taps into its latent urge to begin productive work on its purpose by exploring how the members might wish to put their cohesive feelings and interactions to use. Raising questions about future goals and actions, while supporting the cohesion and affective tone of the group, helps it use the cohesion to proceed to more difficult tasks.

Illustration   *Male Batterers Group*

A group of male batterers has been having a lot of difficulty defining their behaviors as abusive. They have argued a great deal with the practitioner and one another. After much conflict and many power struggles, including threats of violence, they have had to swallow feelings of entitlement and personal hurt derived from their own abusive family experiences. They have had to face up to their view of the practitioner as a more perfect and less impulse-ridden fathering male. They have come to a point where they see themselves in a more positive light, and feel they can overcome their problems through each other's support.

At this meeting, they are talking about how they feel they can suppress the anger they've turned on their significant others. Al says, "All I have to do is remember that you guys are here supporting me and I won't strike out at her." Mel agrees. Rick says, "My wife left me and has an order of protection against me. She'll never take me back."

The discussion continues with members talking about how nice the group of guys is, and how if they had this as kids maybe things wouldn't have turned out like they did. The practitioner is quiet for a while. Then he says, "It's true, it would have been nice if you guys had a warm group like this when you were younger. But what about now, how can you use this atmosphere to help better your difficult situations?" There are some angry reactions at first, then Mel yells out, "We gotta cut the crap. We gotta stop feeling sorry for ourselves." The group is quiet. Then Al says, "Mel is right. We can't go back. We have to try to get it right this time. I've got children. I've got to get it right for them before I lose them too."

Discussion

The members of this group are experiencing the hurts and letdowns of their family situations, as well as their current feelings of loss of their partners and children. They have been able to acknowledge the group as a nurturing milieu—one that they currently need and would have needed in their own childhoods. The closeness they feel in this sanctuary can provide a second chance for them to extract a newer set of behaviors from this sustaining environment.

With the practitioner as part of their process, they have had to acknowledge his less impulsive behavior. With this in mind, the practitioner has affirmed the group's caring and support and permitted himself to be part of that process. His silence during their idealization of the group permits the members the time they need to feel good about themselves and their accomplishments, and to experience the wish for this sustenance in their childhoods. The practitioner directly affirms their need for the group as a nurturing milieu, agreeing with their perception that this atmosphere was necessary but sometimes lacking in their childhoods. He gently takes the opportunity to direct them toward thinking about how they will use the group to improve their current situations. Though reluctant to move ahead, the group is sparked by the quick response of one member to the practitioner's intervention. Another member follows suit. If he had not, the practitioner would have had to support the dissident member in pushing the group to newer arenas, and given affirmation to the other members as well.

Stage Theme 5: "This Isn't Good Anymore"

Boston Model Stage 4	T-Group Stage	Values and Norms
Differentiation	Disenchantment-Fight	Accept differences
		Accept deviance
		Right to self-determination

When group members find themselves unable to take the risks necessary to change, some become angry—disenchanted with the group and disparaging of one another. While some members may continue to try to stem the tide of group dissolution, others distrust the attempts and risks members are taking, at times denying their sincerity altogether. Eventually, the negativity of some members prevents others from moving forward, because purposeful movement requires everyone's involvement and cooperation. This results in a loss of faith in the capacity of the group to work together toward reaching its goals. When the members are in an extreme form of this conflictual mode, they may move to disband the group—saying that "this isn't good anymore." While it is uncharacteristic for the members to blame the practitioner for their current lack of progress, they do compare their activities and attitudes to the practitioner's—and as is the risk of comparisons, their efforts often appear futile. If the group ends at this time, members are bound to be left with lack of resolution that results in feelings of anger, frustration, and disappointment with the group and group life in general. (It is less frustrating and more positive, however illusionary, to end at the point of sanctuary than at this juncture.)

Practitioner Issues

A practitioner may experience the blame the group places on its members as a sign of his or her own ineffectiveness. Feeling unnoticed or peripheral to the struggle results in a sense of helplessness rather than helpfulness. Afraid of addressing the negative reaction in the group—and of interpreting the latent fears and avoidance—the practitioner may become overanxious, jumping in to rescue the members by a frantic affirmation of their accomplishments. The practitioner might also become angry and punitive toward them because of their lack of productivity. All in all, when the practitioner fails to recognize the imperative of this theme, he or she inadvertently may stimulate the group to disband rather than assisting it in actively developing interpersonal and practical means for working with the practitioner.

Practitioner Role

An attitude of confidence in the group's capacity to continue with its work is required. To accomplish this, the practitioner must address the members' negative reactions by identifying them and exploring them rather than through direct confrontation (the latter might be experienced as punitive). Refocusing the members on their objectives, while actively affirming the reality and normalcy of the difficulties, is necessary. The practitioner helps the members restore their visions about the future and their abilities to continue effective work.

| **Illustration** | ***Family Members of 9/11 Victims*** |

A group of family members of 9/11 victims has been meeting for nearly a year. They have dealt with many issues regarding their losses, including rage at terrorists and at the government for not having prevented these attacks. Now they are angry that still there is no memorial at Ground Zero. Another of their recent issues has been the mixed feelings of wanting to let go of the bitterness, yet at the same time not wanting to violate either the memory of the loss of their loved ones or the truth of their own anger.

At this meeting, Dimitri begins by saying, "I don't think there is anything more that can be said in this group about this horror. The truth is that it has ruined our lives. I left Russia for a better life for my family, only to have my child taken from me here in this country. How can I go on?" Joe agrees with Dimitri that "Yes, it's a terrible fate to have left one's country for this dream of America, only to have it come down on us." Mariana agrees and talks about her brother who was a sous chef at Windows on the World. "He was so hard working and full of life. He died for this country, and now all they want to do in return is keep out Mexicans. Our people are in the military and they're not even citizens. It's okay to die here for America but not to live here."

They go on, some of them arguing and reflecting that nothing is going to be done about a memorial because "we are so busy in Iraq." Others are fuming that no one cares where Osama Bin Laden is. "He did this, not Saddam Hussein." Dimitri says. "You have no idea what it's like to have lived under a dictatorship like his. Saddam was the worst of them. And Osama? America did that." More political discussions continue, intermittently reflecting a sense of futility and despair.

Frankie, a fireman who lost his brother in the towers, says, "I wanted to just give up. I knew so many who died. But Dimitri, I'm going to say something you're not going to like. Do you have other children?" "Yes, I have a daughter." "What are you doing for her life? I don't ever hear you talking about her. She's alive. How do you think she feels knowing that you are more wrapped up in your son who died than in your daughter who lives? It's been over 5 years now. How old is she? 26? She was 21 when she lost her brother. Did she finish college? Is she on drugs? That's all I can say to you Dimitri." Andrea says, "Each of us has to do what we have to do. I can't tell you how to run your lives and you can't tell me how to run mine."

The group falls silent. The practitioner wonders, "Does that mean that some of you have given up and there is no point in trying to find more positive productive ways to deal with your grief and anger? It feels like you are moving forward and backward."

Members talk about how hard it is to go forward. Andrea talks about her friends having children and feeling sad knowing that her own children never will have cousins since her only sister died. Dimitri acknowledges Frankie's point, "I try with my daughter, but you're right, I can tell she doesn't want me to keep talking all the time about Alexei to her. Maybe if she were married and I had a grandchild I could feel better." Mariana says that "We all want life to go forward, but for each family member, it has to be on terms that are good for them. If my mother put pressure on me to have a child because my brother died, that would make things even harder for me right now."

The practitioner acknowledges how hard it must be to go forward "when you have so many angry and hurt feelings. I don't blame you for being stuck. I don't know where I would be if I were in your shoes. Angry and stuck, too, I guess."

Discussion

The practitioner here is not afraid to react to the negative and fearful feelings. Rather, he points them out empathically in the hope that members will start to reconsider their own obstacles to getting on with their lives. The acknowledgment about how difficult it is to go forward when one harbors so many feelings of anger and hurt might provide support and impetus for members to turn their feelings into constructive action rather than having them remain frozen in time only to cause feelings of refusal. By identifying and empathizing with these feelings, the practitioner does not become caught in self-blame or in distancing himself from the realities of the members' past and present grief and anger.

Stage Theme 6: "We're Okay and Able"

Boston Model Stage 4	T-Group Stage	Values and Norms
Differentiation	Consensual Validation	Open communication
		Difference is enriching

In the process of working through ambivalence toward the group experience, members develop a deepening confidence in their abilities to attempt more difficult work. A range of difference among the members is valued as important for enriching the experience. As they assume more responsibility for sharing their perceptions and conflicts, these feelings are more readily accepted as essential for the problem-solving process. The members learn to choose from among options and reactions that reflect the different styles and capacities of each person in the group. A fuller ability to present their feelings, perceptions, questions, and views of one another's contributions in reaching their goals is evidenced. The members feel capable of encouraging and assuming collective and individual leadership in caring about one another. They are better able to assist one another in meeting their objectives.

The practitioner is implicitly expected, and explicitly requested, to explore and clarify members' interactions and emotional efforts. The members can be spontaneous in asking the practitioner for feedback, advice, and assistance in defining alternative roles, forms of expression, and options. The members also readily ask the practitioner to share feelings, opinions, and real-life experiences.

Practitioner Issues

The practitioner is affected in positive ways by the group's open ambiance and productivity. The group worker's opportunities to fully use skill and empathy without meeting resistance and fear, along with the members' activity in looking back on their own and the group's change processes, yields a feeling of professionalism and competence. One risk the practitioner faces at this time comes from feeling lulled into a sense—albeit a positive one—of not being needed anymore; this may result in relaxing involvement and directiveness. The practitioner is also at risk of being unable to admit to a lack of resources and to professional and personal limitations.

Practitioner Role

At this time the practitioner is in a position to confront the members and their processes to motivate action geared toward dealing with their issues and meeting their goals. The group is strong enough in values, norms, and structure to work on itself while being aware of the changes everyone is going through. The practitioner assists the members in enhancing their abilities to explore and clarify issues that will help them to focus their efforts in more productive directions; helping the group explore and resolve its conflicts is also needed at this juncture. Sharing feelings of vulnerability and frailties, as well as capabilities and successes, that relate directly to the members' needs is necessary. This heightens mutuality and closeness in order to enable even more detailed and complex processes to unfold.

| **Illustration** | **Male Alcohol and Substance Abuse Treatment Group** |

As the members in a male alcohol and substance abuse treatment support group are coming into the meeting, they are talking animatedly. Ralph, the practitioner, enters the group and finds a seat. He runs this group as part of an independent employee assistance program (EAP). These men have a range of blue collar and white collar jobs, and are mostly minority members, including the practitioner, except for two white guys. Greetings are exchanged. Bob, looking to Ralph, says,

"We've all been talking about the shit that goes down at work where some people who know we're in rehab still have a hard time hanging out with us." Tom echoes, "I used to think it was racial—the white guys with the white guys, the Hispanics with each other." Andy says, "Well, it's true—they talk Spanish a lot of the time. So, I was talking to my girlfriend, and she said that it's about having been an addict. What do you guys think?" Joe says, "I met a guy on the train I work with, he was talking Russian. He said, 'Good morning,' then went back to talking. I could have punched him. But I also realized I'm into my own stuff too, with you guys, and if I was with you, I'd want to talk to you—and in this case it's not about color." Terry reflects, "It's that old anger and short fuse. Are we ever going to be free of that?" Members talk about how the past never will disappear, and that losing all that time to drugs also won't change.

Albert says that he and his wife went to a jazz club with Rick and Eleanor, a white couple. "We had great fun. Of course there were the usual jokes about them being in the minority in that club. Rick and I work together and when we found out we both were addicts, we would check in with each other on the job for support. Going out socially is easier with them than some of my black friends, especially in a jazz club. It was understood that we would not order alcohol, no questions."

Ralph wonders if it's not a whole lot of different commonalities that cause people to hang with each other, and maybe it's true that "having been in rehab is one common theme also to bring you together, but also scares others who don't know about it. Perhaps it's not just race and religion alone that connect or separate people. Look at the mix in this group."

The discussion goes on, with the men—including the practitioner—talking about whether it's worth it to try to cut through barriers, with some of the bitterness surfacing, and more discussion about how to try for the ideal because then there is no bitterness. Andy says to Ralph, "I know that you had to deal with all kinds of people to be in the position you're in." Ralph nods, saying, "When I was younger, it got to me, but I learned through many mistakes that if you try to give people respect, most people respond."

Discussion

The practitioner is easily a part of this process. At the beginning the members spontaneously tell him about their perceptions concerning how they might be separated from white or Hispanic people. They express comfort with his role as practitioner and an ease in talking with him openly about what they are feeling. As they continue, they are challenged to deal with the fact that some people might distance themselves from the men because they were addicts. The theme of bitterness about lost time and being labeled is raised, but it does not incur defensiveness on the part of the members. In this session, despite a couple of white men in the group, the central topic begins with black people, and there isn't any defensiveness about that topic either.

When a group member points out that the practitioner too must have had a difficult time as a black man becoming successful in the work that he does, he is able to use himself by reacting honestly to the observation, using his own feelings to nudge the group into further work. As the work continues, the practitioner remains part of the process.

Stage Theme 7: "Just a Little Longer"

Boston Model Stage 5	T-Group Stage	Values and Norms
Separation	Consensual Validation	Self-determination
		Difference is enriching

As time approaches for the group to end its experiences together—to disband—the members may spend difficult amounts of time in interpersonal forms and themes that appear to be like those of earlier stages. The latent objective of this particular process is to convince the practitioner that they need the group "just a little longer," that more work is yet to be completed and that things are not as good as they seem. As anger and disappointment mount, both members and the practitioner become targets. Members may directly and indirectly act as though their interpersonal skills, problem-solving capacities, and abilities to be close are not as well-integrated as they appeared to have been.

On the other hand, when the members connect to the processes and the fact of ending, facing the disappointments and anger, they also come to terms with their accomplishments. They take pride in their experiences and relationships. The practitioner is asked to provide support and to reinforce their capabilities to use what they have learned in order to move ahead into enhanced interactions and new experiences.

Practitioner Issues

In this period, a practitioner with a strong attachment to the group and its members is vulnerable to difficulty in separating from them, colluding with the members' doubts about their accomplishments and competencies. The practitioner may also regress to using earlier types of interventions to deal with the group's reaction out of the fear that the group really is regressing and/or unaccomplished, that it really has had a fragile learning experience. The practitioner may not recognize the members' doubts as their symbolic expressions of not wanting to end. The practitioner also may not recognize his or her own desire to remain within this group setting is a reflection of anxiety about other challenging and unpredictable professional experiences. An additional dimension is brought about by fears regarding unfinished issues— have members been sufficiently helped to do well?—as well as the concomitant vanity that the process has not had a perfect ending.

Practitioner Role

The practitioner's role during the ending phase should be governed—as with all practitioner responses at any point in time—by the values and norms of the humanistic group work method. Its values and standards of interaction continually lead to a recognition that people are interdependent in mutually supportive ways, and that each is as purposefully motivated as the other. How and if members will remember each other after the group experience will be quite individual and personal, and unknowable.

The practitioner acknowledges how all participants—practitioner and members alike—are approaching and avoiding, and how all are having difficulty going on to other situations. The practitioner also helps members accept the imperfections of endings. The importance of valuing the memories of the experience is stressed as well; the practitioner shares his or her own feelings about the meaning of the experience, about ending with these particular people, and about plans for future professional projects.

| Illustration | **Adolescent Psychiatric Unit Discharge Planning Group** |

The discharge planning group is in its ninth (and next to last) session on the inpatient adolescent psychiatric unit. Marsha, the practitioner, has spent the past 2 hours contacting schools, workshops, residences, and families to help develop plans for each girl when she leaves. The girls, too, had been asked to find out information from staff about places where they would be going. Marsha walks in, clipboard and lists in hand, greeting the girls. She begins the meeting by telling them she's got more information to add to what they already know.

As the practitioner is about to continue, Hilda falls to the floor, with head between her legs and sobbing. Marsha and a couple of the other girls crouch to hold her. Hilda sobs, "It's there again. My brother and his wife won't let me come to live with them in their house. I have to go to the group residence in Queens. I hate that place. I will be back here again in 2 months, you can be sure of that!"

Sara and Rose help Hilda get up, hug her and say (almost simultaneously), "Look, Hildie, you and I and Rosie here, and Toni too, we will see each other weekly in the aftercare group, and at Gregory's karaoke where the cutest 'bods' hang out." "Come on, Hilda, don't get sucked into your brother saving you and giving up his wife for his younger sister, please don't. The judge at family court also said you couldn't go there. They both work."

Silence falls on the sound of this poignant and defensive issue that Hilda has been on for years. Hilda remains silent. Marsha does not focus on this painful issue; she lets the silence continue, then says, "Rose, what have you found about the aftercare program?" Rose talks about the chance to live in supportive apartments when she gets stronger. More members share information; Hilda is paying attention.

Near the end of the session, the girls sit in pairs, identifying chores to carry out for next week's information-gathering assignments. Marsha asks the pairs to report back to the whole group as to their individual assignments, whereupon she writes a note for each member with her assignment on it.

After the session, Marsha somewhat anxiously runs to her office to call the residence that Hilda is going to. She leaves a message that she will call back, "But Judy can try to call me too. I'm here all day." Marsha goes on to supervision.

Discussion

In this meeting, the practitioner is very much a part of the group's ending process. She has helped them maintain their autonomy, in spite of the possibility that they may regress at the group's end and upon discharge from the hospital, by structuring assignments for each girl that involve partial planning for her own aftercare.

The practitioner chooses to allow Hilda to remain silent after her outburst and not focus on her sad feelings of abandonment and rejection by her brother that have been triggered by the discharge from the hospital. Her threat to return validates her special vulnerability when she is faced with endings. The practitioner recognizes this vulnerability when, at the close of the meeting, she puts in the call to the referral site. The group members, recognizing Hilda's recurring issue, help her face her present reality and offer their support to her in the new program. Thus, it is not necessary for the practitioner to intervene. In fact, during the "just a little longer" period, it is most necessary for members to experience their abilities to take responsibility for one another so as to foster confidence in their autonomy and capability in their future enterprise.

For clarification of stage themes, practitioner issues, and practitioner roles, see Table 3.2.

Table 3.2 Stage Themes and the Practitioner

Stage Themes	Practitioner Issues	Practitioner Role
Stage Theme 1 *"We're Not in Charge"* Members look to worker for cues; size up worker and members.	Invests in group's success and in own success. May relinquish own responsibility to avoid anxiety.	Sanctions expression of feeling toward worker and group. Connects talk about past group and worker to present group. Invites trust. Identifies common needs.
Stage Theme 2 *"We Are in Charge"* Looking to each other for cues; ignore worker; vie for leadership. Pecking orders emerge.	Feels tense, ineffectual, anxious in reaction to group battle for control. Asserts authority by overcontrolling or abdicates to placate.	Helps group own its needs, conflicts. Helps group see frustration of struggle to control group.
Stage Theme 3 *"We're Taking You On"* Develops strength to ask worker "What are you doing here?"	Doubts skill; fears group; sidesteps by recontracting or redefinition of worker's role.	Encourages exploration of feelings toward worker. Presents stake and role in group.
Stage Theme 4 *Sanctuary* Members feel good about group; "This group is wonderful."	May avoid intimacy by withdrawing; may over engage in feelings of cohesion and intimacy.	Encourages exploration of direction of intimacy; reflects good feelings; recognizes differences.

(Continued)

Table 3.2 (Continued)

Stage Themes	Practitioner Issues	Practitioner Role
Stage Theme 5 *"This Isn't Good Anymore"* Members feel disappointed in group; move to disband.	Rescues group; sidesteps negatives; blames self or is angry at group.	Encourages exploration of negatives. Exhibits confidence in group's capacity to deal with obstacles.
Stage Theme 6 *"We're Okay and Able"* Members feel hope; work to achieve goals.	May relax direction in face of positive; may fear sharing positive and negative options and feelings.	Focuses, guides group desire to work; encourages ownership of experience; shares in effort.
Stage Theme 7 *"Just a Little Longer"* Members try to stay; doubt accomplishments. Consider future options.	Joins in doubts about accomplishments. Joins regression to earlier forms of behavior; prolongs the end; fears separation.	Encourages exploration of regressive trends; shares feelings about leaving; identifies future options; makes referrals.

❖ SUMMARY

This chapter has established and identified seven stage themes as patterned and sequenced changes in group life that impact the feelings and roles of the practitioner as part of the process. These stage themes of group development are as follows:

1. "We're Not in Charge"

2. "We Are in Charge"

3. "We're Taking You On"

4. Sanctuary

5. "This Isn't Good Anymore"

6. "We're Okay and Able"

7. "Just a Little Longer"

The chapter has delineated practice principles associated with each of the themes. These include taking responsibility for helping members affiliate at the start, helping the group challenge the practitioner's authority, supporting and taking part in closeness with the members, prodding the work effort, accepting negative feelings, and helping members end the group.

The chapter has made the point that worker reactions and vulnerabilities are not idiosyncratic countertransferences, but engendered by the group's process. These special vulnerabilities the practitioner may expect to experience during each stage theme have been identified. These include the desire to avoid responsibility for his or her own membership in the group, subverting the group's challenge to authority, denying professional limitation, and avoiding endings.

The humanistic values and democratic norms as enriching forces in the process were shown during each of the stage themes. These stage themes also have unique applicability in short-term and open-ended groups (see Chapter 10 for fuller explication).

PART II

Dual Objectives
and Techniques of
Humanistic Group Work

4

The Dual Objectives

In the description of the humanistic method of group work, emphasis has been placed on the importance of the practitioner compre-
hending, owning, and expressing humanistic values through attitudes
and interactions. Given this state of affairs—the relation of values and
norms to degrees of interpersonal expression—it is important to recognize that it is by design and practice skill that the group work practitioner helps members have experiences and attain resources that are
meaningful for them and others in their lives.

❖ THE DUAL OBJECTIVES: DEVELOPING
 THE DEMOCRATIC MUTUAL AID SYSTEM
 AND ACTUALIZING GROUP PURPOSE

The practitioner of humanistic group work attempts to accomplish two
complementary objectives (Glassman & Kates, 1986a). The first is the
development of the democratic mutual aid system; the second is the *actualization of group purpose.* These objectives are addressed, worked on, and
worked through during the entirety of the group's life. Their interactions
occur with different intensities in the different stages in the group's
evolution.

Developing the Democratic Mutual Aid System

The first objective, developing the democratic mutual aid system, addresses the domain of process and the multiplicity of transactions that evolve. To foster the development of a democratic mutual aid system, the practitioner assists the members according to their capabilities and needs in developing genuine and productive ways of interacting. It is important from the first contacts with the members for the practitioner to express humanistic values and to exemplify democratic forms of interaction as powerful contributions to the change process.

It is not to be taken for granted that people will employ values and norms that are expansive, inclusive, and considerate of one another's differences. These abilities will depend on their prior social experiences, and current social skills and limitations. This is a crucial fact to comprehend. The practitioner must work with the members, taking their social skills into account, filling in with professional, institutional, and technical support when necessary. The members' attentions are drawn to the effects their interactions are having in providing one another with opportunities to gain from experiences, while making certain that the nature of their interactions is not at any one member's or the group's expense.

The evolution of a democratic mutual aid system as a series of helping experiences occurs earlier in group life than the actualization of group purpose (Lang, 1981). This milieu provides the medium within which purpose is elaborated. In her classic article, Lang supports this view. She suggests that the guiding, building, and owning of a democratic group occurs in the early stages of group development, during which members and the worker are concerned with affiliation issues including those of power, authority, and trust. Lang further proposes that the practitioner must pay careful and sensitive attention to helping the members develop norms that foster democratic values and egalitarian sharing so that a democratic group can form, rather than one where the most powerful dominate.

Lang (1981) further suggests that—lest a group form with norms destructive to the human spirit—the practitioner must not rush the process or it will be affected by anxiety and arbitrariness. The early formation stages should not be rushed. The practitioner should directly point out when the group is speeding the process, and empathically temper the group's pressure to move too quickly and deeply into working on the members' needs without attending to the effect of values that are extant in the group's interpersonal process. The practitioner helps members to consider how they are valuing one another, directing them to open up their modes of interaction for the scrutiny and participation of all members. In helping the group to be patient with its process, the practitioner recommends, exemplifies, and supports the use of humanistic values and democratic norms. The practitioner may also help members face interactional limitations that inhibit social cooperation. Time should not be the main consideration used to rush the group's decision-making processes. When there is a need for speed, as in the short-term group, members usually meet that need. However, the worker has to recognize the impact of imposed time limits on the members, especially with regard to sacrificing democratic processes. (See Chapter 11 for a discussion about short-term groups and which parts of the process can be appropriately hastened to achieve group goals.)

When members move too quickly to meet their needs without having developed different media for the experience, the group may meet the needs of some members—to certain degrees—without truly challenging all of the members to real efforts and changes. The group may begin to disband after the first few sessions, because the members can neither protect themselves from one another's demands, handle their anxieties, nor meet their needs.

Important in developing the democratic mutual aid system are the members' abilities to gain understanding of themselves as a group and their relation to the authority of the practitioner. In a humanistic group the members develop and enhance their abilities to view, question, and challenge the professional role, position, and functions of the practitioner in an open manner. This subsequently enables a distribution of power between the practitioner and the members (Glassman & Kates, 1983).

Other group forms addressing themes familiar to social group work omit or pay little attention in their design to the specific and purposeful development of a democratic mutual aid system. For instance, the structured group—where agendas are brought to the group by the agency, program, grant constraints, or the practitioner—is not built on the group's ability to develop its own power and participation dynamics, design its own agendas, question the leader's authority, and extend its life outside the auspices of the group's meeting time (Papell & Rothman, 1980b). While these groups may utilize discussion methods with a high level of member participation, they do not address the issue of the distribution of power in, and ownership of, the group experience in its complete form. (See Chapter 11 for discussion of humanistic group work approaches in structured groups.) Some of these groups are for parent effectiveness, anger management, and psycho-education. Special interest groups or those designed primarily to meet political action goals also do not systematically establish democratic processes. While some mutual aid occurs in these several group types, the active examination of power and authority relationships is not explicitly built into their designs.

There are also those groups that are antihumanistic, such as cults. While on the one hand, members will feel very high degrees of belonging, they will be involved usually with a particularly charismatic leader professing to have answers to all questions. One further sign of a destructive antihumanistic cult group is that it will encourage externality of members only within the confines of the cult group rather than with the world at large. In extreme situations, members will actively be encouraged to sever connections to family and friends outside of the cult system.

After the resolution of power and authority issues that revolve around the practitioner's role, as well as some members' needs to control, members in a humanistic group experience stronger attraction to one another. Leadership issues among the members of how they will allow and encourage each other to take initiative—and when they will follow, yield, and lead—will become more resolved. This becomes a turning point for the members and practitioner. Establishment of patterns of working together then permits the group to move on to purposeful change.

Actualizing Group Purpose

Actualizing group purpose, the second objective, centers on the individual and collective goals to be worked on in the process. From the start of the process, the members try in different ways to pursue the issues that brought them together. After the practitioner's efforts have focused on establishing a democratic arena for caring, mutual aid, decision making, and participating, the practitioner's efforts turn to helping the members meet their needs for personal and environmental change. Now group and member goals are more explicitly examined by the practitioner and the members.

As the practitioner pursues the actualizing of group purpose, he or she draws the members into dealing with issues related to group purpose and group process in order to work on their goals using their already established interactional abilities. Groups lacking a clear sense of how they are pursuing their purpose use the supportive environment they have constructed as a sanctuary, shielding them from the role responsibilities of life. For example, a group composed of abusing parents that is a safe haven but has no focus on inhibiting acts of abuse, will be what Shulman (2006) calls an "illusion of work" (p. 153). The safe haven must be used purposefully and productively to help members take steps toward more effective role performance. By the same token, a support group for alcoholics will not meet its objectives if the norms and actions that are necessary to help maintain sobriety are not part of the process.

The practitioner helps the members further their purpose by helping them experience meaningful types of interactions in a variety of ways and situations. The humanistic group is constituted to examine and enhance members' psychosocial functioning and quality of life in relation to selected psychosocial phenomena such as aging, parenting, employee relations, community relations, mental or physical illness, and life-cycle socialization issues. The commonality of theme and interest brings each group together and motivates its work. Members experience an enhancement of role abilities in the middle phase processes when purposes are actualized. Prior establishment of democratic ways of interacting now assists the members in working on and through purposeful and focused change. Members gain clarity through examining each other's life-space issues and behaviors. This helps them to take risks and experiment with changing unhelpful patterns and actions. Members can accept their own and each other's weaknesses and strengths in the group, as well as transfer these attitudes and abilities into their life-space situations.

The more traditional psychoanalytic therapy groups, wherein psychosocial issues are secondary to personality change, are aimed at heightening and working out transferential reactions to others, rather than working on adaptations in effective social life. These groups rely less on the group as a social and democratic entity to promote participants' changes and more on the group as a vehicle for fostering and heightening the individual (idiosyncratic) transferential distortions that come up among the participants and therapists. As a rule, members are discouraged from seeing one another outside of the psychotherapy group in the "real social environment" (except perhaps in a structured "alternate session" without the therapist). This is done so that the transference is not diluted.

In humanistic social group work, the "real" milieus are the central foci of the group's experience within, as well as external to, its formal sessions. The group's ability to plan and produce programmatic events that enhance social functioning and quality of life is a special feature of the group work method. This feature has been defined as the group's "externality" (Papell & Rothman, 1980b), that is, its ability to exist outside of the meeting time.

Practitioners of multifaceted group approaches make efforts to develop groups grounded in values that are humanistic and democratic. Groups such as T-groups, leadership training groups, and education groups are quite concerned with members' rights, due process, decision-making abilities, abilities to cope with group pressure to conform, and diversity as a positive value.[1] Other group approaches—more oriented toward treatment, rehabilitation, or remediation—use processes of acceptance, belonging, and inclusion as a means for helping members grow and change, but do not systematically propose these processes as central to the organization of group experiences. What is unique in humanistic group work is the explicit development of a democratic group form *in conjunction with* the actualization of group purpose.

This unique combination of group process and group purpose has significant practical implications. For the social action group, it places negative sanctions on overly rigid and dictatorial attempts to develop change tactics that are at the expense of members' feelings, due process, collective decision making, and rights. Rather, both democratic process and purpose-related outcomes go hand in hand in a means-ends relationship. In the social work clinical treatment group, members examine what is dysfunctional in their self-expressions to actualize purpose. Simultaneously, they review and modify relationships with each other and the practitioner as a responsibility of group membership. This effort is immediately brought into relationships with significant others in the members' own lives.

❖ ACCOMPLISHING THE DUAL OBJECTIVES

There is also a relationship between the dual objectives and stage themes of group development. Members in the processes of Stage Themes 1, 2, and 3—"We're Not in Charge," "We Are in Charge," and "We're Taking You On"—in effect end up evolving and strengthening their interactions for developing and sustaining their mutual aid systems.

Throughout this process, the members essentially focus on building cohesion, with less concentration on the more difficult issues of personal change in the group and the environment. Once the group basks in the intensely felt safety of Stage Theme 4, Sanctuary, there is a turning point and members' efforts shift from group process to purpose-related efforts. The myth of the group as deity (Bion, 1961) is relinquished as members move on to the current realities of the work at hand. The dynamics of Stage Themes 5 and 6—"This Isn't Good Anymore" and "We're Okay and Able"—are related to the frustrations and accomplishments of undertaking personal and collective efforts to change the dysfunctional behaviors and interpersonal arrangements that comprise the members' collective purpose. In the ending phase, as the issues of prolonging the end become manifest through Stage Theme 7, "Just a Little Longer," the members struggle with solidifying and owning what they have learned so they feel confident and better able to function without the group.

❖ DUAL OBJECTIVES AND THE CHANGE PROCESS

The change process involves a continuum of trust, risk, and experimentation. This continuum encompasses the helpful dynamics of the members' working-on and working-through efforts. It results in successes and failures in the members' attempts to change and to master change. It is repeated any number of times as different aspects of interaction are worked on and through. In the development of the democratic mutual aid system, the continuum occurs as the members build and sustain milieus of cooperation and caring. In actualizing group purpose, the continuum occurs as the members, trusting one another, risk changing ineffective actions and patterns.

In the long-term group, the change effort is a complex of events and experiences, usually dealing with personal and group issues that revolve around a panoply of role-enhancing experiences and interactions. In time-limited groups, agendas are less complex, usually relating to one or two specific behaviors. The change process nonetheless involves trust, risk, and experimentation, albeit in a more clearly delineated process within a narrow frame of reference (see Chapter 11).

In the change process, members are held accountable to one another, and they experience doubts and disappointments, regressions and hurts, and joys and successes, all in an atmosphere of cooperation, effort, and mutual aid. Conflict and confrontation are enacted by the members in a group strong enough to take on difficult issues that are not to be avoided or denied because of fears and anxieties about retribution and rejection.

❖ INTERACTIONS OF THE DUAL OBJECTIVES

As the group is woven with threads of humanistic values and democratic norms, its members develop interactions that are characteristic of the achievements of the dual objectives. The practitioner may use his or her awareness of these interactions as a barometer to evaluate the ups and downs in the process and members, and identify strengths as well as difficulties that occur in meeting these objectives. Members may be acquainted with these interactions in order to widen their spectrum of choices and enhance their autonomy. While each of the following interactions occurs throughout the entirety of group life, the two typologies of group member interactions are distinct to each of the dual objectives, having salience to addressing different dilemmas associated with each of them. Table 4.1 lists the interactions of the dual objectives.

Table 4.1   Interactions of the Dual Objectives

Forms of Group Interaction That Foster the Democratic Mutual Aid System

- Developing and appreciating democratic norms, which include rights to belong and to be heard, to freedom of speech and expression
- Making decisions and developing rules
- Developing the leadership and followership skills of cooperation, yielding, listening, and flexibility
- Respecting differences among members
- Expressing feelings about the practitioner with particular attention to power and authority issues
- Collectively developing and setting goals that enable the group to move toward purpose
- Developing a beginning expression of feelings toward members, laying groundwork for future expressions
- Developing affective bonds and furthering cohesion

Forms of Group Interaction That Foster the Actualization of Group Purpose

- Identifying themes to be worked on (e.g., making agendas, prioritizing efforts, and dealing flexibly with new issues)
- Taking risks in expressing and experimenting with role-enhancing behaviors
- Sharing perceptions and feelings about each other's behaviors
- Creating activities in the milieu and external environment to actualize the group's externality
- Identifying group process issues and structures to heighten the group's self-awareness
- Identifying projections and self-fulfilling prophecies as they interfere with collaboration and role enhancement
- Reflecting on and reinforcing member and group change in order to motivate change in life-space situation

Forms of Interaction That Foster
the Democratic Mutual Aid System

The interactions expressed as a product of the mutual aid system are reflective of the members' efforts and are consonant with the theme-centered issues of the first three stage themes: "We're Not in Charge," "We Are in Charge," and "We're Taking You On."

The following interactions help the members develop a democratic mutual aid system.

Developing and Appreciating Democratic Norms. These include rights to belong and to be heard. A humanistic group needs to develop conscious understanding and an ability to enact democratic norms as the reflection of the explicit values of the method (see Chapters 1 and 2). These values become the property of all—the members as well as the practitioner. The more conscious the members are of the necessity for establishing and safeguarding democratic principles, the more they enhance each member's autonomous functioning. Being heard is reflected when members feel "We're Not in Charge," as well as when they think "We Are in Charge." Their appreciation of democratic norms as the culmination of accepting that all members have rights to belong in an egalitarian and cooperative system becomes more intensely highlighted. Members put some of their internal power struggles to rest, adopt standards during their normative crisis, and gather strength to confront the practitioner ("We're Taking You On").

Making Decisions and Developing Rules. Whether implicit or explicit, the members' abilities to make decisions and play by rules govern how they deal with one another as the group goes on to actualizing purpose. Members come to terms with issues of cooperation and compromise to enable them to meet essential needs of every member rather than just some members' needs. As democratic norms are established that center on equality and participation, decision making requires the members to stay focused, to draw together, to integrate implicit and explicit demands, and to choose helpful experiences. Effective decision-making processes guard against the surfacing of unbridled interpersonal conflicts during the middle phase, when purpose is being worked on.

Developing Leadership and Followership Skills. At the onset of the normative crisis, the members are faced with the problem of developing a flexible leadership structure, rather than solidifying a rigid and inflexible one in which leadership resides in the hands of a powerful member or clique. In a humanistic group, leadership and followership skills become reciprocal and flexible; they are collectively used. Members take initiative. All can respond according to their needs and the requirements of situations. A preordained, rigidly fixed pecking order (Garland, Jones, & Kolodny, 1973) is antithetical to the values and interpersonal objectives of a humanistic group.

Respecting Differences Among Members. This attitude is reflected in the members' abilities to listen to, respond to, and incorporate different opinions, values, cultures, and personalities without requiring adherence to a narrow ideology or to a narrow spectrum of permissible behaviors. Veiled reactions or avoidance of differences are brought to the members' attentions.

Expressing Thoughts and Feelings About the Practitioner With Particular Attention to Authority Issues. In all groups, members will have a multiplicity and range of feelings about the practitioner. In many types of groups, these feelings rarely surface, thereby remaining underground and affecting the level of intimacy among the members (Levine, 1979). In the humanistic group, this "taboo area" (Shulman, 2006), which includes the feelings about the real and imagined power of the practitioner as well as the practitioner's expectations of the members, is surfaced and aired. Exposure and examination bring about deepened work and feelings of integrity and autonomy from the point of first confrontation (with "We're Taking You On") and thereafter.

Collectively Developing and Setting Goals. The ability to move toward defining and carrying out group purpose is reflected in the humanistic group when the group members can work on their relationships with the practitioner. The newfound integrity, autonomy, and strength are then used by the members to focus their collective attention on establishing goals related to the needs of each member. Members engage with the practitioner and one another in sharing leadership, which enables goals to develop.

Expressing Feelings Toward the Members. This newly developing ability is also a direct result of the members' efforts to engage with the practitioner regarding issues of power and authority (Bennis & Shepard, 1962; Garland et al., 1973). Basic acceptance of one another and support of each person's membership and contributions ensure future support among members. These dynamics set the stage for future relationships and experiences as the group moves toward actualizing purpose.

Developing Affective Bonds and Furthering Cohesion. For the group to work on difficult tasks related to group purpose, the ability to function together and affective bonds have to be substantially in place in the process. With collective well-being, members take the necessary risks to further their activities in the group and in their role relationships outside of the group.

Forms of Interaction That Foster the Actualization of Group Purpose

These interactions occur more noticeably throughout the middle and ending phases of the group's life, after the members have successfully developed and sustained the interactions of the mutual aid system. Herein, Stage Themes 4, 5, and 6—Sanctuary, "This Isn't Good Anymore," and "We're Okay and Able"—are reflections of the intense desire and frustrations of working and changing. Stage Theme 7, "Just a Little Longer," is a reaction to the members' concerns about moving on in new ways into future experiences without the actual external social supports provided by the other members and the group milieu.

The following interactions help the members actualize group purpose.

Identifying Themes to Be Worked On. Group agendas that reflect a blend of group and individual interests are identified and refined through the participation of all members. Without harnessing productive problem-solving efforts, members will "muck around in the work phase" by finding comfort in relating and belonging, but lacking motivation to change themselves and their situations. Members begin to accomplish more results than the internal time they are in the group would suggest.

Expressing Role-Enhancing Behaviors. It is especially crucial for members to be motivated to carry out different and effective ways of interacting with significant others. Anticipatory planning, role playing, and the programming of in vivo experiences—such as the teen group undertaking a community service project—should occur. These offer the member cognitive, emotional, and interaction opportunities for experimentation, observation, and changes of forms of expression that have inhibited as well as have enhanced their abilities.

Expressing and Identifying Feelings That Help the Group and Members Work on Change. The change process for members is significantly enhanced by their abilities to identify feelings and actions that are obstacles in situations and in the group experience. At this point, a significant level of trust has developed along with self-confident feelings that encourage taking initiative. This condition is sustained into the work phase. This helps members to express their difficult and threatening feelings, motivated and supported by a group norm for change and independence.

Sharing Perceptions and Feelings About Each Other's Behavior. The feedback process is a unique opportunity of group membership. Focusing on the here and now, members learn how their behaviors affect others, and how they in turn are affected by others. This helps them to deal with how they really come across outside of the group. The immediacy of feedback does not support avoidance of face-to-face engagements; it fosters opportunities for concerned change efforts.

Creating Activities in the Environment. In their classic article, Papell and Rothman (1980b) note that one of the distinguishing features of the social work group is its externality. Its members design group life and their relationships within the group to be a part of their actual lives beyond the group meetings. To fulfill the group's objectives, the members develop programs in their actual social environments for the group, subgroups, and significant others. Programming is an important part of the group's expanded effort to enhance and transform social functioning. In planning, members work on anticipatory anxiety and misperception. The program activity itself is an opportunity for role rehearsal, experimentation with different behaviors, and the creation of new environments for experiencing different types of interactions.

Identifying Group Process Issues and Structures to Heighten the Group's Self-Awareness. Interpersonal learning and enhanced role functioning occur when the members examine and clarify the meaning of the group's process and social structures that result from and affect change in their interactions. Looking at ongoing processes provides the members with opportunities for clarification of their perceptions, heightening of empathy, and the development of skills in understanding each others' different feelings and opinions. The members' collective abilities to reflect on their history and themselves, as well as their content and their allegiances, contribute to their growth. Members can see how allegiances are made for behavioral enhancement or for stagnation and inflexibility, which often is disguised as subgroup agreement that subgroup members are doing well when in fact they are not.

Identifying Projections and Self-Fulfilling Prophecies as They Interfere With Collaboration and Role Enhancement. Projections and self-fulfilling prophecies are more frequently identified and confronted in interactions, so they do not fester as distortions that interfere with the group's efforts. The ability to sustain meaningful, purposeful relationships will be impeded by a member's projections and self-fulfilling prophesies. The members' negative experiences and unmet needs now become central to interpersonal and inner conflict in group life.

Reflecting on and Reinforcing Individual and Group Change in Order to Replicate Change. Much of the work related to the group's purpose involves members' experiments with new behaviors in and out of the group. The change process involves personal struggles to alter dysfunctional or uncomfortable behaviors in the interest of role enhancement and the development of abilities; members give one another mutual support for these undertakings. Members review change processes to identify progress and personal agendas and to consider the various forms of thinking, feelings, and behaving that have gone into the change and its process.

❖ SUMMARY

The dual objectives of humanistic group work have been identified as *developing the democratic mutual aid system* and *actualizing group purpose.* It has been emphasized that the development of democratic processes of mutual aid has to occur before the group works deeply on achieving its purpose.

The relation of the dual objectives to stage themes of group development was delineated. The *development of the democratic mutual aid system* is related to Stage Themes 1, 2, and 3: "We're Not in Charge," "We Are in Charge," and "We're Taking You On." The actualization of group purpose is related to Stage Themes 4, 5, 6, and 7: Sanctuary, "This Isn't Good Anymore," "We're Okay and Able," and "Just a Little Longer."

Interactions among members that reflect the group's achievement of each of the objectives were identified. Forms of interaction that foster the democratic mutual aid system are developing democratic norms, making decisions, developing leadership and followership skills, respecting differences, expressing feelings about the practitioner, setting goals, beginning to express feelings toward members, and developing cohesion.

Forms of interaction that foster the actualization of group purpose are identifying themes to be worked on, taking risks and experimenting with role enhancement, expressing feelings that help the group work on change, sharing perceptions and feelings about each other's behavior, creating activities, identifying group process issues for group self-awareness, identifying self-fulfilling prophecies that interfere with growth, and reflecting on change in order to replicate it.

❖ NOTE

1. House Plan Association (1965). Group work programs were conducted by the House Plan Association of City College of New York, which emphasized humanistic values and democratic norms.

National Training Laboratory (1966–1967). These summer programs in group dynamics and group development held annually in Bethel, Maine, focused on the development of leadership in groups along with group norms.

Jewish Community Relations Council (2008). JCRC of New York City conducts a range of intergroup relations programs for youth through its Intergroup Relations Program.

5

Techniques for Developing the Democratic Mutual Aid System

Group work techniques are patterned professional skills the practitioner uses within the guidelines of the values and norms of humanistic group work to achieve the dual objectives. These techniques represent the collective experiences of group work practitioners who have shared in their development.

Though techniques provide important means of practice, it is necessary to understand that in order not to be prescriptive, the use of technique is informed by empathy and knowledge of social group work values. Schwartz (1961) addressed this concern, stating that the development of skillful use of technique comes about in the interplay between intuitiveness and technical skill:

There is nothing in the conception of a professional methodology which denies or subordinates the uniquely personal and artistic component which each worker brings to . . . the helping function. On the contrary, the concept of a disciplined uniqueness is inherent in the definition of art itself. In a broad sense, we may view artistic activity as an attempt . . . to express strong personal feelings and aspirations through a disciplined use of . . . materials. (p. 29)

The concern about prescriptiveness centers on the application of skill without values and the resulting effect of techniques on the well-being and performance of the group members. The concern that members will be manipulated, coerced, and controlled by the practitioner's use of technique is an important one. By focusing on the artistry of the practitioner, Schwartz (1961) indirectly addresses this concern. Within this frame of reference, the social work practitioner operating out of the framework of professional values can be both disciplined and creative, unique and individual. By modeling the practitioner, members also can share these characteristics.

That techniques can be used incorrectly and dangerously is important to consider, especially with the pressure of increased accountability requirements from funding sources and school and agency accreditation standards in the form of identifiable competencies and measurable outcomes. For instance, the expression of ingratiating attitudes or aggressive emotions by a practitioner can stimulate threat, anxiety, and submission. The expression of technique within an attitude of neutrality and scientific curiosity can also elicit anxiety and concern. The combination of technical patterns and procedures, along with attitudes of conceit and superiority, can have a powerful numbing or controlling effect on group members. Safeguards built on sound ethical practice are important to the practitioner's methodology and use of techniques.

Techniques in the humanistic method of group work have safeguards. These are the feelings, ideas, and interactions that result from humanistic values and democratic norms. These govern the practitioner's self-expression and view of the members. The application of techniques requires cognitive, affective, and purposeful use of self within the values and norms of the method. In humanistic group work, the explicit and sanctioned values and norms are humanistic and democratic.

Techniques for practice are the product of views about people, what they are like, how they can handle themselves, what they will become, and how they should treat one another. Authoritarian or utilitarian values will yield techniques and their expression that may limit people's potentials and, even worse, denigrate and control them. The process and outcome in group work are reflections of both the practitioner and the setting. Technique, then, is one among a number of significant features of the whole of the method of humanistic social group work. The values, norms, unique dual objectives of the method, and stances of the practitioner are fundamentally significant features, as well.

❖ USE OF TECHNIQUE

A practice theory of technique is also related to professional and methodological imperatives. First, professionals practicing a humanistic group form need to attend to the quality of their work: to be responsible for it, monitor it, criticize it, and convey it to others. Developing and conveying techniques creates a medium for criticism, refinement, and accountability. Second, the use of technique creates a self-awareness on the practitioner's part about the various and multiple effects that his or her behavior is having on group members. This ensures that the practitioner's uses of techniques are neither mechanistic, impersonal, nor unempathic.

With a constellation of techniques that is transmittable and refinable follows the ability to discern the details of members' responses to them. Techniques are responded to by the members, who contribute to and propel additional aspects of the process as well as the use of different techniques. Because techniques are a creative blend of acts, ideas, and feelings, they can be flexibly and creatively expressed and applied. Techniques are used to assist in shaping the group members' processes of interaction and self-expression.

In the humanistic group method, techniques are both the means and ends of interpersonal processes that assist the group members in becoming effective. Techniques are not mechanical devices to manipulate, control, or condition behavior. They are used by the practitioner to focus members' interactions with one another in cooperative and differentiated ways and will provide a model for members to emulate within the group and in other social environments. Techniques are meant to be used in ways that are empathically sensitive to and actively responsible to the expectations and needs of the members. They can be expressed in full or partial forms, as well as in combination with one another. How techniques are expressed is a function of the needs of the members as felt and perceived by the practitioner through his or her spontaneous, conscious, intuitive, and empathic interaction with the members.

❖ CATEGORIZING TECHNIQUES

A practice theory of technique that is directly related to the goals of helping members attain flexible and satisfying forms of interpersonal expression is related to social scientific and practical observations. Therefore, techniques have been identified and categorized according to their use in achieving each of the dual objectives (Glassman & Kates, 1986b).

The first set includes the techniques for developing the democratic mutual aid system. These techniques assist the members in being attentive to and developing the process of mutual aid, which is discussed in this chapter. The second set, techniques for actualizing group purpose, consists of those that are used to assist members in focusing on and changing the characteristic patterns of interactions and environmental circumstances that have brought them to the group. These techniques are discussed in Chapters 6 and 7. While each of these sets of techniques is primarily related to developing the specific interactions of the dual objectives, they occur in interrelated ways throughout. Those techniques related to developing the democratic mutual aid system will be used more frequently earlier on, and those related to group purpose later on. Several additional techniques are ubiquitous throughout the group's entire process. These techniques serve to develop the democratic mutual aid system and actualize group purpose. They are discussed in Chapter 8.

Twenty-nine techniques that practitioners use to achieve the dual objectives of the humanistic group have been identified; these are shown in Table 5.1. The intent of the technique is presented. The behavior of the

Table 5.1   Techniques in Relationship to the Dual Objectives

Techniques Related to the Mutual Aid System	Techniques Related to Actualizing Purpose	Techniques Woven in Both Objectives
Facilitating collective participation	Role rehearsal	Demand for work
Scanning	Programming	Directing
Engaging group as a whole	Group reflective consideration	Lending a vision
Modulating the expression of feeling	Interpretation	Staying with feelings
Facilitating decision-making processes	Feedback	Silence
Processing the here and now	Conflict resolution	Support
Expressing feelings about practitioner role	Group mending	Exploration
Goal setting	Confrontation	Identification
Good and welfare	Data and facts	
	Self-disclosure	
	Dealing with unknown	
	Taking stock	

practitioner in enacting the technique is described. An illustration demonstrating the use of the technique in a group situation is presented along with a discussion of the group and practitioner's process.

❖ TECHNIQUES FOR DEVELOPING
   THE DEMOCRATIC MUTUAL AID SYSTEM

The earlier discussion of the dual objectives of the humanistic method pointed out that the practitioner's primary activity at the start is to help the members develop a democratic mutual aid system. Among the 29 identified group work techniques used by practitioners, nine have been developed and are used to assist the members in achieving this objective. These are *facilitating collective participation, scanning, engaging the group as a whole, modulating the expression of feelings, facilitating decision-making processes, processing the here and now, expressing feelings about the practitioner role, setting goals,* and *good and welfare* (see the "Techniques Chart" at the end of the chapter).

Each of these techniques also has a relationship to the interactions of the democratic mutual aid system. For clarification, see Table 5.2.

Facilitating Collective Participation

This technique is used to foster the acceptance and right of all members to belong, as well as to acknowledge their special importance because of their unique qualities.

The practitioner openly invites members to participate by encouraging opinions from all, with careful attention to those who have not yet offered them. By pointing out to the group when someone is trying to interact, the practitioner creates emotional space for all, while at the same time helping the group see that making space for each other is the group's—not just the practitioner's—responsibility. By redirecting members to speak to one another, not about each other, the practitioner places further emphasis on the group's responsibility for including each other and in valuing each member's expression. The practitioner also points out when members are inattentive, thereby avoiding risks of misinterpretations and misunderstandings. The practitioner fosters participation by asking the members to build on what is being expressed and systematically inviting members to take part in relation to things that have been expressed by others.

Table 5.2   Techniques in Relationship to the Interactions of the Democratic Mutual Aid System

Technique	Interaction
Facilitating collective participation	Develop cohesion and affective bonds.
Scanning	Develop cohesion and affective bonds.
Engaging the group as a whole	Develop cohesion and affective bonds.
Modulating the expression of feeling	Express feelings. Respect differences. Develop rules. Develop cohesion and affective bonds.
Facilitate decision-making processes	Enhance decision making and development of rules. Develop leadership and followership skills. Collectively develop and set goals. Respect differences.
Processing the here and now	Foster the expression of feeling. Develop cohesion and affective bonds. Develop democratic norms—belonging, inclusion, being heard.
Expressing feelings about the practitioner role	Foster expression of feelings. Develop affective bonds and cohesion. Develop democratic norms—belonging, inclusion, being heard.
Goal setting	Collectively set goals. Develop cohesion and affective bonds.
Good and welfare	Respect differences. Develop cohesion and affective bonds. Develop democratic norms—belonging, inclusion, being heard, owning the group.

Illustration   Latency Age Boys Group

In a socialization group of 9- to 10-year-old boys at the child guidance clinic, James is telling everyone how bugged he gets when the teacher yells at him to stop talking, when it's usually his neighbor who gets him into trouble. Dave, the practitioner, notices that the boys want to participate, but they don't know whether to interrupt James. He says, "James, stop a minute, I think there might be others who have similar problems." Several boys give James support and share similar experiences about their relationships to their teachers.

The practitioner notes that Joey, who is Hispanic and usually rather shy but attentive to the process, is exhibiting his usual quietness during this time. He turns to Joey and says, "I noticed you've been listening quietly. Do you have something about this topic that you could tell us? How is it with you and your teachers?" Joey tells the group that he didn't like his teacher at first because she was strict, but now she has been nice. And she's not that bad; she just has to be strict because of some of the children's behavior. The practitioner asks the group, "How do you react to what Joey said? Is this similar for any of you? Can any of you see yourselves changing your minds about your teachers?" The members talk more about how they have gotten to like a couple of their teachers better and what they could do to improve their relations with them, such as "being quiet, doing homework, listening in class, and not fighting." One member, Ivan, the child of Russian immigrants, makes a comment that is bypassed: "My teacher is mean to me, even when I am good." The practitioner says, "Wait, you guys didn't respond what Ivan has just said. How do you react to that?" The children talk about how hard it is when they are judged unfairly. The practitioner asks the group to "tell Ivan, because you sound like you're talking about him, not to him, although he's here."

Discussion

This use of the technique sets the stage for the group to learn to include each of the members by responding directly to them through exploratory questions, affirmation, or just acknowledgments. The practitioner stops James from talking too much and possibly losing the group, which might make it more difficult for him to feel commonality with others. Upon hearing the members' experiences, he elicits more responses directed toward James and among the others.

In this group of mostly black and Hispanic children, Ivan is the only child of Russian background in the group. It is possible that he was feeling different, as well as being perceived as different by the other members. Such feelings and perceptions may make it harder for a member to feel included and to be included. Thus, the practitioner makes a special effort to foster the inclusion of Ivan by not permitting his concerns to be bypassed. Inclusion of Ivan may turn out to be complex, due to his unique ethnic origin; by using this technique to involve Ivan, the practitioner sets the stage for helping members respond to him.

Scanning

Scanning is used to help the group practitioner focus on and become more sensitive to the entire group, beyond any one person who happens to be the center of focus at the moment. It is used also to strengthen cohesion and affective bonds. Perceptions gained from scanning may be shared with the group either at that moment or at a later time.

To enact this technique, the practitioner looks from person to person, sometimes to the person being addressed by the speaker, and then around the room to observe, acknowledge, and incorporate the group's full nonverbal expression. Leaning forward, listening attentively, responding to outside distractions, being tuned out, and talking to each other are some of the behaviors the practitioner makes sure to note. By looking around, the practitioner tries to take in the dominant affect of the group at that moment, as well as the possibility that several affects may be concurrent. This technique enables the practitioner to be in touch with the person who is talking, and to be with the group as well (Shulman, 2006). It is used in all forms of group life—during discussion, silences, and activities. The practitioner may be selective about when to make or not make eye contact with members. Eye contact may stimulate the member to respond to the practitioner, when that was not the intention. The practitioner may also test out to see who is willing or not willing to make eye contact with him or her, but usually does not hold the eye contact.

If the practitioner feels vague or confused about the process, scanning can often provide the stimulus for a new empathic awareness. Eventually, members learn to imitate the practitioner's scanning and therefore to tune in more sensitively to each other as they conduct their work in the later stages of the process.

| *Illustration* | *A Community Planning Group* |

A community planning group, made up of a cross section of residents and professionals in a large urban setting, was developed to explore the housing crisis in the area created by gentrification (i.e., the conversion of affordable housing into condominiums) and destabilization of rental guidelines. The group convener, Annette, is the director of the local nongovernmental agency serving the homeless. Three members are talking busily about trying to get one of the community churches to develop a temporary day program for the homeless. This would give the small but dedicated staff a visible setting where people who might have been overlooked could receive needed services and entitlements while also obtaining some long-range planning options.

While slowly looking from person to person, Annette notices two members looking at each other and still another one silently withdrawing, conveying opposite feelings from the tenor of the three-way discussion. She becomes sensitive to their anxiety about being able to take part and draws in those members by saying, "I notice some of you are more involved, others are less involved. Any sense of what this means to you and our process?"

Discussion

The idea of a temporary day program for homeless persons was an action that the group convener favored. However, for it to happen, the full support of this group would be necessary. Thus, as a group convener with an executive leadership role as well, Annette had to bring everyone aboard, make room for their doubts and concerns to be expressed, and, if the idea was to materialize, to enable everyone to own the results by participating in the process. On the other hand—even after full discussion—the withdrawing silent members might never have come around to liking the program idea, thus forcing it to be dropped. While this might be a disappointment to the group convener, it is better to drop the idea now than to ignore the disapproval, get it passed now without discussion, only to have it aborted later on, and possibly be embarrassed by a public display from disapproving factions.

Scanning the group is necessary, whether or not the group convener or practitioner is positively oriented toward the topic being discussed. Scanning helps the practitioner to accomplish the purpose of strengthening the development of a democratic mutual aid process. Had Annette been swept away by the threesome's agreement with her own goals, she would have lost her potential to be with everyone in the group, rather than just those who represented what she wanted to accomplish. In the long run, her leadership capability and credibility may be strengthened by her show of commitment to including everyone's ideas and participation in the process. With this kind of leadership, members in this task force may more easily become aware of her demonstration of respect for their perceptions.

Engaging the Group as a Whole

In many instances, beginning practitioners with groups experience great difficulty in engaging with and addressing the group as a whole. They address only individuals, leaving out a spectrum of connections that may be used and processed by the entire group. As a result, members imitate the practitioner's behaviors, hardly ever addressing the group in its entirety. An intent of the technique that follows is to establish and strengthen the identity and cohesion of the group in order to draw on its energy as a collective.

The practitioner uses pronouns that serve as metaphors for the humanistic social work group. Sometimes the practitioner uses *we* and *ours*; at other times, the practitioner uses *you* and *yours*. Through the use of this technique, the members are helped to differentiate between the domain of the group including the practitioner and the domain of the group excluding the practitioner. The use of *we* and *our* refers to and strengthens the feelings of the group's members, including the practitioner, and connotes a common stake in the process and life of the group. By using *you* and *yours*, the group practitioner acknowledges the reality of the uniqueness of the members' experiences and their separateness from his or her own experiences.

It is not uncommon for group work practitioners to use only *we* and *ours*, avoiding the use of *you* and *yours*. While many do this from an egalitarian or humanistic perspective, rather than from a manipulative one, it appears that this strategy represents a failure to differentiate the uniqueness of the practitioner's role within the domain of his or her membership in the group. When the practitioner conceives of himself or herself only as part of the collective, then *we* is used manipulatively, disguising the practitioner's power in the group and diverting the members from dealing with the different status, power, and authority issues the practitioner's activities yield. On the other hand, some group practitioners use only *you* and *yours*, as if they are not members or have no stake in the group's outcomes. This represents an inauthentic differentiation that does not account for the intersubjective nature of the group's experience for both the practitioner and the members. Falck (1988) has noted that all are members in the group, sharing a stake in the process. Simultaneously, though, each person's membership is unique. Not only does the practitioner have a special role and unique stake in the process, but in that role the practitioner also carries more power and authority than any other single member.

This group practitioner consciously uses the humanistic group work method toward fulfilling members' collective needs, not the practitioner's needs. Therefore, the practitioner is sometimes part of the *we* of the group, and sometimes part of the *I* and *you* of the group.

| *Illustration* | *Teen Group in a Community Center* |

The members of a teen group in a community center are talking about how they want to run a fund-raising program so they can collect money to go on an overnight trip to the state capital for a special program hosted by legislators. Many ideas are bandied about—a cake sale, a dance at the center, a talent show, or a combination of these. The practitioner, Tim, says, "You've got lots of good ideas for raising money so we can get to this legislators' meeting." The kids then begin to talk about trying to include another teen group. The practitioner says, "One of us needs to talk to them about it. Shall I talk to their worker, or do you want to talk to their worker, or to the group? If it's really going to happen, then I guess we'd need a joint meeting."

Discussion

The first statement made by Tim acknowledges the group's collective investment in going to the state event, while at the same time noting that the practitioner plans to go with the group in his role as a group worker. In this case, the practitioner does not offer the ideas for the fund-raiser—rather, the teens did. It is not the practitioner who needs funding for the event (the agency covers his fees); rather, it is the teens. On the other hand, for the practitioner to have said "You can get to the legislators' meeting" would have been unreal and inappropriate, because the person from the agency who usually accompanies the teens on outings is the group worker. Here a *you* statement would have stranded the teens, because it could be seen as an abdication of role responsibility. At least, it would have required an explanation.

Not only does the use of *we* and *you* differentiate the teens from the worker within the group meeting, but it also accounts for the agency's participation in the life and activities of the group. Since this group exists in a community center where many aspects of the life of one group may be intertwined with the life of another group, the domain of the agency invariably will be a factor for the teens' consideration. Thus, the practitioner takes note that he is part of this group in entertaining a cooperative venture with another group at the center. He does not deny membership in the group; at the same time, he does note a difference because of his professional role.

Modulating the Expression of Feeling

Practice wisdom (Yalom, 2005) points to the need to "balance self-disclosure" and suggests that "it may be necessary to slow down the pace of a client who too quickly reveals deeply personal details before establishing engagement" (p. 234). Those who reveal too much or too little early on are more apt than others not to return to the group. Anxiety and embarrassment tend to result from premature self-disclosure, rather than the desired feelings of well-being and catharsis. Therefore, caution needs to be exercised, especially by the beginning practitioner who might be relieved by self-disclosure (thinking that self-disclosure might be a means for rescuing the group from ambiguity and anxiety about how to work together). In other words, the group worker should take, and not avoid, responsibility for tempering the amount and nature of members' self-disclosures in the early stages of group life.

The practitioner sees this as a nonthreatening atmosphere for collective emotional expression. When a member presents personalized material, the practitioner should not probe or encourage the member to go on. The practitioner stops the disclosure from unfolding and becoming a purely affective and personalized presentation. He or she identifies its meaning and then generalizes it to the feelings and perceptions of other members, as well as to the collective significance for the group as a whole.

Illustration   *Women in a Domestic Violence Support Group*

The women in a domestic violence support group meet in the hospital clinic on a weekly basis. It is a newly formed group, meeting for the third time. The practitioner has been concentrating her efforts on helping them build mutual support; she hopes to get them thinking about alternatives for themselves and their children. Some of the women have moved out of their homes; others have not.

In this meeting one member, Barbara, begins to tell how her husband has violated her sexually. She seems to want to share many of the details of her sex life. The practitioner notices several members looking away; one sighs and another frowns. Before Barbara discusses more of the details, the practitioner interrupts her and says, "I have a feeling you're not the only one here that's felt sexually violated. It's positive that you want to share, but I'm not sure people here are ready yet to look at some of the details of these painful experiences. There will be so many feelings and reactions you will want to share as the group progresses and we get to know each other better." After a brief silence, the practitioner says to the group, "I noticed some of you were having a hard time thinking about Barbara's experience and some of the material it gives us to work on. I was thinking that for some of you, taking each part slowly might make it easier to cope. I am curious what your thoughts are about that."

Discussion

It is tempting to help a member talk about personal issues in detail. After all, it might be cathartic to talk about the pain one has experienced; others are also in the same boat. But at this time, allowing this level of intensity to be aired is more apt to overwhelm all the members than to help them. For a group to be truly helpful, there has to be a collective feeling that the members are ready to listen to and help one another share intimate details that will trigger some of their own negative experiences and painful feelings.

The practitioner responds to the subtle feedback of the members—the sigh, the seeming movement away from the member. The practitioner does not avoid or deny the validity of this member's experiences; rather, she takes note of the effect this topic has on the others. She responds to it directly, and reflects on the varied opinions and reactions about revealing themselves quickly.

Facilitating Decision-Making Processes

The intent of facilitating decision-making processes (Lowy, 1973) is to help the members arrive at junctures that move them to newer and different productive courses of action and expression, in order to develop their sense of mastery. This technique also involves members in a face-to-face laboratory for learning democratic process wherein people have full expression and can listen to each other. Learning decision-making processes enables members to meet needs in ways that do not result in rejection and censure. This essential technique is built on several interrelated activities. Though complex, its parts make up one unique and important technique in helping make use of demo-cratic processes to increase collective experiences (Klein, 1953; Trecker, 1972). The technique includes the following three aspects.

Checking for Interest, Feelings, and Opinions. This is used to air the alter-natives and the majority and minority views about directions the group can take. In the course of exploratory discussion, the practitioner periodically asks the members to state their feelings and opinions regarding the issue. The practitioner discourages them from arriving at premature closure by directly inhibiting fixed conclusions. Maintaining the fluidity and flow of opinions and ideas is necessary; therefore, voting and silent, head-nodding agreement methods of deci-sion making are not supported.

Weaving Collective Perceptions/Consensus. Herein, the effort is to bring the members beyond fixed and narrow sets of alternatives. The practitioner identifies, summarizes, and clarifies the different sources of the threads and themes being expressed. The members are encouraged to do the same. The practitioner asks them to select common themes prevalent in their opinions in order to focus the group on its new commonality. Consensus is reached if and when the reweaving of collective perceptions brings forth a new approach that is acceptable to all of the members.

Compromise. Compromise can be used to help members give up vested interests on behalf of collective interests and experiences. The crucial behaviors for the practitioner include asking members to accept the realities of the situation and requesting—as well as eliciting—members' willingness to give up what appear to be their vested interests. Compromise is used after the members have discussed options and thought that consensus is impossible. Voting is an appropriate model of compromise; it must come only after discussion, however, and only if everyone's needs have been considered. The opinions of the minority must be respected and members must discuss willingness to abide by forthcoming decision. The practitioner asks these members how they would feel about going along with the outcome. This is done so that the members do not remain or become more split after different views are expressed and a compromise is agreed on.

Illustration   *College Students Planning Committee*

The student programming committee of a college residence hall is discussing how to go about supporting a strike of clerical workers on the campus. The residence director runs these meetings. The group is meeting to talk about what to do about a forthcoming party they have scheduled for the weekend with a live band and a disc jockey (DJ). Many faculty members are supporting the strike by trying to hold classes off campus so as not to cross the picket line. In this atmosphere, some students do not want to hold the event on the campus. Mark thinks that "the students need something and programs should not be taken away from them." Several vocal members state their views, and one member suggests they vote on it. The residence director says, "I don't think voting will help us understand the group's needs. Let's hear from more people regarding thoughts about what to do next."

The thought about supporting the strikers is clearly positive. The student members talk more about not wanting to cancel an event. Some are strongly in favor of moving the event off campus, while recognizing the difficulty in securing space. For others, there is a strong desire not to cross the picket lines to come into the dorms or to eat in the cafeteria, let alone have a frivolous party on campus. Denise talks about her mother's membership in a union and how important it has been in getting her good health benefits. The salary scale of the clerical staff is also mentioned; students become upset.

The residence director says, "Some of you want to have the event off campus and some of you feel okay about having it on campus. It seems that no one wants to cancel the party, is that right?" Much vocal agreement is expressed. Denise suggests that the community center or nearby church might support the event. She asks her roommate Erin to "help me call these places to see if the group can hold the party off campus." The residence director wonders what they will do if they cannot find an off-campus place. Several members say they don't want to have the party on campus. The residence director wonders if anyone has spoken to the band or the DJ, reminding them that union musicians will not cross a picket line, "and the decision might be made for you." Sherry says she will call her friends in the band right away to see how they would feel about coming on campus. Mark says he has already put out publicity on campus and invited the local colleges; quick actions and corrections are needed.

The residence director says, "It sounds like most of you want to go off campus. How would you feel, Mark, if we did that? And are you prepared to handle notifications to other schools?" He shares his reluctance, but also a willingness to accept the solution. The residence director asks the others, "Denise and Erin, how would you feel if there's no place off campus to have the event? Will you want to have it on campus?" Denise is adamant: "I will not be involved in the event. I will also not be part of the committee until the strike is settled." Erin is not sure; more talk ensues. Some people feel it's a mistake to hold it on campus and let students from nearby schools be faced with a picket line. The group eventually agrees to make every effort to hold the party off campus. They decide that if no off-campus site is available, they will hold a small event (without a band or DJ) just for students who will be around on the weekend, but they will cancel the invitations to other schools. Denise says, "I feel better about this decision. I still won't attend if it is on campus, but I will understand."

Discussion

The practitioner here faces a difficult and emotionally charged situation. First, the idea of a strike can bring about many intensified feelings among group members. There is obviously much to be learned in this situation, as well as a great potential for conflict. This group consists of one member, whose mother is a committed union member, who will not cross a picket line. The group has many responsibilities to consider: to fellow students, to the college community, and to the strikers.

First, the practitioner does not permit the group to come to a premature decision. This is a very complex issue that needs to be sensitively and carefully considered to include the opinions of all the members. Not voting allows the members to go forward in expressing various views and feelings. They can also examine consequences and begin to develop some strategies for action. When the practitioner discusses contacting the band, the members see themselves as action oriented and begin to mobilize an effort to go off campus. A more or less implicit decision is made that going off campus is the preferred plan. Without efforts at the inclusion of the spectrum of feelings and opinions, the group might have fragmented and the members would have come away feeling bad, disoriented, and alienated.

Processing the Here and Now

The here and now is that aspect of the group's life that occurs in the present, moment to moment, and is focused on experiencing the group (Yalom, 2005). According to Yalom, when the group is in the here and now, "the immediate events of the meeting take precedence over events both in the current outside life and in the distant past of the members" (p. 141). However, for understanding to come about, there needs to be "an illumination of process" wherein the "group . . . also doubles back on itself; it performs a self-reflective loop and examines the here-and-now behavior that has just occurred" (p. 142).

Processing the here and now (Bradford, Gibb, & Benne, 1964; Schwartz, 1976; Yalom, 2005) is a technique used by the practitioner to engage the group in an immediate and active examination of members' self-expressions and group interactions in order to raise conscious awareness of the process. It is also used when the practitioner wishes to focus the members' attention on latent processes that are occurring simultaneously with manifest ones. When the members can turn attention on themselves, understanding of relationship, communication, and other dynamics is heightened. In the course of group interaction, the practitioner points out particularly significant events and reaction patterns, describing them and asking for the members' collective efforts at observation and consideration of the feelings and dynamics that are occurring.

| Illustration | *Divorced and Separating Women's Group* |

In a group of divorced and separating women, there is considerable talk about the emotional harassment and anger many have felt and even feared from their husbands. Several of the men are already out of the homes, while others continue to remain. This results in a stressful situation for all concerned, including any children. Regardless of the living arrangements, the women are experiencing financial pressures as well, such as no money for groceries and constantly having to figure out ways to get the former husband to provide some money to buy necessities for their child. The women are talking about the hurts they are experiencing and how some of the children are reacting as well.

Several of the women—Dora, Judy, Beatrice, and Myra—continue talking about the difficulty they experience with their husbands in the house. Judy's husband has a girlfriend in another state, but still will not move out; Beatrice's husband won't move out because he "wants to have his cake and eat it, too. We have nothing to say to one another. I wish he'd just go to his mother's house."

Eventually the practitioner says, "I've been noticing how those of you who are talking still have your husbands in the house, and the rest of you who are living separately are being quiet. What's been going on here today?" Several of the women who have been talking say they haven't noticed this. Then some begin to talk about how hard it is to speak to those who have already "gone through with it." The practitioner says, "Is this what's been going on for you today?" Dora responds that it has, and she says, "I don't understand how you were able to separate so easily, while some of us seem to be having such a difficult time." Myra says that she had a hard time, too, but having no children made it much easier: "I don't want to sit in judgment of you. I've just been listening today trying to figure it out with you." Indira agrees and reminds the group that she ran away with her son to a shelter. "If you think that was easy to do, you are wrong. I was so scared, but I had to get my baby out of there." Lauren talks about how having a job made it easier for her to split up with her husband. Her children were so miserable with the fighting that divorce had to be a better alternative.

Myra tells the group, "My children think I'm a wimp for not being able to throw my husband out. He makes a fool out of me." She then asks Mary and Lauren, "Do you think I'm a wimp for still being with him?" They offer her support, saying how hard it is to leave. Then Myra continues, "But you really seem to want to take the next step. You took the first step in joining this group." There is more talk about the difficulties in splitting up and the need to have good legal help.

The practitioner points out, "Right now, more of you are participating. I had a sense there's been a pattern to the sharing here, perhaps cliques forming of those who have left or whose husbands have left, and those who haven't." Linda says, "Maybe that's true, I do find myself talking to Judy more because I know she's still in the same situation of not leaving. Maybe I should also talk to Lauren." Beatrice says, "Indira, I never realized you were so scared until now." Indira acknowledges what has just been said. More discussion follows on the different views of the meaning of separating from their husbands. Discussion moves to comparisons about which women are stronger or more independent than others. The women start laughing and crying together.

Discussion

In this meeting, the practitioner uses the here-and-now technique to help the members establish a broader level of commonality to enable a wider use of support. The practitioner has focused the group's attention to the process as it is unfolding in the meeting. Certainly the content being discussed is important, too. But without the practitioner's intervention, the equally important process itself would not be considered and made part of the content. Here is a group of women who need help and support in expanding their abilities to deal with and examine various aspects of interpersonal relations with each other, as well as with other women, men, and children. Yet they show signs of falling back on the safety of sameness, which for them will undermine necessary interaction and independence.

In this interaction, the practitioner does not respond to the individual member's concerns. Rather, she takes note of a subgroup of people not participating and that this may indicate the formation of a status hierarchy of two different subgroups. If they become fixed, the subgroupings will serve no useful purpose in meeting the members' goals. Focusing attention to the here and now helps the members appreciate the significance of their own behavior and the meta messages of their interactions. This results in an expanded ability to ask for help from others who are perceived as stronger.

Expressing Feelings About the Practitioner Role

The intent of this technique is to help the members directly express the latent and manifest feelings they have toward the practitioner. These usually remain or go underground, and they will not be a significant part of the process. The practitioner is a member with a special position and a professional role and stake in the group; as such, he or she is perceived by the members to be different than they are. Directly discussing their feelings about the practitioner strengthens the group's capacity to take direction and to disagree with the practitioner. Expressing these feelings and perceptions alters distortions that occur when members' projections and idiosyncratic frames of references remain unexpressed. While expression of these types of feelings may be thought to be taboo (Shulman, 2006), not expressing them colors and masks the group's spontaneity and depth of intimate relationships (Levine, 1979).

The practitioner encourages the group to express feelings and opinions about him or her. The practitioner asks the members how they are responding to his or her efforts and interactions. The practitioner may point out when members are avoiding responding to direction from him or her, or when the members seem to want to hear, talk to, or look only at the practitioner rather than the other members, seeming to overvalue the professional and devalue one another.

This technique also requires addressing and interpreting the members' expression of feelings about other helpers (Bennis & Shepard, 1962; Shulman, 2006), such as when they are talking about teachers, doctors, or supervisors, as a reflection of their feelings and perceptions about the present practitioner. Additionally, by owning up to errors and encouraging the group to react to these, the practitioner further demystifies the aura of power and potency unrealistically attached to the person carrying out the professional role.

| Illustration | **Adults With Developmental Disabilities** |

Members in a group of moderate- to high-functioning adults with developmental disabilities are talking about their experiences in the sheltered workshop. Martha, Hubie, and Earline are part of an assembly line that makes desk items. Pandit, Chuckie, and Lorinda are in a print shop. Zoe and Terry are on a housekeeping crew in a nearby office building. The print crew begins talking about the foreman of the print shop and how he "blew his stack today" because they didn't get a job out to one of the schools on time. Talk continues about the different bosses they have. Some tell them exactly what to do, and other bosses "overdo it because we are retarded." Chuckie, Lorinda, and Hubie are quite active in this discussion.

After some time Larry, the practitioner, turns to the others and asks, "How about your bosses, how do you feel about them? I'd like to hear form Earline, Zoe, Terry, and Pandit." After some encouragement, these members also talk a bit about those who supervise them on their work sites. Larry then says to the group, "I was wondering how you were feeling about me as a worker in this group? Do you think I boss you too much, or too little, or do things you don't like?" Some laughter ensues, with Larry laughing also, and then encouraging their response. "Come on, I'd like to know what you think. There's no point in you not telling me." Finally, Lorinda says, "You're okay, Larry. You don't make us feel dumb and stupid at all." Chuckie says, "At first I didn't like you asking us to say what was on our minds. In the other group I was in, we did exercises. We didn't talk or sit in a circle. You make us talk a lot and it scares me." Larry asks, "Is anyone else scared?" Earline snaps at Chuckie, "You're always scared. You always want your mother around. You're such a pain. You love to play retarded." Larry says to Earline, "You don't like it when other people are scared." She says that she doesn't, "especially when they don't keep quiet about it and try to get everyone else worried." The practitioner asks Earline, "Were you scared here? Did I ever scare you?" Earline admits that she has been afraid in the group, "when you said we would talk about our feelings in here, and about how to have better relationships on the job and with friends." Zoe chimes in, "You treat me like a person even though I am slow. You should see how they treat us when we clean—like we don't exist!" The practitioner says, "I'm sorry about that, Zoe. Please let me know if I ever insult you, okay?" More talk continues about the practitioner and the group's experiences with one another.

Discussion

In this group, the practitioner moves slowly toward helping the group look at his self-expression and interactions in his role. When several of the members are talking about their bosses, he does not immediately ask them to talk about their reactions to him as practitioner. This is because they need special assistance to make certain that all are included in the conversation and that everyone understands the theme that is being discussed. With three members talking, the practitioner had to make certain all were involved in talking about their bosses, so that all could become involved in talking about how the practitioner was acting in his role.

Many professionals would not broach the subject of the practitioner role with people with mental retardation. This is an error, a result of the practitioner's stereotyping and stigmatizing the members. Talking about the practitioner offers the members opportunities for autonomy. It furthers their ability to deal with the many people in authority roles they always have to interact with and to whom they have to answer. It helps the members deal with the hurt about their limitations that is ubiquitous in social situations.

Goal Setting

This technique is used to capitalize and build on the emerging collective ownership of the group experience. It is also used to crystallize cohesion and group identity. Use of goal setting marks the beginning of the group's transition from working on developing a democratic mutual aid system to working on actualizing group purpose.

When the members question the group's format and objectives, the practitioner focuses their attention on identifying and setting their goals. The practitioner points out different ways in which individual and collective needs are emerging and merging, and how these are a reflection of newer and deeper characterizations of the group as a mutual aid system. This provides motivation and support for the members as a collective in terms of their objectives. The practitioner asks the members to begin to explore the different types of needs and interests the group might work on, given the group's stated purpose.

Illustration	Middle School Children at Risk

The 10- to 13-year-old children identified by the child guidance clinic and child protective service, because they were removed from parents, have been meeting for 6 weeks with a clinic social worker based at the school. They have been talking about spending trial time with a parent and about not liking to leave their foster home and friends to go to a different place that's not in the neighborhood. The practitioner says, "I guess whichever way you look at your situations, they're not smooth and easy, right? And there are lots of things not to like about them." Davy says that he doesn't like to visit his mother because "it's boring. She keeps watching soaps and not taking us anywhere." Mara says that she has more fun when her mother lets her bring a friend for the visit. The practitioner asks the member who lives with a paternal grandmother, "What about you, Hazel? Your dad is far away. When do you see him?" Hazel says she flies out for long weekends and vacations. "I have a new set of friends there, so it's okay. But it costs a lot to go there, so I don't get to go too often."

The practitioner says, "Some of you are complaining about going. How would you feel if you didn't go?" Several say they'd miss not seeing their parent. Some members begin to show anger at one or both of their parents. Laura says she hates her visits because her mother makes her run errands with her. Susan, who lives with her grandmother, announces that "I'm going to move in with my mother soon. My little brother is driving me crazy and my grandmother can't handle all of us." The practitioner asks, "How do you feel about that, Susan?" Susan says she's not sure—she doesn't want to cause problems for her grandmother, but she doesn't even know if they will let her go with her mother. Laura says she'd rather live with her foster family and can't imagine why Susan would leave her grandmother. Silence follows.

The practitioner says, "You've all got lots of feelings, and it's hard, for sure, but as you've been talking it seems there's a lot we can discuss together. What do you think you can do here?" "I want my mother to make things fun for us," says Davy. Laura echoes, "Me too." The practitioner says to Davy, Laura, and the group, "It sounds like you guys might have things you want to say to your parents. Do you talk with any of them about what you want?" Some say that they do and some that they don't. The practitioner says, "Maybe we can also talk about that, too—how and when you can talk to your parents and what to say." Many of the children agree.

Then James, who has been quiet most of the time, says, "I want to know how to get my mother off drugs." Everyone becomes quiet. The practitioner says, "I guess that's one of the hardest topics, talking about your hopes that she can recover. You realize it's not up to you to get your mother off drugs." Members nod in agreement. "But we can definitely talk about that here."

Discussion

The practitioner begins by pointing out to the members that their situations are not easy and that whichever way things happen, they have mixed feelings. The practitioner also relates to the many difficulties they are experiencing in going to different homes, with different friends, and spending time with a parent who may be disappointing. For some, getting parents to hear their needs more clearly is potent.

For still others, learning how to have a good time will be essential. The practitioner is careful to include the member whose father is living in a different state.

As talk continues, one sees that the members feel angry, and they displace this anger onto their situations. Abandonment and disappointment are major issues in this group. The practitioner raises their themes and issues as possible future topics. The subject of missing other family members is pointedly asked about to heighten feelings and test reality. Learning to speak directly with parents is offered as an option for members to consider. Coping with feelings about parental limitations needs to be addressed. The practitioner is focusing the members' attention on their future work in the process.

Good and Welfare

This technique is used to help the group members gain closure of a meeting, whether or not there is unfinished business. By providing the members with this structure for expressing their reactions to a meeting at its conclusion, the practitioner's intention is to prevent dissatisfactions and interpersonal tensions from festering between meetings and into the next one. Good and welfare sets the stage for future decisions about issues to deal with through the members' collective efforts. By hearing how others have just experienced the meeting, members can more constructively respond to one another after the meeting time and consider issues for forthcoming meetings. The assumption is that members will carry reactions out of the meeting and may deal directly with one another outside of the meeting. Furthermore, whether or not members meet one another, the current meeting and the next one can be more productively considered as they leave and prepare themselves for future interactions.

The practitioner introduces good and welfare right before the close of the first session. In a go-around structure, each member states what he or she liked or disliked about the session. The practitioner explains the purpose of good and welfare and asks that members succinctly share reactions to "how the meeting went today," telling them not to respond to what is being said, but to just listen to one another. This structure is maintained because the good and welfare, which takes place near the close of the meeting as time is running out, should not kindle issues that cannot be handled. To further enable the group, the practitioner also shares reactions to the session and process. The practitioner offers encouragement to the members to begin the good and welfare process. If no one does, the practitioner can start by modeling positive and negative reactions. As each person finishes, the practitioner looks to another member to stimulate movement and sharing.

After several meetings, the group may well initiate this process without the group worker's recommendation.

Illustration	Cancer Support Group

The members in a cancer treatment support group are in the midst of their first meeting. They have been talking about the effects of treatment on their families. They have also spoken about the need to discuss treatment procedures with their doctors and about aftereffects of those as well.

Near the end of the session, the practitioner, Gloria, introduces the idea of the good-and-welfare process. "It's usually helpful," she says, "to take some time before leaving to just go around, briefly saying how you've reacted to the meeting." There is a pause, and then encouragement by the practitioner: "Does someone want to start?" Murray starts, saying, "It's often hard to talk to your family about having cancer. But here, it's been much easier to talk." The practitioner looks to the next person, Fran, who begins, "My daughter doesn't understand that I don't want to talk with her about my cancer. It just depresses me, but today I started to see other ways, especially from what Sally said." Sally nods in acknowledgment. The practitioner looks to the next person, Eva, who was quiet during the meeting. Eva says, "I don't want you to think that I wasn't listening even though I was quiet. I learn a lot just from listening. I feel I would like to say more next time. I am seeing how some of our friends find it hard to bring up the subject unless we do."

After everyone has shared reactions, the practitioner summarizes and ends the meeting by offering her view of themes that seemed prevalent: "I guess people are saying we can get together here and be helpful. Some of you think you didn't say all that you wanted to, but that's often how people in groups feel at the beginning. For myself, I'm feeling positively about this meeting; you've already mentioned ways you might provide help and support to one another, family issues, friendship, talking versus remaining silent, and how to deal with doctors."

Discussion

Several times in this illustration, the group worker could have been drawn into beginning or encouraging exploration of issues and themes presented by members during the good-and-welfare process. First, when one member (Fran) specifically identifies the contribution of another member (Sally) the practitioner—rather than turning to Sally—holds to the structure of the technique and provides for the process of the group by looking to the next person (Eva) and encouraging her to go on. Otherwise the group, never having done this before, could have been drawn into trying to find out what specifically had been said by Sally that was helpful to Fran. Eva, who was quiet today, would have been likely to yield the floor to a discussion between Sally and Fran. In this case, Eva takes the opportunity to indicate to the group that she knows she has been quiet. This helps the other members consider her specific feelings and thoughts, and also keeps them from viewing her as mysterious, withdrawn, or secretive.

The practitioner does not respond specifically to Eva's concern about her quietness. Rather, during her time to sum up, the practitioner takes the opportunity to universalize the concerns about members not having said all that they might have wanted to say. She also gives the group food for thought for the next few meetings. In addition, by letting them know how she feels as a practitioner, she motivates their interest in developing a positive commitment to the group effort.

❖ SUMMARY

In this chapter, the stage was set for the practitioner's use of techniques that will achieve the dual objectives of the humanistic group. It was established that using techniques without values is mechanistic.

Techniques were defined as behaviors the group worker uses to achieve particular intents. Twenty-nine techniques were identified and categorized according to the objective to which they were connected.

The nine techniques that were used specifically to establish the democratic mutual aid system were discussed. Four of these assist the members in being a collective; these are the techniques of collective participation, decision making, engaging the group as a whole, and processing the here and now. They are called in to play to help members develop a "we" feeling and identity; they can also be used when the members are over reliant on the practitioner for an identity and controls.

Modulating the expression of feeling technique helps all members stay focused on what is possible (and not possible) to do within the context of the group's current identity, cohesion, and implicit decision-making processes.

The technique of expressing feelings about the practitioner role is distinguishable from the others for several reasons. One is the assumption that the members can function cohesively and effectively as a whole at the same time as they deal with the practitioner's participation. From these points of view, the practitioner anticipates a sense of purposeful unity and integrity.

Goal setting and good and welfare are techniques that relate to particular aspects of the process; the members collectively develop goals, and they react to the group's unfolding process. Scanning is essentially a sensory means used by the practitioner to perceive the group and its manifest and latent processes.

The following two chapters discuss techniques for actualizing group purpose.

Techniques for Developing the Democratic Mutual Aid System

Technique	Intent—Used to:	Practitioner Behavior
Collective Participation	Foster valuing each other; foster acceptance and right to belong.	Reflect to group when others want to speak; elicit responses directly from quiet members; encourage members to talk to each other.
Scanning	Perceive mood of entire group.	Look around from member to member.
Engaging the Group as a Whole	Establish group identity and cohesion.	Use *we* and *our*, and *you*, *yours*, appropriately.
Modulating the Expression of Feeling	Temper premature self-disclosure; prevent overwhelming of group.	Neither probe nor support flow of personalized material; stop story from unfolding so as to identify and universalize parts of story for entire group.
Decision Making	Enable owning of group, democratic participation, mastery; prevent premature self-disclosure.	Check out feelings, majority-minority opinions; reweave collective perceptions; help compromise or consensus; ask members to bend.
Processing the Here and Now	Open up group's immediate awareness of itself; foster ownership of process.	Ask for identification and consideration of group's salient events as dynamics unfold.
Expressing Feelings About Practitioner Role	Enable understanding of practitioner's stake and role; demystify role.	Ask group to share feelings about practitioner; respond directly to indirect expressions; solicit feelings toward worker mistakes; own up to mistakes.
Goal Setting	Enhance conscious ownership of group; crystallize cohesion and identity.	When group questions format and goals, help group reweave individual needs into common quests.
Good and Welfare	Summarize individual feeling at end of meeting to prevent dissatisfaction from festering.	At end of each meeting, ask members to sum up reactions, without discussion; practitioner also takes part.

6

Techniques
for Actualizing
Group Purpose

Actualizing group purpose is the second of the dual objectives of humanistic group work. Techniques the practitioner uses to actualize group purpose are aimed at assisting members to focus on the issues, situations, and interpersonal patterns that have brought them to the group.

Relationships that have been built on humanistic values and democratic norms provide the basic frame of reference for self-expression. The group is governed by the principle of externality (Papell & Rothman, 1980b), which fosters its functioning outside of the meeting. Members and significant others carry out needs and interactions in and out of the group's actual meetings.

The practitioner recognizes that the processes related to purpose will vary in their intensity, duration, and frequency. These differ in relation to how comfortable the members are in working together and their ability to use democratic norms productively. Purpose-related processes vary in relation to prevalent stage themes and external events.

While some beginning behaviors do erupt in the middle phase, especially in instances when group members lose their bearing while working on new forms of self-expression, they usually do not alter or divert the members' focus on purpose. The members are able to maintain useful and helpful forms of cohesion, motivation, and energy. When the members recognize the practitioner's knowledge and skill, strengths, and weaknesses, they do not revert to authority issues presented earlier in the group's process.

During a group's later stage themes of Sanctuary, "This Isn't Good Anymore," and especially during "We're Okay and Able," members will turn attention to more intently working on their purpose. The practitioner becomes more often involved in using techniques to help members actualize their purpose. As they increase their interpersonal work, the members incorporate and use these techniques, too. When this happens, the practitioner joins in the group's process.

Shulman (2006) and Yalom (2005), focusing on the middle phase of the group, speak to the members' increased interpersonal intensity and productivity, as well as the members' increased and more intense demands on the practitioner. The practitioner must actively help members steer their own course. At the same time, the group worker may experience discomfort at the loss of control, as well as feelings of envy or exclusion when realizing that intimacy and mutuality are developing among the members. Levine (1979) writes as follows:

> The [practitioner] can no longer gain political control of the group or offer professional opinions that will not be questioned and countered by the group members. . . . While the [practitioner] may continue providing insight and opinion as well as empathy, the danger of [the practitioner's] competition with the members is high. . . . The [practitioner] who is reasonably secure in his [or her] professional identity will be able to value the mutual helping of the group members while still providing professional input into the discussions. A here-and-now focus during the mutuality phase provides the major source of growth and change for the members. (p. 200)

Participation through helping to actualize purpose demands that the group worker consistently examine his or her interactions and emotional self-expression. When actualizing purpose, not only are the members' behaviors more consistently connected and apparent to one another, but so, too, are the group worker's. The practitioner has to be emotionally mature, possessing the ability to be unguarded and

undefensive, thereby serving as a model (for the members) for participation and change. The practitioner qua member is accepting of the
discomforts and misperceptions that make empathic communication
what it is—difficult and satisfying. Attitudes and stances such as these
help to prevent social defenses such as stereotyping, scapegoating,
and stigmatizing—which are connected to inferiority and superiority
feelings—from becoming a part of the group's operations.

There are 12 techniques specific to actualization of purpose. Of
these, the following—*role rehearsal, programming, group reflective consideration, interpretation,* and *feedback*—are discussed in this chapter (see
the "Techniques Chart" at the end of the chapter).

Each of these techniques is related to the interactions of actualizing
purpose. For clarification, see Table 6.1.

Table 6.1   Relationship of Techniques to Interactions That Actualize
Purpose

Technique	Interactions
Role Rehearsal	Express role-enhancing behaviors.
Programming	Create activities in the milieu.
	Express role-enhancing behaviors.
Group Reflective Consideration	Identify themes to be worked on.
	Identify feelings that help work on change.
	Identify projections and self-fulfilling prophecies.
Interpretation	Identify group process issues and structures to heighten group's self-awareness.
	Identify projections and self-fulfilling prophecies.
Feedback	Foster sharing perceptions and feelings about each other's behavior.

❖ TECHNIQUES FOR ACTUALIZING GROUP PURPOSE

Role Rehearsal

Some behaviors may be members' habituated responses to their
situations. Other enactments may be fraught with conflict and anxiety,
causing the individual to have unstable and unhappy relationships.
Change requires acquiring and learning new patterns of interaction and
emotional expression, whether undoing old responses or developing

new ones. Fear of the unknown is often related to the inhibition of repertoires of interaction and self-expression to meet expectations.

The intent of role rehearsal is to help members in changing dysfunctional behaviors and in developing new ones within the group, as well as in other significant relationships. Role rehearsal may be facilitated by the practitioner in a few ways. In one of these, the practitioner engages the group or member in imagining and talking about feelings and actions they are anticipating in a forthcoming situation. The group's collective imagination is focused on detail in order to develop strategies and emotional reactions that widen the options available to members. As members consider consequences of emotions and interactions, the practitioner further encourages their efforts.

In another approach, the practitioner identifies scenes that may occur between group members to help them try new role behaviors. Members are assigned to try out parts they usually do not enact in significant relationships or situations.

Still another approach involves a more formalized role rehearsal: role playing. From the situations discussed and collectively (or individually) expressed concerns in meetings, the practitioner asks the group to develop a role-play situation based on the anticipated events. Role players are selected, characters are assigned, and the practitioner has the players make a circle inside the group—a fishbowl structure. The players are encouraged to begin quickly so as not to overrehearse or intellectualize the situation out of expected embarrassment and reluctance they may be feeling. A nonevaluative experimental tone is set, within a 5- to 15-minute time limit. The practitioner stops the players and involves those not actively role playing in a discussion of their observations and feelings. There is opportunity to reflect back on the important behaviors and feelings that surfaced during the action.

| *Illustration* | *Substance Abuse Residential Treatment Group* |

A group of substance abusers in a residential treatment program is talking about the rules in the program that prevent them from maintaining contacts with people from the outside unless given formal permission. Delia complains, "I want to call my husband, who is in a different program now. I've been told I can't until I'm ready for my discharge plan, which will include couple and family therapy." Fred tells her he knows that she and her husband did dope together and that it makes no sense for her to talk to him now. He also says he doesn't trust her to do things differently: "You'll talk to him and immediately figure out how to bullshit us. I know. I've been there." Leila concurs, but doesn't see the harm of Delia calling her husband just to talk about their kids. Geoff reminds everyone that "since Delia's mother is taking care of her kids, there are no decisions to be made from in here." Delia tells the group that her mother wants her to end the marriage. "She says neither of us has the will to stop doing cocaine when we're together, and that she doesn't want to turn on the T.V. one day and see us all strung out."

The practitioner, Virginia, asks, "Is there truth to that?" Delia says, "We got rich in the music business. There's less money in it now, but hey, the drugs are still there." Larry and Geoff talk about how they did time for dealing drugs and how "drugs sure are a lifestyle of people weaving a web around each other." Larry says to Delia, "Being in jail—it's worse than humiliation. I saw it was my life I was ruining. You've got a big problem, because you and your husband earn your living in an environment that is full of temptation. But when I did coke, no one could count on me."

The practitioner asks, "Larry, is there someone you want to have count on you now?" Larry responds, "My partner, who helped me come to the program, I don't want to lose him—he put up with a lot." The practitioner says, "What Larry just said really relates back to you, Delia, how you get to work on the things that need to be worked on so you can be counted on again—that's the big question." Delia talks a bit about her children not counting on her, though she made believe she was available to them. Fred reminds her, "No, your mother always bailed you out with the kids!" More discussion follows about how their important relationships get sacrificed.

The practitioner then asks Delia, "Would you think about which are the hardest couple of steps you have to take next to help your recovery?" After some silence she says, "I have to start to talk to Richard honestly about what was happening between us as a couple, and as parents. I have to tell him how I let myself be lured into the glamour, the glitz, and the hype." Fred asks, "Can you tell Richard that?" Delia says she is afraid to tell him, afraid he won't accept it. Fred chimes in. "That's why they don't want you to call Richard. You're not ready."

The practitioner says, "Perhaps you, Delia—and you, Fred—could role-play out how Delia might react even if Richard didn't want to listen at first. Sometimes it helps to playact it first. We can all look at what happens and give you our reactions and opinions. Do you want to try it?" Everyone agrees. The practitioner says to Fred, "Remember, Richard is also in a treatment program. They're probably getting on his case, too, so don't play him too rigidly."

During the role play, Delia tells her "husband" how she knows it will be hard but they have to resolve to work on their relationship to be good parents. She tells him, "My mother has been too generous. We have used her to avoid responsibility, to go out all the time, to party and act like we have no kids."

After 10 minutes or so, the practitioner says to the players, "You can stop now," praising their effort. He asks the members to share their reactions.

Different members note that when Delia has responded in a straightforward manner to "Richie" he seemed taken aback, but attentive. One member points out that Delia rushed in too quickly to yell at him for not being available to his children, which closed him off, placing parental responsibility on her. Generally, members felt that when she took time out to explain how she felt, she was better understood.

The practitioner asks Delia how and when she felt in charge of herself. She discusses more about the need to be honest, that she had not been, and how she has never told him how important it is for her to be a mature parent. More discussion follows. The practitioner finally says, "It looks like when you do get to talk with Richie, there's a lot you're both going to have to start to work on. What do you think?"

Discussion

The practitioner notes several important events. First, with the help of the group, the member is put on the spot regarding her collusion with her husband to continue to take drugs. Her reluctance to accept the observation of collusion needs work. By providing a chance for her to consider future directions and practice new behaviors, the practitioner helps her see the pitfalls of meeting with her husband now. The future directions their work together can take are also identified. When offering the member a chance to experiment in the role play, the practitioner does not let the group get too confrontational, thereby enabling the members to develop an empathic (as well as sympathetic) interactional way of helping Delia. Not dwelling on the need to call her husband propels Delia to think abut her role as parent. This is done when the practitioner, focusing on Larry's need to be counted on, brings her attention gently back to her role as a parent and as an adult daughter.

It is then, and through the subsequent role play, that Delia begins to see how she avoids parental responsibility by using her mother to get her off the hook. As the role play unfolds, it becomes apparent that Delia wants to take on her parental obligations and wishes for the strength to get her husband to do that with her. Rehearsing in the group further solidifies for Delia the observation that she needs to do much about her interaction and emotional expression in her marriage. Whether or not to end the marriage is a premature consideration, and is not dealt with directly. The issue is her adulthood, regardless of whether she is mature in this marriage or in another intimate relationship.

Role rehearsal here is drawn around the group's functional purpose. The group members are kept away from the usual drug culture in order to discover new ways of functioning drug free in the community and in one's significant relationships.

Programming

The practitioner uses programming (Ciardiello, 2003; Middleman, 1968/1981, 1983; Vinter, 1985; Whittaker, 1985) to involve members in a joint venture or organized activity during or beyond the group's actual meeting time. Participation in programmed activities enhances relationships and members' skills. Programming is the most completely active, interactional, and experiential technique of all. Programming is the technique that epitomizes the humanistic group's externality. The practitioner focuses on developing programs that can take place among the members themselves, with important persons in the members' role set or with a wider range of people both in and out of the meeting environment. Though some program activities may develop spontaneously in the process, more often they will involve a series of planful actions. Some groups plan programs before resolution of their normative crisis—children's groups, because they are experiential from the outset, and groups whose basic purpose is to be action or activity oriented. The development of programs in the group may be used to catalyze the establishment of group norms and cohesion. Readers should refer to the technique of decision making (Chapter 5) for a discussion of those processes. When programming occurs following some significant resolution of the normative crisis (usually occurring during Stage Theme 3, "We're Taking You On"), its goals center more on role enhancement than on developing decision-making processes. At this point, the practitioner and members become more focused on the members' needs in the actual group experience.

Through planning and participating in a program, members experience and learn how to actualize themselves, further their goals, and enhance their potentials with significant as well as unanticipated others in their natural and formal milieus. The program is a proving and improving ground. The total programming process focuses on and reflects the actual experiences that bring the members together. The program reveals and brings to life the group's objectives and goals, as well as the members' actual forms of interaction and self-expression.

The program event the members undertake is a central way in which the group as a whole can meet members' needs to take action to affect their social environment. Group programs are some of the most significant statements of what makes this type of professionally guided group a unit of social work. Through the program, members experience the gamut of opportunities for experimenting with new behaviors more than would be possible within the confines of a meeting's usual process (Ciardiello, 2003; Seitz, 1985). Members can experience mastery and enhanced role responses and repertoires.

The practitioner uses five interrelated acts in carrying out the programming technique. These are (1) initiation, (2) discussing options, (3) tasks and tools, (4) program experience, and (5) evaluation.

1. *Initiation.* The practitioner introduces one or several program ideas, or responds to program initiatives from the group. Assessment of the members' current skills, abilities, and limitations is required in the initiation process (Vinter, 1985). The practitioner also informs the members that conducting a program enhances group pride and mastery through the collective group experience, while providing a unique arena for specialized change and experimentation for any one member.

2. *Discussing Options.* The practitioner offers his or her own ideas or motivates members to consider other program options. The practitioner helps members consider the range of complexity of a program event—the effort that each undertaking will take. Some programs might be simple, requiring little prior preparation and minimal competence for performing the activity (Vinter, 1985). Others, more complex, will require a higher level of group organization, member skill, and preparation. Some programs will be only for the members themselves, others will be for specific significant others, and still others will include a wider spectrum of participants. The members' attention and decision making (see Chapter 5) is directed to ways in which potential program efforts will meet particular group needs. The practitioner helps the members choose a program and develop a commitment to assume responsibility for program tasks and participation.

3. *Tasks and Tools.* When the members have selected a program event, the practitioner directs his or her efforts toward the nitty-gritty of the tasks of planning and implementing within the confines of physical space (Vinter, 1985) and time. The practitioner may have to be the first to secure additional space and make lists, with the goal of turning tasks over to members. In some groups, the members themselves will have the capacity to develop their own leadership and subcommittee structure for carrying out a program. Program tools may require collection and storage. All phone numbers and e-mail addresses will be confirmed again. The practitioner ensures that the network for extrameeting communication is in place. The practitioner encourages members to volunteer and accept responsibility for carrying out the

tasks. Through the process of assigning and volunteering to undertake tasks, the practitioner also helps the members identify outlets for sharing strengths and developing newer abilities.

Members will want to know if the practitioner will be present at the program itself if it is not taking place during the regular meeting time; this will have to be directly dealt with in the group. The practitioner's participation will be determined by the practitioner and members in the context of agency policy, group need, and professional role constraints. The practitioner relinquishes varying degrees of control by participating in the program.

Whether or not the practitioner is present during the program, the result of his or her efforts and disciplined approaches will be in evidence during the members' experience.

4. *Program Experience.* Once the program experience is occurring, anxieties and hesitancies will arise. It may be necessary for the practitioner to actively initiate the start of the program. In some groups, because of their feelings and abilities, the practitioner may be required to take a very active part in the start-up, lending support to the members' efforts until things get well underway.

During the program, the practitioner encourages and sustains members' efforts, taking special note of peripheral or floundering participants. The effort is to appropriately move to the background; during the experience, this practitioner is not the primary social and emotional connection for the members. The practitioner circulates throughout the program, modeling for the members an active and engaged participant. There may also be times when the practitioner fills in to help complete tasks and keeps track of the beginnings and endings of events within the program.

5. *Evaluation.* Once the program event is over, usually at a forthcoming session, the practitioner engages the group in rehashing the experience. Discussion includes a focus on how the program met the members' and other participants' needs. The practitioner may also initiate discussion about how the tasks were or were not achieved, and whether different resources would have improved the event. The practitioner helps the group take appropriate pride in accomplishments and accept its failures. The future is considered at that time, with the practitioner helping the group move toward entertaining new ideas about future options and plans.

| Illustration | *Young Adult Relationship-Focused Therapy Group* |

At this group meeting, Sally, Dan, Josh, Harriet, Bernadette, Claudia, Fred, Lee, and George are in the process of planning a party. They have been meeting for almost a year with the practitioner, Tom. Several of the members have discussed the difficult personal and social experiences of their adolescence, including drugs and dropping out of school. Others are looking for a wider range of friendships and social relationships. Many have admitted that their social events had been characterized by pot smoking and some secretive binge drinking at parties where people did not really get to know each other. Several express concern about being able to mingle comfortably with people they do not know.

The practitioner, Tom, sensitive to their fears and aware of their proclivity to intellectualize and avoid experiences, sees a program option. He has encouraged them to have a kind of party that will be more likely to occur as they become more adequate young adults. Issues related to whether doing anything outside of the meeting would contaminate the process and their relationships were discussed at prior meetings. The group decided to take a chance because improving social skills was a major priority.

The members want this party to have a relaxed atmosphere, where people talk to and get to know each other. They decided on a party theme—celebrating the beginning of the summer. Some members and their friends have been taking high school equivalency or welfare-to-work classes that have led to college classes, and the end of the semester seems like a good time to celebrate. The group has decided on a menu. Everyone is bringing food. They decided they will not drink any liquor, but if friends brought it, they will put it out for the others. Josh designed special e-vites, and each member will invite five friends. Fred and his roommate, Alex, have volunteered their house for the party. Claudia, Sally, and Dan have helped Fred set up his house.

When the practitioner arrives at the party, it is well under way. There are many new people, and several members greet him with food and drink, taking him around to meet some of their friends, girlfriends, cousins, and colleagues. Several are people talked about in the group, and the practitioner makes a mental note of this. Claudia wants Tom to meet her fiancé, whom she had described as skeptical about her belonging to the group; Tom finds him to be somewhat formal with him.

Sally can be seen in one corner talking very seriously with a young man. Dave comments to Tom that "it looks like Sally and my friend Pete are hitting it off." Then Dave continues, "This is a great party. The chemistry is great. I've been talking to some very nice people. Did you see that gorgeous woman over there? She is Fred's sister. I have to be careful with a group member's sister, right? I can't try to hook up with her like I would usually do." Tom laughs and asks, "Did you talk to her, Dave?" Dave says that he discovered she was going to law school and "that makes her too much out of my league." The practitioner comments, "Come on, Dave, it's just a conversation."

The group made a small dance floor in one corner of the basement. Bernadette walks over to Tom and asks him to dance with her. While they are dancing, Tom notices several of the members taking note of this. Members are laughing and joking about how "you dance almost as good as we do."

After more time passes, Tom tells Claudia, Fred, and Dave, "I really have to be going. I have some plans for later." Claudia catches the eye of George, who quickly comes up to Tom and says, "Wait 5 minutes, we just want to bring out a cake, okay?" Tom agrees, "Just 5 minutes, sure."

While Fred brings out the cake, Claudia asks for the group's attention. She says, "We are happy to bring all our friends together to celebrate our great group, and the end of a rough year of classes and work, and the beginning of summer." Lots of cheers are heard. Then George talks about how the group has appreciated Tom's efforts and "for putting up with us and encouraging us." Tom affirms his pleasure with the members and acknowledges the opportunity to bring friends together saying, "I'm going to take my leave now, before you guys get busted!" Everyone laughs; Tom leaves with, "See you Thursday night."

Everyone is present at Thursday night's meeting. The practitioner begins, "Let's go over the events and experiences at the party." Everyone talks animat-edly, expressing enthusiasm about the party, the food, the music, and the fact that Tom could attend. Fred, noticing that Claudia is quiet, reaches out to her. She tells the members that her long-standing fiancé put down her friends, and she was so upset and hurt "at his lack of understanding, I just broke up with him." The members express shock at his lack of support. "He just wants me to be dependent on him, not on anyone else. This is not a new issue, as you know." Bernadette tells her, "I saw it coming." Claudia admits that she saw it coming, but was having a hard time accepting the truth. She expresses disappointment in herself. After a lengthy supportive discussion with Claudia, the members and the practitioner turn their attention back to the party.

The practitioner asks the members to consider what it felt like for them to be at this party. Several talked about the ease with which they met new people. The practitioner reminds them "you planned it that way." Dave jokes with Sally about her interest in his friend, Pete. She smiles and says, "Oh! He Is really nice. But I'm not going to say anything else, because I don't want to now." Tom wonders, "How do we handle the issue in the group if Sally wants to talk about herself and Pete, with Dave being his friend?" Sally agrees that she is feeling uncomfortable. Dave says, "Whatever you say won't go back to Pete. And I won't talk with him about you, either." Sally says, "Thanks, that's hard to do, I appreciate it."

After some silence Sally continues. "What was so good was being able to be myself with someone in a cozy and healthy atmosphere. That's all for now. That's the best part." More talk ensues about the opportunity the party gave them to feel comfortable socially. George admits it was the first time he didn't get drunk at a party. The practitioner asks, "How was that?" George admits it was "new and different, but I'm getting used to it—pretty good."

The practitioner asks, "Any other feelings?" Dave cuts in, "Okay man, I got nervous about talking to Fred's sister. She's beautiful, she's smart—she's out of my league." Members talk about how they want to be careful about entering into relationships with each other's family and friends. The practitioner wonders, "Isn't that true about entering into all relationships?"

Discussion

The young adult group's party illustrates a program execution. It was partially the result of the practitioner's use of initiation, discussion of options, and tasks and tools in a partly directed, off the cuff, yet professionally guided process. It had started several weeks earlier, when members talked about their wish to celebrate the end of the year differently than they previously might have celebrated an event.

One key aspect of programming is its flow with the organic psychosocial needs and interactions of group members. While the technique appears clearly ordered to remind the practitioner of necessary business, it is not designed to lock the members into a fixed agenda and process. In fact, programming can start spontaneously. It has to be encouraged by the practitioner, who in this situation helps the members seize the moment.

The break up of the member's engagement is precipitated by the learning that takes place through the avenue created by the program. This severing of an important relationship will need further consideration by the member in the group. Another member discovers a newer ability to be herself with the other sex in the ambiance created by the program. One member attends the party without getting drunk. Another raises the question of how people will relate to others they meet. Finally, learning to be expansive in the member role tests the group's maturity. Through future events, members will be provided with still further opportunities for social and personal enhancement. The practitioner is supportive in this process, focusing on particular issues of the experience for the members and significant others.

The practitioner chooses to attend this event for part of the time and to conduct himself in the professional role in a relaxed fashion throughout. He meets the members' friends and accepts one member's request for a dance. To accept that dance is part of the program; not to dance might be taken as a sign of rejection. He does establish and protect the professional boundary between himself and the members by leaving the party early, indicating that he has other commitments. This is accepted by the members, who easily adjust the schedule to include him in the presentation of the cake.

See Ciardiello (2003) for a comprehensive set of activities for children, all of which are grounded in group work development theory.

Group Reflective Consideration

The intent of group reflective consideration (described as valuable in case work by Woods & Hollis, 2000) is to assist members in considering recent experiences that relate to their purpose. This technique is used in group work as a refocusing and reframing device to help in the formation of new ideas, attitudes, and perceptions.

The practitioner asks members to recall the aspects, contexts, and effects of particular experiences. Attention is paid to the sequencing of events and to feelings, interactions, and moments of choice. This serves to assist members in reconstructing actions, feelings, and thoughts. Effort is made to keep the discussion focused on specifics rather than muddied generalities. The members are able to distinguish helpful and unhelpful patterns. The practitioner asks how the moment-to-moment awarenesses are affecting the members as they reflect on and bring to the surface insights, intuitions, and facts.

Illustration   *Lesbian and Bisexual Support Group*

Women in a group who are lesbians or bisexual have been talking about how certain members have experienced some negative reactions when letting coworkers know about their sexual orientation. The pros and cons of keeping this information hidden are also considered. Leila starts to talk about her job in a bank and her friendship with another woman there who is a manager. She says that when she told about her life and her current relationship with her partner, the woman stopped having lunch with her. Others say they are discreet at work. Some say that everyone knows and they don't care.

The practitioner, Eunice, says to Leila, "Hold on, let's go back over the events at lunch. Where were you? How did it all start?" Leila says, "We had gone to the coffee shop, and then were going to take a quick look in some of the nearby boutiques." The practitioner asks her how the topic of her sexuality came up. Leila tells the group that she was preoccupied and anxious about letting this woman know about herself. She wanted to feel less guarded and more friendly toward her, and she thought telling would help. Some members interrupt: "Not everyone wants to hear." The practitioner says, "Go on, Leila, tell us how you started to talk." Leila describes how she just told her, "You know, I am gay," going on at length to talk about her current relationship: "I didn't want her to get the wrong idea, that I was interested in her. But I think she did anyway." "Wait a minute," the practitioner says, "How do you now?" "I don't know for sure," Leila replies.

Diane then asks what the woman's response was. Leila can't recall, saying, "She didn't say much." The practitioner asks her, "What do you think was going on for her?" Leila says she doesn't know. The practitioner asks, "What did you do then?" Leila says, "I started to talk about my significant other." The practitioner asks, "So what do you think is going on for her now?" Leila says, "I must have scared her." The practitioner asks the group, "How are you reacting to what Leila has been telling us?" Vivian's response is that Leila is anxious and tells too much too quickly. Margaret thinks she wanted to go shopping, not hear about Leila's love life—whether with a woman or with a man—just then. "I don't think you checked out with her what her reaction is," Diane says.

The practitioner asks Leila, "How do you react to what was just said to you?" She responds, "I see their point. I didn't ask her to react or give her a chance to. I just talked a lot." Eunice asks, "How are you feeling now?" Leila admits that she is anxious, and she had been eager to get this off her chest. The practitioner wonders if these feelings were similar to what she was feeling at lunch. Leila admits that they are similar. Diane says, "And you had a hard time listening to us, too, but we interrupted you. Everyone can't do that to you."

The practitioner points out that what happened to Leila seems common in this group: "Sometimes you're just not sure if you're being rejected because of your sexuality or because of other reasons." Members begin to talk about how to clarify this issue.

Discussion

This technique is used to deal with actual situations the members have been in. The practitioner knows that the member is moving headlong into a rush of ventilation and feeling that will not be productive for her. In addition, all members' learning will be intertwined with their abilities to develop vantage points from which to appraise situations while they are in them. The practitioner, by cutting into the venting of the member, slows the process down and turns it into one of reflection. By doing this, other members are given impetus to also cut in, slowing down the story and giving themselves and the member a chance to think about it. A chance to think about the interaction anew is provided.

The practitioner stops the members, redirecting them several times. By asking Leila what she thought was going on for her coworker, the practitioner redirects her toward developing empathic awareness of others. Her response—"I'm not sure"—points further to her own self-preoccupation, which gives impetus to others in the group to focus Leila's attention on this trait. Eventually, with everyone's help, the member does begin to think that she might have overwhelmed her colleague in this situation, and that she has the tendency to steamroller over others in the group as well.

Interpretation

Interpretation is used to expand awareness of the latent content and hidden agendas that play out between members and their significant others in and out of the group. By bringing the meaning of covert topics to light, members are able to learn more about themselves and their situation in and out of the group.

In using interpretation, the practitioner reaches beyond what is presented on a manifest level by "reading between the lines" to bring aspects of latent levels to awareness. The practitioner goes below surface presentations to the point where a new perception can be experienced by the members. The practitioner does not go too far beyond the group's conscious awareness; this is done to avoid defensiveness that may result from overstepping members' comprehension, feelings, and defensive boundaries.

An interpretation is offered when the practitioner judges that the member is ready to benefit from looking at particular behaviors with more complete insight. This may be done when the member continuously repeats dysfunctional or unsatisfying behavior, creating a stumbling block to his or her efforts to change, or when the member is seriously examining his or her motivations.

The practitioner offers an interpretation about the underlying meanings of the behavior with an empathic affect, speaking about feelings regarding hidden intentions, fears, and expectations. These perceptions are related to stereotyping, self-fulfilling prophecies, and the members' family-symbolic representations of others.

The practitioner may use interpretation in conjunction with role rehearsal, aspects of programming—especially during the evaluation time—or along with group reflective consideration. While the practitioner is not intent on having interpretation immediately change the member's form of expression, it often begins the process of change because of the support and discussion members provide for one another. Interpretation occurs most often, and most valuably, when the members are reflecting on their differentiated (Garland, Jones, & Kolodny, 1973) patterns of interaction and emotional expression.

Illustration	**Adolescent Boys in a Group Residence—Hip-Hop Music Studio**

A group of 14- to 17-year-old boys write and produce their own music and lyrics in the hip-hop studio at their residence. They have been having difficulties with the residential director and other staff. It seems they have been singing loudly and repeating the profanities from their lyrics all over the place. The staff is furious because it has disrupted the other kids. The director of all the residences has threatened to close down the studio.

The group worker, Betty, has been meeting with the boys and runs the studio with them. She has come to the meeting to tell them that there is a problem with the studio and the way they have been behaving at the residence. She tells them that the "People downtown know I am talking with you about this. They have made it clear that no matter what happens they most likely will close down the studio."

The impact is devastating. The silence is deafening. The practitioner sees that the boys have rage and hatred in their eyes. She says, "This must be infuriating you. It must really piss you off and make you want to tell off Mr. Lamont." Boom! Yelling and screaming. This goes on for a while, with foot stamping and table pounding too. As it subsides, the practitioner asks, "How will you go about stopping this from happening?" More anger and frustration. Betty says, "You're not talking about what is happening, what you think about it, and how you feel. The only chance you have of stopping it from happening, if you can, is to understand what's going on. Understand means to stand under, to look at all aspects, at what people are into, what they might not even be aware of themselves. Maybe then you can be effective. Leonard?"

Leonard responds, "I hate Mr. Lamont. He's a big fuck, always getting all riled up about the music." Carlos adds, "He will make me run away. There is nothing I can do." The practitioner says, "So, he is lashing out, and you are his victims? This is just how you set me up when we started this program months ago. I would control the program, you would be dependent, then you'd act all pissed off, remember?" Mel shakes his head in agreement. Victor says, "I'll run away before they ruin our program. Just another nightmare brought to you by the foster system. No one gives a fuck about us. All they want to do is tell us what to do. But they're never there for us." The practitioner is aware of the connection between Mr. Lamont's rejecting behavior and the boys' need to run away from the residence as an enactment of flight from painful relationships with fathers and mothers. She chooses to let it lie because she feels it would be too difficult for the members to explore at this time.

Someone says, "Those miserable directors. All they do is criticize our music. But they have never listened to our words." Betty asks, "How can you get them to listen to your lyrics, to show them how you feel?" The immediate answer is, "We can bring Mr. Lamont here and let him hear some of what we wrote." Eddie interjects, "Some of the stuff that isn't 'eff this' and 'eff that' for starters."

The practitioner says, "Your assertive tone sounds good to me—to be here in the situation." Some feel it won't do any good. No one will change. She continues, "Guys, maybe you can figure out ways of explaining yourselves and the reactions Mr. Lamont caused so he can hear you. I will help. I'll be in the room." Victor says, "I'll tell him he is just like my mean father." Others agree. Betty adds,

"So, the agency is mean to you when they make threats to take away something that helps you, and you have to find ways to say this with strength but without sounding persecuted." Talk continues.

Betty interjects, "One more thing, how are you guys going to deal with one big fact, that they are mostly upset with you because you have been cursing all over the place? Why are you doing that?" Ben says, "Because it's our music, man." Lots of agreement and high fives. Betty continues, "Come on, is that all there is to it? It's your music?" Silence. Stevie says, "Well, because we like pissing them off." Gary and Leonard talk about how great it is to get a rise out of them. Others agree. Betty notes, "Remember we talked about negative attention here?" Many nods in agreement. "Why piss them off and jeopardize something you want?" Betty continues.

The members ask why they should have "to give in." More talk ensues with Betty wondering why they wouldn't try to do something someone asks of them? They decide they would do something if Betty asked them because she is kind to them. There is more talk about compromising at times and doing something even if the other person is not being kind. Betty notes it might be more effective if they let people hear their lyrics on their terms, when they wanted, "Not because you were in their faces. This just turns them off, and then you don't get what you want. How will they give you a chance if you do that?"

Discussion

In this example, the practitioner is very careful to highlight certain latent issues without surfacing others. She does not explicitly link Mr. Lamont with a rejecting parent at the start. It didn't matter if it ever came out, though when it did it was helpful. She showed concern that their wounds might become too raw in the face of the underlying mother and father story. She stayed, however, with the latent (but close to the surface) theme about their positions as victims, rather than as rejected sons.

What emerges is that their loud cursing is about seeking negative rather than positive attention, something the group had already discovered and reviewed at a prior session. While this behavior has its origins in prior parental and other authority relationships, its history could not be examined at this time. First, they had to deal with the hurt in the present context.

As a female, the practitioner appeared cautious in allowing herself to be pitted against Mr. Lamont, though she let the boys keep certain illusions about her as a good mother and friend. The practitioner used the interpretation of the aggressive-victim role to empower the boys to act on their own behalf.

She chose not to move the process into slow motion and reflection, or to engage the boys in interacting with one another to address their disappointments and abandonment issues with their parents. Rather, she focused on helping them understand the impact of their negative attention seeking behavior so they could redirect this into behavior that would more effectively meet their needs.

Feedback

Feedback (National Training Laboratory, 1966–1967) is a technique designed to assist members in maintaining their boundaries, eliminating assumptions, and expressing their reactions to one another's behaviors. For the receiver, feedback offers understanding of how one is perceived and reacted to in the group process. For the giver, feedback provides a chance to clarify and express one's feelings and reactions to others' behaviors. Through the feedback process, the group as a whole learns that no two members will perceive or feel exactly the same way—a most humanistic observation.

The practitioner slows down the interaction when members are reacting directly to one another to clarify the "I perceive and I feel" perspective. Or the practitioner may decide to introduce feedback more formally by teaching it to the group. In clarifying, the practitioner notes frequent uses of accusatory statements such as "You are acting hostile," by questioning, "What did she do that gave you that perception?" Another question is, "How did you feel when you thought she was hostile?" The practitioner may ask members to share perceptions and reactions to interactions, or encourage two members to demonstrate the process by asking one to begin by sharing a feeling about another's behavior ("When you do x, I feel y"). If the members are reluctant or unclear, the practitioner demonstrates his or her own perceptions and feelings in feedback form.

Illustration	**Drug Rehabilitation Group for Members With HIV-AIDS**

A group in a drug rehabilitation program, made up of members with HIV-AIDS, is involved in expressing angry feelings toward drug-addicted lovers who gave them the disease. Some of the members, who were substance abusers themselves and contracted the disease, are quiet. Justine says, deliberately looking away from some of the quiet people, "Damn them, they're quiet." The practitioner, Laura, asks, "What are you trying to say?" Justine answers, "I hate the quiet. I know it's drug users like them that gave it to me." Lee responds, "I'm quiet because I feel like you won't let me be angry that I have this disease. I gave this to myself. Do you think I knew I was getting it? I have no one to blame. At least you do. You can blame me."

After some angry outbursts, then calm, the conversation shifts to talk about how there is no use blaming anyone. Darryl begins to cry silently and Ivory reaches out to him, saying, "I'm sorry if I hurt your feelings and got you upset. Is that why you're crying?" "No," he says, "it's because I don't want to die. But it's no use, I might as well go back to drugs. What irony. I give up drugs only to find out it's too late anyway." Lee says, "I know, but when you say that I start to feel hopeless also. But then I say it's better not to be hopeless. I don't want you to feel hopeless either. The drugs we are taking now are really keeping us going." Todd adds, "Hell, no, this group is supposed to help us get support." Ivory says, "But what if it's an abyss and there's no hope." Todd says, "Come on, Ivory, look at all the people with HIV who are living productive lives now, with the cocktail. We have no right to go into the abyss. We are lucky. We get the most current drugs. Look at Africa."

Others chime in, offering support, and the talk turns toward wanting to continue living a productive life and taking care of themselves. After some time, the practitioner says, "There have been some really heavy things said. It might help if you could look at how you have been responding to what others are saying." After some silence, Felicia begins, "Well, I feel Ivory laid a trip on some people here, and I don't like it." "Tell Ivory," the practitioner urges. Felicia continues, looking at Justine: "Like you are so angry, you just have to lash out." Justine is quiet. The practitioner says, "Ivory, how do you react to what Felicia just said?" "I know you have a point," Ivory answers. "No one likes to be told they laid a trip on someone else. Do others feel I did that?" Marion says she feels that Ivory is less tolerant of the drug users than the gays. The practitioner says, "Marion, it would help if you could pinpoint how she shows that." Marion says, "It was just in this meeting that I became aware of this." The practitioner says, "When you saw her do that, how did that make you feel?" Marion says that she felt upset because everyone in the group is trying to cope with terrible luck, and she tells Ivory, "You undermine that and get sneaky. I know it hurts. It hurts me too, for myself and for all of us." Darryl points out that he feels "glad you said it hurts you too, Marion, because I was feeling we were just picking on Ivory because we couldn't look at our own stuff." Heads nod, followed by quite for a few moments.

The practitioner wonders, "What other reactions have you all been having to what's being said tonight?" Todd tells Lee that he appreciates what he said about feeling he could blame no one but himself: "I didn't realize until then how you felt." "Sort of made you feel closer to him?" the practitioner asks. "Yes," Todd answers, "and I see how much I am like you, Lee, because whether you did drugs or are gay like me, you end up blaming yourself for getting it. I hadn't quite realized that before."

The practitioner says, "I've been feeling particularly connected to all of you today. You've said so many things that hit me. I value your courage to find hope. Todd, Felicia, and Marion, I value all of your strength. Ivory, Darryl, and Lee, I appreciate your sharing the sadness and feelings of futility you are experiencing."

Discussion

The group begins by moving quickly toward a high degree of intensity. At this time, with many feelings being expressed, it is not appropriate for the practitioner to ask members to pause and reflect directly on how they are feeling about what members are saying. Too much is being said; rather, the practitioner merely asks for clarification early on. After it becomes apparent that the members have expressed what they needed to, the practitioner begins to try to help the group look at the meaning of their interactions, trying to make sense of the impact of one another's contributions and intense affects. The initial expressions of anger and despair are not typical of this usually supportive group; this is another reason why the practitioner does not intervene in it. When a member seem to have finished venting, the feedback instruction and focusing begins.

When Felicia attempts to offer feedback to Ivory but does not address her directly, the practitioner intervenes with "Tell Ivory." From there on, members speak directly to each other. The next intervention the practitioner makes to is to ask Marion to be specific regarding what Ivory has said. It is at this time that Marion, too, realizes that Ivory has presented this negative affect toward drug users only at this meeting. This intervention prevents the group from globalizing from one incident. Asking Marion to tell how she felt about what Ivory said enables her to accept responsibility for her own hurting reactions. By asking the group for additional reactions to each others' behaviors, the practitioner takes the focus away from Ivory, opening up channels for others to give and receive feedback.

Finally, as the process seems to move toward a natural conclusion, the practitioner offers her own perspective and feelings about the members' behaviors.

❖ SUMMARY

The practitioner's judgments and emphases in using the 12 techniques for actualizing group purpose were discussed. Specific attention was centered on five techniques. Role rehearsal and programming are two techniques that are directly experiential in their aim. Through these, members and significant others can interact completely in the framework of meetings, as well as in contrived and actual situations, to meet their needs. These more experientially oriented techniques lead to the examination of members' interactive patterns.

Group reflective consideration, interpretation, and feedback come into play in relation to role rehearsal and programming. They are used to focus attention and efforts on group and member scenarios and idiosyncratic reaction patterns that are interfering with the change process.

The next chapter discusses seven more techniques that are used by the practitioner to help the group actualize its purpose.

Techniques for Actualizing Group Purpose		
Technique	**Intent—Used to:**	**Practitioner Behavior**
Role Rehearsal	Enable member change and experimenting with new roles in group and milieu; prepare for new situations.	Ask group to imagine their behavior in forthcoming situation, focus on detail, develop strategies. May set up role plays by asking for volunteers to enact character and theme.
Programming	Further ability to change in milieu; foster role taking and mastery.	Introduce or respond to and explore ideas vis-à-vis purpose/needs. Discuss and choose from options. Define tasks; secure tools. Enable execution or program and participation of group members. Take part in event. Foster evaluation.
Group Reflective Consideration	Clear up distortions.	Ask for recall of aspects and affects of relevant experiences. Focus on sequences, interactions, specifics to enable reconstruction of events. Ask group to consider their effect in present.
Interpretation	Expand awareness of meaning; bring about change in patterns; bring latent content to conscious awareness.	After group is stimulated to further understanding, redefine meaning of interaction. Call for consideration of more basic meaning of an issue.
Feedback	Enhance affective relationships; clarify distortions about how members feel about and are reacted to by others.	Describe "I perceive and I feel" perspective. Ask members to share feelings or elicit feelings from others.

7

Further Techniques
for Actualizing
Group Purpose

Seven techniques used by the practitioner to help the group actualize its purpose are discussed in this chapter. *Conflict resolution, group mending,* and *confrontation* are techniques the practitioner uses when there are disruptions in the flow of the group process, or when it is necessary to redirect that flow. The techniques of *data and facts* and *self-disclosure* are used when the members need information that is factual about either events or about each other. *Dealing with the unknown* and *taking stock* are used to help the group move to newer levels (see the techniques chart at the end of the chapter).

Each of these techniques has a relationship to the group interactions that actualize group purpose. For clarification, see Table 7.1.

❖ FURTHER TECHNIQUES FOR
ACTUALIZING GROUP PURPOSE

Conflict Resolution

Conflict is an important feature of group life. Conflict among group members may revolve around differences of opinion, ideology,

Table 7.1   Relationship of Techniques to Interactions That Actualize Purpose

Technique	Interaction
Conflict Resolution	Identify themes to be worked on. Respect differences.
Group Mending	Identify feelings to help group work on change.
Confrontation	Identify issues for change. Identify projections and self-fulfilling prophecies.
Data and Facts	Identify themes to be worked on.
Self-Disclosure	Identify feelings that help group work on change. Foster sharing perceptions and feelings about each other's behavior.
Dealing With the Unknown	Express role-enhancing behavior. Help members work on change. Identify projections and self-fulfilling prophecies.
Taking Stock	Reflect and reinforce member and group change in order to replicate change.

or bias. Some group conflicts may occur in a highly suspicious and untrusting atmosphere in which members are unable to enter into the point of view of the other (Gruber, 2006). Other group conflicts may be due to lack of communication and problem-solving abilities needed to work toward compromise. Still other conflicts will be the result of competition, power struggle, or personality clashes (Deutsch, Coleman, & Marcus, 2006). The successful expression and resolution of conflicts facilitates increased creativity in problem solving, which involves the ability to "illuminate collaborative synthesis of disparate points of view" (Gruber, 2006, p. 392).

Conflict resolution (Bernstein, 1973; Deutsch et al., 2006) may be employed in response to processes that are related to the group's interactions, programs, and role rehearsals, as well as involvements in environmental situations. This technique is used to define and bring to the surface conflict-causing issues so that differences are respected and worked on before they fester, go underground, and become so irreconcilable that they cause the dissolution of the group.

The practitioner has to be prepared to use conflict resolution in the group. Using this technique requires self-awareness and self-discipline in exposing conflicts and dealing with them The practitioner—like the members—may want to avoid conflict, thereby becoming unable to retrieve interpersonal relationships and establish truces. Conflict resolution also requires the ability and vision to entertain and introduce a novel point of view that will help members reframe the conflict (Coleman & Deutsch, 2006).

Four interrelated activities are used in this technique. The first is surfacing and defining the conflict; the second is clarifying themes, feelings, and stakes in the conflict; the third is reframing and offering new perspectives; and the fourth is enhancing creative problem solving.

1. The intent of *surfacing and defining the conflict* is to identify conflicts early enough to prevent the members from becoming engulfed in negative and hateful feelings. Rather than letting conflicts go deeply underground, the practitioner pursues them early on by identifying the issues and feelings that surround them.

2. The intent of *clarifying themes, feelings, and stakes in the conflict* is to help members view the issues through varied lenses and develop empathy for the other point of view. The practitioner probes through request and even through insistence, inviting the full participation of all members—whatever their alliances or their intensity of investments in winning and in being right. Asking members for specificity around their feelings and stakes in a conflict, as well as checking for intentions and misperceptions, brings about clarification of issues and needs. This aspect of the technique helps members partialize their many concerns in an effort to provide flexibility and enhance understanding where there once was rigidity.

3. The intent of *reframing and offering new perspectives* (Bernstein, 1973) is to help members to reexperience the issues in novel, unique, and constructive ways (Coleman & Deutsch, 2006). The practitioner helps members view conflict in a different way by redefining the members' experiences of the problem, by building on the clarification of themes and feelings that has just occurred, and by capturing its emotional and interactional dimensions. Reframing helps develop processes for resolving conflicts so as to gain perspective and enhance interpersonal skills. The objective sought through offering new perspectives is to reestablish the "we" feeling in the group as a sign of work toward resolution.

4. The practitioner must view the existence of conflict as potentially positive and as an opportunity to *enhance creative problem solving*

(Coleman & Deutsch, 2006). The members can see that surfacing conflicts and seeking direct means to resolve them alleviates fear and anxiety, and may result in the development of creative solutions that would not have been possible without the conflict.

Illustration	*Interfaith Young Adults Visiting Holocaust Sites*

An interfaith young adult group visiting Holocaust sites in Europe has been traveling through Poland, the Czech Republic, and Germany for 2 weeks. The final part of the trip will be to Israel. The group met formally with the social worker before and after visiting a concentration camp. They have been airing concerns about vulnerability and at times became angry and disagreed about whose historical or personal situation had been more painful. For the past three days, their process has been woven around communicating in areas where members disagreed with one another. At times, there have been heated disagreements that have led to valuable activities and discussions. The practitioner, Frank, has used various techniques to accomplish this.

At the end of the meeting after visiting Bergen-Belsen, the practitioner saw two Jewish members, Ellen and Rhoda, leaving together and whispering to each other. He noted that others saw this as well. Remembering that Ellen and Rhoda were central in the group's power struggle, having ultimately been rejected as group leaders early on, the practitioner decides to surface this dynamic in the next meeting.

As the members enter the meeting room, the practitioner notes that Ellen and Rhoda are uncharacteristically late. They arrive together, talking on their way in. The practitioner looks to them and points out the difference in their actions over the past sessions, indicating that it is reminiscent of behavior that occurred in the first few meetings: "Are you aware of it? Are others?" Others admit to having noticed it at yesterday's meeting. With some furtive glances, Ellen and Rhoda agree to the patterns. The practitioner wonders if the behavior might not be in reaction to recently surfacing themes of whether slavery or the Holocaust had a worse impact.

Heated talk ensues, with some members seeing the common theme as being annihilation of a people, atrocities, survival, and courage. Some feel that the atrocities committed in the Holocaust outweighed those of slavery. Dave, remembering that Morris had been going over his struggles as a black man and how this conjured up his rage and hatred about slavery, asks Morris how he is reacting now. Morris talks about how pained he feels every time he sees a death camp, and he has attempted to understand the history of slavery as a parallel. The practitioner asks Ellen and Rhoda if Morris's anger relates to how they feel. Rhoda becomes noticeably uncomfortable and, looking to Ellen for nonverbal support, doesn't respond. Ellen avoids answering also, saying "You make such a big deal out of everything. Can't I just talk to a friend?"

Sal says to Ellen, "We all know the Holocaust happened, even if there are deniers, and all that. History has protected the evidence. But in Turkey they still won't admit they massacred 2 million Armenians. Today I feel that you get to have a voice in the world and I don't. It makes me so angry." He pauses, "It's not at you." There is quiet. The practitioner notes, "Indeed, there are the genocides we know about that are always highlighted and those we know less about." Dave wonders about himself as a Jew—can he be empathic enough about other genocides besides his own? Morris says to Dave that "white people don't want to understand what our people suffered as a result of slavery. And now that it's further away, they want to deny its impact." Rene, also black, agrees, stating emphatically that "this is going to happen with the Holocaust. And there will be some other genocide that will make them forget about this one!" Lots of feelings surface. "I don't even know where I lost my relatives," says Sal. "Imagine, I don't even know. And I can never go there to find out." Some try to offer advice and invoke caring attitudes. Others fall into their own space.

"My mother was born here at Bergen-Belsen," Ellen says. The group is totally silenced by the impact of that. "Well," Morris says, "that certainly brings it very close to us. But despite the horror—your mother lived!" Then Rene says, "My great-great-grandfather was born a slave. I know the plantation." Morris reflects, "As I am listening, it feels to me that our common humanity is about how a people survives, and about their legacy." Some nod in agreement. Carina adds that "You're right, Morris. My parents and grandparents were hidden in a cellar in Hungary—in fact, by a German soldier."

The practitioner says, "You have presented so many painful issues and so openly that everything you have said I know will stay with me. But I have to add that what is happening here is significant to your recognition of how a loss of empathy in the heat of deep feeling separates people unnecessarily. Ellen, you've withdrawn and run away from us because being here in this town today must be so painful for you." Ellen notes that once she could be open with the group she could "understand what you mean, Morris, about having the connection with the plantation—that place is a tomb, but also a place where people passed their lives and even bore children."

Further discussion opens up about vulnerability, and Dave points out to Rhoda that it feels like she shielded Ellen from telling her story. More talk continues about how they each have a story that these Holocaust sites will surface. The practitioner asks the group, "Does it help to talk about these things, to find another way to support each other and show vulnerability? Or is it too hard?" Rene notes that these issues must be talked about, otherwise Ellen will withdraw and then we will not see her more fully. The practitioner says, "So, it's all about taking the chance of being open with each other, across all of the differences, and beyond the need to compete for who suffered more. In the end, if we talk to each other truthfully, we will have done our small part to heal."

Discussion

The practitioner first picks up nonverbal cues and decides to cite them in the forthcoming session. This is done directly, leading to a surfacing of difficult and painful feelings. The practitioner also offers some ideas on motives for the tension in the group, focusing the members on their need to compete for which of the group they represent suffered more in its history.

It was necessary for the group worker to feel comfortable enough and knowledgeable enough to air the issues in the conflict related to genocide, slavery, and the Holocaust, and to hold the belief that some resolution could occur through the raising of such highly painful issues.

This group appears to be on the way toward recognizing and accepting the role honest communication plays in understanding each other empathically beyond the need to compete.

Members are given tools to air the conflict and painful feelings, as well as recognize that showing vulnerability openly will require further efforts. Had the practitioner not helped the conflict to surface, this group could easily have disintegrated into a fight-flight mode wherein members used fighting and conflict as a way of fleeing from the painful feelings the surroundings evoked. Due to the length of time they are spending with one another in this intense experience, there is much potential for this group to use their conflict creatively to develop a host of interreligious approaches to commemorating and combating genocide. These interreligious approaches would further the goals of their group.[1]

Group Mending

It is a fact of group life that as the members move forward to meet their needs and interests they will encounter varying degrees of failure along with success. Some of the members' experiences with their own and others' limitations will result in feelings of vulnerability and ineffectiveness. Group mending is used to help members own and get beyond feelings of failure, rejection, and humiliation to restore the group's ability to function in an affirming, goal-oriented manner despite disappointments.

In the face of these reactions, the practitioner reaches for and actively initiates discussion of the interactions and feelings that are causing group members to feel hurt and uncomfortable. Denial, threat, and avoidance of talking about failures and negative reactions also are bound to occur; the practitioner helps bring about the talking out of these difficult feelings while at the same time causing the group and members to examine and affirm their strengths.

| Illustration | *Gay, Lesbian, Bisexual, and Transgender Teens in a Residential Program* |

A group of gay, lesbian, bisexual, and transgender (GLBT) teens in a residential program have severe social and emotional difficulties along with being stigmatized because of their sexual orientations. The group has been organized with the goals of improving their social interaction, self-expression, and effectiveness in school, along with the possibility of repairing strained family relationships. Their school careers have been marked by failure and underachievement. Randy, the group worker, has made some inroads into their schooling by identifying and reinforcing their strengths. By and large, their families have been quite rejecting of them. Many of these youngsters have been sexually abused and have a history of trauma. Through the energetic support and vision of Randy, they have been writing a book of poetry and essays for the purpose of building self-esteem and self-expression.

This meeting is taking place immediately following the weekend when two members visited their respective parents. Both came back to the residence devastated. Neither went to school that day.

Just before the meeting, Randy goes to the meeting site, where she finds Andy and Stephania asleep on the couch. She wakes them and reminds them of the meeting. They ignore her. Andy has his hair in braids and tied up with orange ribbons. He is wearing purple tights and a silver bracelet. Stephania (aka Steve) wears platform heels and false eyelashes. They try to ignore Randy. Eventually the rest of the group come in, some appearing to look quite "cross dressed" and others rather nondescript in jeans and T-shirts. Randy tries to start the meeting, but Andy and Stephania are still sleeping. She cajoles, "Okay, nap time is over." She pleads, "Come on guys, wake up time." Finally, she yells some feigned profanity at them and says she will give them "milk, cookies, and green nail polish." This makes them laugh and they finally open their eyes.

A lot of banter follows. Then Randy begins, "Okay, Andy and Stephania, tell us what happened." Andy starts talking about how horrible it was to visit his family. He was wearing the same tights and braids, and when his aunt and grandmother saw him they could not hide their disgust at his appearance. Andy describes missing them, and recounts how when his mother and stepfather burned him his aunt and grandmother lovingly took care of him. His present disappointment is profound. He begins to cry that he has no one and what's the point of trying. Willie and Doretha try to console him, "You have us. We will always be here." Randy affirms, "How awful and disappointing this is for you. But, oh my gosh, it would be even worse if you stopped trying and just stayed down on yourself."

She then asks the group what they can share with Andy. Manuel points out that he finally learned not to wear ribbons in his hair when visiting his mother. "Why are you doing that, Andy?" He replies, "I want to be accepted for who I am."

"Me too," says Stephania. "I visited and the same thing happened to me. My mother was the drug addict, not me. She was the one in jail, not me. She wants me to be Stephen. She didn't raise me. She doesn't have that right. What she did was give me a positive drug toxicology. That's what she gave me. That's why I am dys . . . whatever—dyslexic." Randy says, "We all see how sad and terrible you feel. But you know, you're the person who overcame the positive drug tox—you learned to read and now you write beautifully." The rest of the group affirm that.

Randy points out, "Hey, Andy and Stephania, together, with everyone's help, we'll try to figure out what you can do next. But, whatever goes on, this cannot be the reason you stop going forward, nor for any one of you when this kind of painful rejection punches you in the gut." Randy continues, "Manuel, I'll come back to what you asked in a minute. But I was wondering what other members have had failures in seeing family and old friends?" Barry says when he visited his father and stepmother they were so pissed off they could hardly talk to him. He left before dinner. "Oh how sad for you," Randy responds. "A whole lot of gut punches when you're trying so hard."

Eleanor adds that she brought her girlfriend to see her parents, and her mother was very nice to them. "But she didn't want us to go where the neighbors would see us. At least she was nice." Randy notes, "It's good that you could accept this, even if it wasn't perfect. Remember you're worth a lot. Remember that. That's why everything positive you do, whether it's in school or elsewhere, is about being worth more than the minimum, for yourselves."

During this time, Randy has been passing around cookies, milk, and juice drinks, and at the same time listening. She smiles and produces a green nail polish for Andy.

"So, anyone have any feelings about what Manuel said?" "I think when I become 18 and go to work because I aged out of the system, I will have to look more conservative," notes Tara. But I'll never wear a dress." Laughter. Andy says, "I want to be who I am right now." "But no green nail polish when you try to get a job, is that what you are saying?" asks Randy. "Yes," Eleanor agrees with that.

The talk then shifts to the group wondering why their family members and others act like they are bad people. Gabriella adds, "We didn't do anything bad to them." More talk ensues about being misunderstood and treated as if they cannot be trusted. Randy notes, "How can you show them that you are all the trustworthy and respectful people I find you to be?"

Discussion

The practitioner employs good professional judgment in starting the group by immediately paying attention to the two members' issue. While parental rejection affected them now, the other members had been dealt the same blow on other occasions. She engages in group mending and reflects the feeling of hurt and humiliation, first by affirming that their pain was deep and second, by asking for more input about other members' painful rejections from family. While she does not ignore Manuel's astute observation, she lets him and the group know that it should be addressed later on.

Throughout, the group worker finds ways to support the members' humanity, goodness, and inherent trustworthiness in order to build their self-esteem and enhance their potential for success. She does not interrogate, nor does she get caught up in what will happen. Rather, she stays with what their needs are for feeling safe, secure, and able to continue working on repairing difficult family relations. The cookies, milk, and juice are part of providing safety and nurturance to young people who have been so impoverished. The green nail polish is her way of accepting what others might consider "bizarre" behavior.

The group needed to regain their emotional resources so they could gather the strength and courage to consider how to work on their own behalf and not sabotage their forward movement.

Confrontation

Confrontation is a very special technique used to change behavior as it is being expressed. It is used when the practitioner has judged that a member of the group has done considerable work on change and is ready to push through a doorway into a different form of expression.

The practitioner uses the technique by indicating that a form of interaction and expression in the present must be altered, right then and there, in the group situation. The practitioner identifies the dysfunctional expression and lets the member know what problems his or her behavior is causing. The practitioner asks for and guides the desired behavior change. Confrontation is done with respect for the members' rights to self-determination, their inherent capacities, and their developing abilities. Members cannot be forced against their wills to change the form or content of their self-expressions.

Illustration	*Iraq and Afghanistan War Veterans Support Group*

In an Iraq and Afghanistan war veterans support group in an urban VA hospital, some members have been bemoaning the lack of educational benefits, the fact the stint they did in Iraq was longer than they expected, and that so many Americans have turned on the war. They are upset at family members' avoidance of their war experiences and their desire to have life go on as it had been.

Felipe notes that unlike during the Vietnam war, the country did not turn against the vets, adding that the reception he has gotten in his urban community has been gratifying, "And they were so nice to my wife while I was away." Nicholas talks with a lot of anger and feeling about not receiving the benefits package he expected would get him to engineering school. He receives a lot of support and empathic responses.

Talk then shifts from anger about benefits to anger about equipment failures and what went on at the front. Kyle talks very emotionally about losing three of his friends on a patrol because their cars did not have the right protection. Linda, one of the two women in the group, adds that she, like Kyle, saw a lot. "They were just great guys . . . it's a jungle out there, and on top of that I left my two little kids with my mother and they are still angry at me." Devon adds, "At the same time that we were patrolling Iraqi homes and being nice to people over there, we were scared shitless because all you needed was one terrorist in their midst and it would be over." There is agreement, a lot of emotion, and then silence.

Then Felipe asserts, "Don't bring up what went on over there. We don't want to relive that now. We have to get on with things." The practitioner, Oliver, responds directly to Felipe, "Every time someone starts to talk about the losses and fears they experienced over there in Iraq, you make them put a lid on it. What went on over there that you do not want to talk about?" Felipe says that he doesn't have to talk about it. Kyle points out, "Fine, fine, but why do you try to get us to stop talking about it?" Nicholas adds, "Anyway, it's better to talk about what went on."

More discussion ensues about post-traumatic stress disorder. Stories are recounted about vets who had seen a therapist and were taking medication to stop reliving the past. The practitioner points out, "Felipe, you don't have PTSD." Felipe agrees that he does not relive what happened. Henry and Dawn push at Felipe: "Then what's bothering you from Iraq that you don't want to relive?" "It's one thing to have PTSD and relive it all the time. It's another to keep avoiding it all," says Dawn. Henry adds, "I think that's why you're having trouble with your wife . . . you're not talking to her like you're not talking to us."

The practitioner says, "Felipe, let's have a look together at what went on. What's so difficult for you to talk about?" Felipe tells a story of a doctor who was trying to help a little boy who they had been told had a cleft palate. He had been part of a special medical team that had been helping children with all kinds of pressing needs and injuries. Felipe's envoy took the doctor with them. Felipe said the envoy was sloppy about the security procedure and so the doctor prematurely entered the house that reportedly belonged to the boy's family, and he was killed. Felipe stops. Oliver reflects, "We are listening. There's more to tell. Go on." Felipe continues to recount that indeed there had been a boy with a cleft palate, but that there were snipers in the house. There was a shoot-out and, along with the snipers and the doctor, the child was killed. Felipe recounts the pain of that day, the horror of losing the doctor, and the guilt about being sloppy about following protocol. He is very choked up throughout, and adds with final-ity, "The doctor was too eager to go into the house, and we weren't fast enough to stop him." After silence and tears, and just as others are about to speak, the practitioner intervenes, "Felipe, it is so important that you told us this."

Kyle jumps in to tell Felipe that he had similar feelings when his friends died, and that some of the dead were innocent children and unarmed civilians. Linda and Henry reflect feelings of terrible painful guilt whenever they witnessed any deaths especially in their units. Oliver asks, "Felipe, I want to check in. How are you feeling about having told us this story?" Felipe says that although it was hard, this is what he hasn't wanted to talk to his wife about. The practitioner con-tinues, "And the rest of you, how is it for you to relive some of this?" The group goes on to talk about the balance between dwelling too much on what hap-pened and not talking about it at times when you just have to.

As the meeting nears its finish, Oliver notes, "So much more was also raised about relationships with family and children, and getting on with your education and lives. We certainly have a lot going on that can be dealt with here. And boy have you all shown you have the strength and fortitude to help each other through these complex emotional issues."

Discussion

In this meeting, the practitioner seizes the opportunity to help one member confront an issue he has been avoiding and to validate what others experienced as a necessity—talking about painful issues so as to move past a difficult stum-bling block.

First, he uses confrontation to direct the member to recognize that he deflects the group's expression of painful feelings in a particular area. Noting that Felipe is not suffering from post-traumatic stress disorder, which would require different interventions, his intervention supports the other members' belief in the impor-tance of talking about these issues. He continues to confront Felipe and asks him to tell the group what he has been avoiding dealing with that went on in Iraq. As Felipe recounts his story, he stops and becomes reluctant to reveal its painful aspects, including the death of the child. Oliver continues to remain in a con-frontational, and at the same time encouraging, mode until the story has unfolded.

The practitioner then lets Felipe and the group know how important it was for the story to be told, cutting in before others could speak in order to empha-size the point.

Once the rest of the group shared their own feelings about their losses, the practitioner expressed confidence in the impact of the confrontation, while at the group's end crediting everyone's efforts and affirming and reiterating the complexity of the agenda that would need to be resumed in the future.

Data and Facts

The intent of this technique (Schwartz, 1961; Shulman, 2006) is to provide accurate information to help people act based on the state of knowledge in the area, rather than on biases that support other popular—albeit uninformed—viewpoints. The focus is to show that knowledge can be used for empowerment and well-being, whereas lack of knowledge can result in distorted conclusions.

The practitioner is called on to improve the members' knowledge regarding relevant subjects. This is done through study, training, and consultations. The practitioner directly shares subject matter relevant to the group's purpose with the members. The practitioner also engages the members in their own efforts at gathering factual information and knowledge. The practitioner, having developed familiarity with the subject areas that underpin the group's purpose, is prepared to help clear up distortions based on incorrect information and biased knowledge. The practitioner carries out this technique within the group's process—in the meeting room as well as encouraging data gathering beyond the meeting.

Illustration	Human Rights Committee in a Developmental Disabilities Residence

A human rights committee, meeting bimonthly, has been formed on behalf of a residential program for people with developmental disabilities. The committee is composed of staff, residents, and community members, including family members. The social worker has been given the role of facilitator to assist them in ensuring the humane treatment of the residents as well as the agency's relationship with the state Office of Developmental Disabilities. This meeting follows one in which representatives of the state's Human Rights Division did a training session for this group. There, the trainer spoke of reports of incidents of sexual abuse of the residents by each other, as well as the challenges of helping people with developmental disabilities with their sexual urges.

At this meeting the committee is very involved with what the trainer said about sexual abuse and concerned about protecting residents. The group is moving toward establishing regulations in the residence that clearly will limit the residents' opportunities for dating and cohabitation. Beverly, the practitioner, has done her homework in an effort to help them make a well-founded, rather than precipitous, decision that includes information gathered from a number of informed sources. She had read extensively about sexuality and people with developmental disabilities, having been involved in consultations with a colleague who

is studying this phenomenon and educating people with developmental disabilities about sexuality. Beverly also took the time to visit five residences, speaking
with various staff in informal ways.

The practitioner says, "Before we decide anything, I know people in other residences who are willing to have us visit them to find out about their experiences
with residents' sexual activity." More discussion follows, along with a sense of confusion about how much information is needed to develop a well-thought-out
policy, some members indicating, "We have the information we need to make a
policy change." The practitioner says, "My experience in counseling some
individuals with developmental disabilities about romance has been okay, that
people know their limits." Mary, the resident member, is nodding in agreement.
The practitioner turns to her and asks, "Mary, isn't there a group at your residence
where you talked about sexual issues?" Mary, somewhat shy and embarrassed,
says that they have several groups on this topic. She says, "In the central office,
they don't trust us like they do at the residence." Beverly says, "This man, Marty,
has a video of a group session on dating that I can bring to a meeting when you
are ready." People agree. She continues, "After gathering the information, then
decisions can be made—perhaps no later than 4 weeks from now."

After a lengthy discussion revolving around the sense of urgency to resolve
the problem, the group realizes that some are anxious and do not have all of the
information. They agree to put off the decision. Some of the members volunteer
to visit several residences.

From subsequent visits to several settings, members learn from informal
chats with residence staff that when people with developmental disabilities are
passionate, they are louder than people who don't have developmental disabilities. The latter then become anxious at the noise and fear for the welfare of the
noisemakers, often assuming it to be sexual abuse.

Discussion

This practitioner is aware of how prone group members can be to making
quick decisions, especially when they believe that their actions are responsibly
based. In this case, the members had two prior training contacts with state officials; through those contacts they had come to believe that sexual behavior
needed to be curtailed. In essence, they were prepared as a majority to make a
decision to limit the rights of residents with developmental disabilities in the
so-called interest of their welfare. However, they were missing data from other
sources. They had not spent time with the residents themselves, learning from
informal sources and staff about the residents' day-to-day activities and how sexuality and romantic relationships had been discussed and managed.

The practitioner had to work against the group's desire to meet its obligations quickly while relying on only one source for data. She had to bring to the

members the necessity for them to obtain more facts, showing them in a non-conflictive way that there was other information to be gathered. While making these resources available to their scrutiny, she was mindful not to hold her own and others' expertise over their heads.

In this process, the practitioner had to help the committee accept the frustration that comes from being unable to reach a decision because the problem has not yet been completely understood. However, by guiding them to the relevant facts and experiences, the practitioner helped them avoid future embarrassment. This could have resulted when the community and residents found out that the committee's denial of residents' rights had come from a lack of relevant facts. Of greater significance, the members in making decisions for other human beings had to make decisions that respected the integrity and desires of those persons.

Self-Disclosure

Self-disclosure is used to convey humanness and fallibility. It shows the practitioner to be integrally related to and affected by the process. Self-disclosure is most often used in the group's middle phase, wherein the members view the practitioner as unique and differentiated, with experiences and perspectives on interactions that can help them understand new aspects of social life and emotional expression.

In using this technique, the practitioner directly shares feelings and reactions toward members and significant others who are involved in the process. Self-disclosure of professional limitations and vulnerabilities is also useful; so is the request for help with certain difficult aspects of the practitioner role in the group. Self-disclosures occur both after reflective periods and in spontaneous ways. A request for help in solving the practitioner's personal problems is not appropriate, because it crosses the boundaries of the professional relationship.

Before the middle phase, while the members are in struggles about their own power and control in relation to the practitioner, self-disclosure by the practitioner may incur distorted reactions and lead the members to negative comparisons with their own abilities and successes. This puts the practitioner into the position of being a hallmark of special ability, often leaving the members feeling incapable by comparison.

Since humanistic group work is based on the group's externality, the practitioner often functions in situations with the members outside of the meeting itself, for instance, at program events. There the practitioner is observed as well, and these observed behaviors disclose his or her handling of feelings and role transactions. In contexts where group members feel something is wrong with them for having to be in the group, self-disclosure helps demonstrate the meaningfulness of interpersonal relationships and prevents one-upmanship among members.

Because it highlights the group worker's feelings as a professional in the group, self-disclosure is wedded to humanistic values of social group work. One sees how the practitioner is called on to develop self-awareness in all types of interpersonal situations and to learn about mutual respect, cooperativeness, and taking care of others' needs. Furthermore, he or she does not violate people's boundaries nor let his or her own boundaries be violated. For example, the practitioner shares what is personal about the self as it relates to the group and not more, and does not set up members to disclose more than they want to. Because these characteristics epitomize interaction in interpersonal relationships, it is clear why self-disclosure as a technique is used when group members are intently working on changing their own interactions in their interpersonal situations.

Illustration	***Support Group of Women Managers***

Carla, Stella, Michelle, En Yeung, Ellie, and Donna are discussing how ridiculous and angry they feel at certain times when they might be the only women in a group of men at business gatherings. They have been meeting as a support group of women managers, under the auspices of the company's employee assistance program. Stella says, "So I started to talk about the sad state of our baseball team and the men looked away as if they didn't hear me. I was ignored. They waited to interact again after I got the message. How screwed up! During the break they were talking about the pitching left and right. But when I make a comment, it's like that was not my place. I should be in the sewing circle."

Michelle turns to Janet, the practitioner, and says, "How is it for you? You sit in the cafeteria with men and women. What is your experience?" Janet says, "At the risk of incurring your wrath, I want to hold off on talking about me right now. I assure you I will. Right now it's your experience, and I want to carry my role and make sure you know what you're working on. If I talk about my own reactions, I am afraid you will be too affected by my experience."

Some members retort, "You're playing games, Janet. You're keeping a distance from us. Tell us what it is like for you." The practitioner says, "I'm not keeping a distance, but I am feeling badly that you believe I am holding out on you." Donna says, "Come on, you're a woman. What do you get out of being with us each week? What do you feel out there at meetings and the like?" The practitioner says, "I have experienced some of what you are talking about, but remember, in social work there are a lot of women, and in here, too. I look for ways to be me with men and women, and I dislike feeling that I'm being stereotyped or discouraged from saying what I want. So I hate these situations, but I try not to personalize them, though at times I do anyway. I've had experiences like you, Stella, where I might as well not have been in the room. I can talk about my daughter and some men will space out—like they're not parents, too. But others don't. What will help you now is for everyone to have a look at what you all feel like when these kinds of things happen."

This explanation triggers the group members into questions and reactions about their own feelings and motives. There is further talk about the difference between being in a profession that has more women in it (though they note the women still are not the majority of managers) and being in their corporate situations where they still are a small minority.

Discussion

In this situation the practitioner does not choose to self-disclose, though she may have a great deal to share with the group. When she is called on to share her feelings, she does not at first. She prefers to have the group understand their own reactions to being rejected. In addition, for her to respond before members react to Stella's predicament can serve for the members to avoid expressing their own thoughts and feelings, making her too central to the process and them too peripheral. By not responding right away, Janet tries to help the members see that their issues matter more than hers and that her solutions can be helpful only as additional material for working on these problems. Though she does not respond to what they are asking right away, she does trust them by giving them her genuine reaction that she is feeling badly that they experience her as holding out on them, as well as her feelings about her professional responsibility with them.

On the other hand, the practitioner has to eventually respond to the request. She tempers her own resolutions and fears they might over idealize her as she points out that social work has many women in it so these incidents may not happen as frequently. She recounts how many men will not respond to her if she talks about her children, sharing similar experiences.

Dealing With the Unknown

Dealing with the unknown is used to help the members take steps into change efforts and experiences when they are inhibited from moving forward. It is more often used when the members are considering their direction than when they are in the midst of an experiential happening. Use of this technique can lead to experiential processes.

Dealing with the unknown may be used when the members have run up blind alleys or are not looking at realities because they are afraid to move toward them. The signs include random, undirected activity where there has previously been directed and purposeful activity. Another sign is the return to old forms of interaction and problem solving after a period of more effective and secure actions (Garland, Jones, & Kolodny, 1973).

The practitioner encourages the members to discuss their views about how change will unfold, what change will feel like, and what risks they imagine. Members also are asked to consider what fears prevent them from acting differently. This technique interfaces with the members' humanistic right to determine their own direction and destiny.

Illustration	Adolescent Boys Group in a Substance Prevention Program

A group of adolescent boys who are part of a drug and alcohol prevention group work program in their high school are complaining about the quality of parties and other similar events. It seems that whenever the high school has a rock concert and party, most of the youths hang out outside the school after the concert and do not go back into the party. Many of them try to act "cool," as if going back into the party itself is "uncool." It takes a toll on them because they don't get to have fun; instead, they spend their time figuring out where they will go next—to the mall, the movies, or the pool hall—who will go with whom and how to arrange the transportation.

At this meeting, several of the boys admonish each other for not getting together the previous Friday night. Jimmy says to Hank, "You said you were going to go to the mall, but when I went over there with Kelly and Joanna, you weren't there. I bumped into Doreen and she said you'd gone into the movies with the guys. Why didn't you wait?" Hank responds that the show was just starting. Pete retorts, "We should have gone back into the party. My mother was real mad when she heard we had left after she had dropped us off there."

The practitioner, Roger, says, "Let's look at what happened Friday night. How come you guys didn't just go back into the party?" Jeff says, "You can't go in, because you don't know if it will be a good party." Mike says, "If you're outside then you can see who is coming and whether it's worthwhile going back in." Greg tells the group, "I went back in and they had a great DJ, but people who were inside really felt uptight because half of you didn't come back. There were lots of girls there, too, and they were really mad at all of you for not staying." Kevin asks, "You guys who left, what did you do?" Several say they spent time looking for kids in the pizza joint at the mall, a couple went to the movies, and Jimmy and the girls went to the pool hall. "How was that?" asks the practitioner. Several mumble "okay" in response. The practitioner continues, "Kids with beer in their back packs?" More mumbles.

The practitioner asks, "What about the guys trying to sell you drugs, were they out there too?" The guys mumble, "Yes," and talk about what a drag it is to have to dodge those guys. Roger asks, "Given the guys in the mall preying on you, what if you had stayed at the party with the DJ?" Hank and Jimmy say it might have been better: "Forget about those guys—Greg said there were lots of girls there." Greg retorts, "You wouldn't know what to do with the girls anyway. You guys won't dance, you just like to act cool, but you won't go into a party and just party." The practitioner asks, "Does Greg have a point, guys? Is that true?" Mike sheepishly says, "Maybe . . . a little bit, we can't dance like you Latino guys."

Roger replies, "Come on, guys, let's look at this 'maybe' business." Jimmy says, "I had girls with me. I just didn't want to go in there." Hank says, "Yeah, but you're just friends with Kelly and Joanna. I know you really like Doreen. And I think she was in the mall looking for you." There are jokes and laughter. The practitioner says, "It sure would have been easier to find Doreen if you all had stayed at the party, don't you think?" Pete says, "It's true, she left with Ellen when she heard us saying you had gone to the mall."

The practitioner asks, "What would have happened if all of you had stayed at the party like you had started out to do?" Pete says, "First of all, my mother wouldn't be threatening to ground me. And second, we might have found the girls!" Jimmy says, "Maybe Doreen would have stayed." Roger asks, "What would have happened if you all had stayed? What would it have been like?" They talk about having to dance and how some of them don't know reggae while others don't know Latin dances; they like to listen to good rock music, rather than dance. Roger responds, "So you guys are afraid that you don't dance so well." Hank tells the group that the girls are always better dancers. Jimmy says, "Yes, at these parties the girls all hang together, laugh, look relaxed, and talk to each other."

The practitioner says, "Jimmy, just for the sake of argument, let's say there's another dance this Friday and you stay and you approach Doreen to dance. What would happen?" Pete butts in, "She'd dance with you. Even if you're a lousy dancer." Everyone laughs. The practitioner says, "Well, Jimmy?" Jimmy says, "I don't know—she'd say she had to go to the ladies room and leave." "What if she did?" Roger asks. Jimmy says, "I'd be embarrassed." Roger says, "She could say no and you'd have to deal with it, but what if she said yes?"

Jimmy tells about how he feels shy and nervous. Roger wonders if other guys would feel that way. The group talks for roughly 15 minutes about feeling embarrassed, shy, and nervous with the girls. Roger supports their efforts by reminding them, "You never know how things will turn out until you try. If you don't try, you'll just be hanging out in the mall at the mercy of the kids who are, for the moment, not going anywhere, not to mention having a beer and then driving." Emphatic retorts of "No, no, we didn't drink and drive!" "Okay, okay," replies the practitioner. "But isn't it better to at least be at the mercy of your own feelings?" More laughter and good-humored discussion ensues. Then the boys start to talk about the local baseball team. The meeting ends with a resolve to go to the next party and to stay inside.

Discussion

Though the use of this technique revolves around dealing with the unknown, exploration and role rehearsal are also used to augment the technique. The practitioner stays with the content, directly questioning what is not clear and instructing members to listen and do the same. First, the practitioner asks the group why they did not stay for the party. This brings about some reporting—and vaguely expressed discomfort—about what the members actually did in their somewhat aimless search that evening. The member who remained at the party is enabled to talk about what it was like to be there.

The practitioner, knowing that the truants and a few drug dealers prey on the young teens at the mall, wants to give them permission to talk about these concerns. He also wants them to know that he is aware they might go to the mall to buy drugs. This elicits their real feelings about their safety from drug dealers and offers the alternative that dealing with the girls at the party is safer than dodging people in the streets.

None of these issues could have been dealt with without the direct efforts of the practitioner. He moves along with the flow of the process, raising new issues for the group to examine. Concerns surface about maleness, shyness, and fear of rejection serving as rationalizations for not making a commitment to go into the party. Concerns about the unsafe environment also surface, and the alcohol and drug issue remains one for future consideration. The boys support each other through this process. When they shift to baseball, the practitioner goes with the direction of the process, banking on the belief that the boys have gone as far as they are able in talking about their behavior, and that the next step involves going to the party with a different mind-set—in touch with their fears and anxieties. Respecting the members' rights to learn from experience, the practitioner does not direct or encourage them to return to the subject, although he does ask if this is not similar to the act of leaving the party in subgroups.

Taking Stock

This technique is used to help the group and members clarify accomplishments up to the present moment so that they can move into future goals. This may be done at the ending stage of the group or during a natural transition to a stage with a newer set of working goals.

At the transition point in the process, the practitioner engages the group in a historical review of important events and crucial themes. The practitioner asks members to clarify the learning and experiences that have taken place and to consider applications of this learning to future situations. This is done to heighten the group's awareness of the meaning of the accomplishments in the group at that place in time, as well as to offer members a chance to consider and integrate the various strategies, approaches, and affects that helped this meaning to come about. The practitioner asks for members to clarify, summarize, and crystallize prior events with a mind toward carry-over and the creation of new initiatives and alternatives.

| Illustration | Young Adult College Students Support Group |

A group of young adults (ages 18 to 25) in a support group in an urban college counseling office is ending after 8 months. The group has faced many issues over the academic year. Included were issues of family, relationships, and academic achievement, as well as various personal emergencies, including an abortion and a death. The members are talking about what it means to leave the group when the academic year ends next month. There has been a range of expression, from fear of leaving to some bravado about the ability to cope without the group.

Marcos and Alexandra begin to talk about how afraid they are to leave the group for the summer. They ask whether it is possible to reconstitute the group in the fall. The practitioner, Dawn, says that "we can talk about the fall later. I think right now it will help more for you to share what you are afraid will happen to you without the group." Marcos talks about how his mother and he get into battles about his stepfather and about how he and the stepfather don't get along. Reggie reminds Marcos how well he has dealt with his stepfather in recent encounters. Jackie also reminds him that he gets pissed at his stepfather because he is really mad at his father for abandoning him. Marcos admits they are right, "but without you, I won't remember all of this." Alexandra talks about wanting to stay in the dorm rather than go home, because she doesn't want to face her parents' divorce. Marcos tells her, "You have to face it one day." She agrees, but says, "I would like to have the group to come back to."

The practitioner says, "Certainly we can form a group in September. Whoever wants to return to it, can. If you don't want to return, or are unable to return, there will be no pressure. It most likely will have some new and different members, too." Several members shake their heads, indicating that they are not sure how they feel about new people joining. The practitioner once again says, "There's time to talk about a future group. I wonder how others are feeling about leaving this group now." Felicia, the mother of a 2-year-old, says, "I welcome the chance to stop everything for the summer and have a chance to be with my baby." She talks about how the group has helped her accept the end of her relationship with her boyfriend. "Now I will try things out on my own." Mara supports Felicia's learning. The practitioner asks Mara, "What are your summer plans?" She volunteers that she has gotten a job in a resort for the summer where she will make a lot of money to help with tuition and books. "I hear there are some great guys at this place, so maybe I can test out making friends and not getting too intimate too fast." The practitioner asks Mara, "Can you clarify when you are in danger of getting too intimate too fast, Mara?" Mara talks about feeling sorry for herself when her father died suddenly and leaning on men to help her feel better. She says, "I'm doing this less, and I'm making friends with women, too," acknowledging Felicia and others. Jose says, "But if you need me, you can call me, and I'll remind you. I'll be here all of June and July." Felicia says, "Mara, really, I expect you to call me anytime you feel down, but you better call me when you feel good, too! I know I will call you." Mara thanks everyone for their special support. The practitioner reminds Mara what a hard year she had with her father dying. "Mara, you learned that your mother is not weak, and neither are you. You didn't have to sacrifice schooling, and you and your mom were able to work out a way to come through for you. You turned out to be stronger than you thought." Mara considers this and agrees.

Dwight talks about how hard the summer without the group will be and his fears about being drawn into a local gang he doesn't want to associate with. Fred says, "Stay away from them, stay home if you have to. That's it. Do you have a job yet?" Dwight says, "I don't, and it makes me uptight." Others advise that it will be easier for Dwight to handle these guys if he is too busy to be seen by them and is involved with college friends. The practitioner asks Dwight how he feels about seeking a job. Dwight talks about how he usually has let things happen on their own and that he learned in the group that this is not a good idea. "I've gone for jobs, and I've even asked people I know for leads." The group supports him for taking the initiative. The practitioner reminds him how taking the initiative with his parents and sister helped the family face his sister's drug addiction. Mara says, "You did the hardest job on them you could have done, and it worked. So of course you can do it for yourself now." The practitioner says, "It seems the more you've all been able to talk openly and face things here, the easier it has been for you to deal with important problems."

The members talk more about how it will be not to see each other during the summer. A couple of members are relieved that they will have a chance to get away from everything related to school. Several are pleased to know they have the option to return in September; some are ambivalent about coming to a different group, still wanting the practitioner to redefine the terms for next year.

Eddie tells the group he is going to see his relatives in Colombia in August. The practitioner encourages the members, saying, "Talk more about how you think the summer will be. What have you learned here to help you handle the summer?" The members talk about patterns of behavior they have been working on.

The practitioner reminds them that four meetings remain in which they can continue talking about future options. Felicia asks the practitioner what she herself will be doing in the summer. She volunteers, "I have a 3-week trip planned with my husband and children to a lake resort upstate. And I look forward to time off, for sure!" Everyone laughs, and jokes about how she must be "relieved to be rid of us for a while." She chides back, "No, you're not that bad, honest. I like this group. We've been through a lot together. And you've put in lots of great work. So it's real hard for me to end, too."

Discussion

The practitioner uses the technique of taking stock in a way that is organic to the group's process. The fears of some members about ending the group surface through their initial desire to reorganize the group for the fall term. The practitioner engages them in talking about the meaning of leaving each other for the summer and the possibility of ending the group. She also involves them in talking about their specific fears and how they have handled them in the past. This enables her to help many of the members appreciate how they have been handling difficult issues and feelings.

The practitioner reinforces the learning of members in cases where it is apparent that special support from her is needed. For instance, she is mindful to help Mara, who having lost a parent exhibited much dysfunctional acting-out behavior throughout the year. The practitioner responds to the situational aspects of Mara's behavior, though it is possible that her problems with men and her mother will require further work. For the moment, however, Mara seems to enjoy the support from the group necessary for her to continue her studies and to stabilize her relationship with her mother, as well as with men. On a latent level, the practitioner uses her own parental ability to reinforce Mara's current strengths.

Members like Marcos, Felicia, and Alexandra have been experiencing personal losses that leaving the group may rekindle. On the other hand, each of these members has demonstrated an ability to handle difficult interpersonal relationships through their mutual helping efforts. Acknowledging the efforts and gains made by them proves useful. Special affirmation by the practitioner is necessary especially for members who need extra support.

The practitioner makes sure to validate the feeling some members have of wanting the group to end. She is careful not to yield to the desire of several members to continue, which might serve as pressure for others to return in September. Thus, the practitioner is careful to say that the group can be offered in a different form in September. Members then can share a sense of freedom that comes from leaving the group, leaving school, and going on vacation. The practitioner, too, validates this feeling by sharing her vacation plans with the group. The humor at the end provides a helpful way for the members to gain perspective, and to work on further issues in the remaining sessions.

❖ SUMMARY

This chapter discussed seven techniques used by the practitioner to help the group actualize its purpose:

Conflict resolution, group mending, and *confrontation* are means for working out differences of opinion, as well as hard and painful feelings about relationships, in the group and in the members' individual or collective experiences in their life situations.

Data and facts and *self-disclosure* are used to give the members objective facts and materials, as well as empathically derived experiences and supports, to use in their own efforts.

Dealing with the unknown and *taking stock* focus the members on what they have come to be able to do, and on how people feel and handle feelings of anxiety and fear as they move on to new aspects of situations and relationships in and out of the group. They are also employed when the group is prepared to end.

The next chapter describes the techniques used throughout the humanistic group work method to achieve both of the dual objectives—developing the democratic mutual aid system and actualizing group purpose.

❖ NOTE

1.   When conflict arises prior to the group's normative crisis, similar strategies help the group develop norms. At that time, it is useful to draw upon the technique of decision making, which is parallel to conflict resolution for the development of the democratic mutual aid system. This technique provides a strategy for coping with the power dynamics that tend to surround conflict during the normative crisis. When the conflict occurs after the normative crisis, the members have an opportunity to add a new dimension to their understanding of each others' differences.

Further Techniques for Actualizing Group Purpose

Technique	Intent—Used to:	Practitioner Behavior
Conflict Resolution	Prevent escalation of conflict. Enable respect for differences.	Upon sensing conflict, surface and define conflict. Foster full expression of issues, stakes, including quiet or uninvolved members. Offer new perspective and new amalgam to reexperience issues.
Group Mending	Help members own and rebuild from failures, hurts, and humiliations.	Reach for and initiate discussion of hurt feelings. Engage group in examining, affirming prior accomplishments and strengths.
Confrontation	Enable group to face painful and divisive patterns. Help member or group step through a doorway after work has been done.	Stop process, clearly, succinctly, and point out to group or member that a change in dysfunctional behavior needs to occur. Use with respect for member's self-determination.
Data and Facts	Increase knowledge. Strengthen resource-finding skills.	Collect information on subject matter relevant to group. Share information. Clear up knowledge distortions.
Self-Disclosure	Display humanness, fallibility, and stake in group. Demystify process.	Share feelings relevant to group process and purpose. Share identifications and differences with group. Share professional limitations and vulnerabilities in practitioner role.
Dealing With the Unknown	Enable change when group is inhibited from pursuing desired change.	Encourage discussion of anticipated feelings and risks. Enable expression of fears that prevent action. Universalize blocks and fears. Help members scrutinize blocks. Give impetus and support.
Taking Stock	Enable passage from one juncture to new agendas.	Engage group in historical review of salient themes. Help clarify learning that has occurred. Plan ways to carry learning to future ventures.

8

Techniques for Developing the Democratic Mutual Aid System and Actualizing Group Purpose

❖ ❖ ❖

The following techniques represent the practitioner's attempts to help members express an array of feelings, ideas, actions, and attitudes. In the actual group process, the group worker will notice that some members need encouragement toward open and genuine behavior, either as a result of unfamiliarity with humanistic ways of participation or out of fear of disapproval. These techniques are used throughout the group process to bring about a variety of social and emotional interactions in relation to the humanistic group's dual objectives. They are *demand for work, directing, lending a vision, staying with feelings, silence, support, exploration,* and *identification* (see the "Techniques Chart" at the end of the chapter). They are generic to social work practice itself and are interwoven in full and partial forms with the other techniques. For clarification, see Table 8.1.

Table 8.1   Relationship of Techniques to Interactions That Develop the
Mutual Aid System and Actualize Purpose

Technique	Interaction
Demand for Work	Includes all experiences.
Directing	Develop democratic norms. Respect differences. Create activities in the milieu. Express and identify feelings to work on change. Express and identify feelings to heighten group awareness.
Lending a Vision	Includes all experiences.
Staying With Feelings	Develop affective bonds and cohesion. Help members express feelings toward each other. Help members express feelings toward practitioner.
Silence	Identify group process issues and heighten group awareness. Test group's autonomy.
Support	Includes all experiences.
Exploration	Develop affective bonds. Express and identify feelings that help group and members work on change. Identify themes to be worked on.
Identification	Enhance goal setting. Respect differences. Express and identify issues for change. Identify themes to be worked on. Identify group process issues. Identify projections and self-fulfilling prophecies.

❖ TECHNIQUES FOR DEVELOPING
    THE DEMOCRATIC MUTUAL AID SYSTEM
    AND ACTUALIZING GROUP PURPOSE

Demand for Work

The technique demand for work (Schwartz, 1976; Schwartz &
Zalba, 1971) is used to encourage and motivate members to examine
process and purpose issues, as well as related tasks. From a humanistic perspective, while respecting the equality and uniqueness of each

member, the practitioner is aware that people may be reluctant to engage with one another. This is true in part because of the newness of the group situation at the start and the ambivalence members face at new junctures in the process when an increase in taking risks and expending efforts is called for. In addition, members may become fearful about expressing their personal issues because they anticipate group pressure, stigmatization, or scapegoating.

Through the demand for work, the practitioner encourages and sometimes insists that the members move forward with the work at hand. The practitioner holds the group to its focus and recognizes when the members' tangential processes may be an "illusion of work" (Shulman, 2006, p. 153). The practitioner also takes into account times when tangential subgroup processes are useful for stimulating thinking and new efforts. Furthermore, when group members become complacent about their efforts up to now, the practitioner acknowledges their accomplishments but reminds them that there is more work to be done.

The demand for work is used throughout the group's life. Further along in the process, it is used when members get bogged down with fears about moving on or in conjunction with the technique of dealing with the unknown. It is also used empathically to deal with resistant attitudes that surface when confrontation is used to help members move into new experiences.

Illustration   *African Immigrant Parents Group*

A parenting group of mostly African immigrants is meeting to carry out its purpose to conduct programs for parents at the school. Early on in the meeting, some of the most vocal members jokingly accuse the practitioner, Vanessa, of being bossy and not really letting them make their own plans. The practitioner asks, "How am I being bossy?" and awaits a response. Frederica says, "Each time we throw out an idea, you lean forward and you look at us." Miriam says, "You ask us questions and give us your opinions like you are reading our minds." Others chime in, "We feel like you're watching our every move." The practitioner says, "Maybe I am, let me think about that," and trails off into thoughtfulness. The members continue talking about the school's rules and regulations in running programs there.

As this topic tapers off and they disengage from the practitioner, who remains silent for a while, the vocal members return to putting out ideas and arguing among themselves. After some time, the practitioner begins moving in and the group becomes uptight again. Noting this, Vanessa says, "I'm just trying to listen. But, actually, I do have a concern. I notice that each time someone has an idea the others react to each other as if that person is trying to be the boss.

When this happens you do not move ahead. Come on, get past this. There are lots of possibilities that can be created through your joint efforts. It won't hurt you to come out the other side and see what you can create."

This demand propels the group into activity. Someone comments that it was different in their various countries because you couldn't create something and that's why they ran away. "Understood," says the group worker, "I know." Many sighs and head nods. No one remarks further about the practitioner's push and she just continues with the flow of the process, joining in and being gregarious with them.

Discussion

The practitioner here is faced with a challenge to her authority. She values this within the frame of the members' right to challenge and question her, all the more because of the authoritarian situations they left behind in their homelands. She also encourages this because she actually believes that she is probably doing some things that are inhibiting them. As she listens, she notes the members' reluctance. Given this, the practitioner sees that they are reacting to power and control issues, as well as to resistance to moving ahead. Not excluding the possibility that her behaviors are inhibitory, the practitioner chooses to stay with the process and her most immediate observations. She identifies their interactions and in the same breath moves ahead to demand that they work. She remains focused on the task at hand, hoping that it works out, but not necessarily needing it to work out. She sees this process as useful for self-determination, whichever way it turns out.

As a result, the members move ahead, reflecting on an old theme that has been aired in the group—the inhibitory role authority exerted at home and the fact that they were able to escape from oppression—and how this surfaces in group life. The practitioner demonstrates understanding of this dynamic and continues interacting with them in the experience of planning. This has the potential of taking the group to another level of accomplishments.

Directing

Directing is closely aligned with the demand for work because it calls on the practitioner to be interactive and expressive rather than reflective and neutral. The group worker's tasks in directing are derived from the metaphor of the director's tasks in the world of drama.

The practitioner verbally or physically helps the group enact new behaviors or interactions. Directing also aims to assist people in communicating directly with one another when they have interpersonal issues to deal with, rather than avoiding the necessary face-to-face interaction. Directing may also call on the practitioner to actively instruct and move group members from position to position within the group environment.

| Illustration | **Boys Social Skills Development Group in a Community Center** |

Jacob, Carl, Paul, Richard, and Saul—boys in a community center group of 11- to 13-year-olds—to develop their social skills are running around the room. Maurice is blindfolded, trying to find them. The practitioner is moving in and around the interactions of this game, trying to stay out of their way while encouraging them. The boys laugh and push each other, fall, and make sounds. Maurice grabs one, holds him, touches his face and body, and identifies him correctly as Richard. Off with the blindfold; they fall to the floor—with the practitioner laughing, too—and just as the boys start putting the blindfold on Richard, talk develops. Carl and Richard are heard to say that after group they are going to a "meeting at their new charter school," that they have to go, and that they hate meeting new people.

The practitioner, Andrew, grabs the moment and says, "Let's get moving guys, Carl's and Richard's new experience fits right in." While he is talking, he is blindfolding Richard. "When you meet new people for the first time, it is just like finding out who they are when you can't see them, like in this game—except you can see them." He goes on, "Richard, run after the others. Boys, move away from him, but let him grab you, slow it down. Good! Richard, you've got someone. Don't take off the blindfold. Hold him." The boys are instructed to watch and listen. To Richard, he says, "Say to him, 'Hi, my name is Richard. What's your name?'" the other boy says, "Jacob." The practitioner says, "Okay Richard, ask him an identifying question, like 'Which school did you come from?'" He does, and Jacob answers.

After several interchanges, Richard says (imitating the practitioner's tone), "Why are you wearing that stupid blindfold and listening to that stupid bush-haired monster?" pointing to Andrew. Everyone bursts out in wild laughter, falling all over one another. Then they calm down and bow to each other stiffly faking polite "Hello, who are you?" greetings.

Discussion

In this illustration the practitioner is using programming activities as age-appropriate forms of communication with youngsters. He is able to seize the moment to use a game to help some members work on a specific need—learning how to find out who a stranger is. The practitioner recognizes the analogy between the game and the situation the two members will be in within an hour's time. The practitioner quickly directs the boys in a form that allows the game to assist in clarifying a situation the members are facing. Their esprit de corps and their previous history allow the members to move into this activity easily, following directions well. The practitioner believes in the outcome of the process as the lesson and does not teach about what is and what did happen; he just lets it unfold. The process develops to where there is a natural ending. The boys enact "getting to know you," which appears as though it will carry over for Carl and Richard, as well as for the others.

Lending a Vision

The practitioner calls on the special knowledge base he or she has developed through being a professional with many groups in order to provide perspective, hope, and a sense of faith about the group's ability to achieve its objectives. The technique of lending a vision (Schwartz, 1961) is used at new junctures in the group's evolution or when the group's members are feeling let down. At the start of the group, the practitioner lends a vision by giving the members ideas about the work they will do and how they will work together. While using this technique, the practitioner draws on his or her professional experience, education, and emotional perspective concerning the nature of the life experiences of people in groups and in other community-based real-life situations. In addition to reading and empathizing, the practitioner seeks out other colleagues and allied professionals to develop the wisdom necessary for the philosophical perspectives provided when lending a vision.

The practitioner directly offers hope regarding the special importance of learning in a democratic mutual aid system, as well as the special importance of accomplishing group purpose together. Drawing from the group's experience, the group worker recognizes what is happening, and provides motivation to continue work by pointing out what can happen between people. The practitioner presents a picture of the members' possibilities and communicates feelings of passion and commitment about the future to help members gain faith in their abilities. The vision that is lent should help the members establish a solid footing as they move ahead into what feels like uncharted territories of interaction.

Illustration   ***Prisoners Group for Maintaining Sobriety***

County jail prisoners in a group for maintaining sobriety are talking about how they will have a hard time going back to their neighborhoods. All agree that it will be difficult to see old friends who will be luring them back into drinking. Some are also talking about the characters they know in the streets who are selling drugs and making big money. Frank says, "It's hard for me to see my brother, who is an active alcoholic. We come from an alcoholic family and we are close." More talk ensues about how they would like to help their families and friends. Then the talk shifts back to their own fear of returning to their communities.

Ed tells them, "The last time I left jail, I ended up coming back because instead of going to AA, I got involved with drinking again, stole a car, and was caught drunk." Charles responds, "I don't want to go through that scene of being in jail again. Once is enough. But I get afraid, because everyone has stories like yours." The practitioner, Rick, asks, "What are you afraid of? Do you know?" Charles responds, "I'm afraid I won't make it, because the temptations out there are too great." Others agree that there are too many temptations on the outside.

The practitioner says, "Hey, wait a minute. I know there are lots of stories about going out and coming back because people get into the same bad scene. I know it's hard, but there are also the other kinds of stories—of success, where people left here and used AA to keep sober. They used therapy also, and went to school, got jobs, and made a life for themselves. Those are usually the people who planned good and hard for themselves to have things work out. Come on, don't just get into a bad place. The temptations will always be there. But you don't have to give in to the streets. Not if you have a plan that looks different from how things have been." Sal retorts, "Come on, man. Prove to me I'll have more money going straight, that it's worth it to stay sober and make a plan." The practitioner says, "Maybe this is not about money. Maybe it's about having a life for yourself that's a real life, not acting cool in the streets, living from minute to minute, just to have the best car you can get!"

Obviously, the practitioner makes his mark, as the group falls back into quiet pensiveness. Finally Sal, now fighting to hold back tears, says, "It's just that I'm afraid I won't make it. It seems easier not to try." Charles tells him, "You have to remember how much it hurts to be in jail and to have your kids know this is where you are." Sal agrees. The group begins to talk, with each member locating a feeling of hope that will enable personal efforts. Charles encourages Sal to use the time in jail constructively by taking high school courses. Ed agrees. "The last time I didn't make any plans while I was in jail, so when I got back to the neighborhood, there I was back with the same losers again." The members continue talking in this vein.

Discussion

While the group talks about the kind of social environments they each will have to confront upon release, the practitioner does not minimize their difficulty. A practitioner with this type of group must recognize that going back to unsupportive communities represents an awesome challenge. Yet the practitioner wants to remind the group that, in spite of difficulties, some have waged successful efforts.

The practitioner has to balance his understanding of the difficult tasks at hand with his desire to give the members further impetus, hope, and faith in themselves to continue the uphill battle to regain ownership of their lives. Rick does this by empathically acknowledging the realities the members face in returning to their neighborhoods, while at the same time letting them know that obstacles can be overcome by planning and development of options. When members challenge him, asking if it's worth it to try to plan at all, the practitioner has to become more passionate in his involvement with the group, reminding them that all does not have to be lost—that all is lost only to the extent that members give up on themselves.

Lending a vision requires a communication of passion and faith in peoples' strengths. It also requires sharing a belief that planned strategies can be used to overcome obstacles. By sharing his faith in their abilities, the practitioner helps the members find the hope and fortitude to continue in the face of actual obstacles.

Much more work will be needed in this group. Each member will have to specifically identify his personal obstacles. The topic of helping families and friends also will have to be worked on before members are about to be released.

Staying With Feelings

The expression of feelings is one of the hallmarks of human interaction, along with the ability to interact with awareness. Thus, group interaction needs to include opportunities for members to express their feelings, to feel comfortable expressing them, to express these feelings in ways that are considerate of others, and to remain focused on feelings when they are being expressed. Humanistic values support this. Each person's emotional and intellectual contributions are sought in a humanistic group. Along with that, the members' joint capacities to remain open and empathic to the expression of feeling by others sustain the group's level of connection and work. It is also recognized that when interpersonal relations are affected by sanctions on the expression of ideas, actions, and emotions, the content and form of expression become noticeably devoid of emotional language. Thus, the technique of staying with feelings is important throughout the entire process of group life. It serves to help members express their feelings rather than to conceal or block them, thereby facilitating an emotionalized, rather than intellectualized, process in the group.

The practitioner carries out this technique by serving as a model for the expression of feeling, speaking in the language of emotions. In addition, he or she asks members to identify what they are feeling, while at the same time acknowledging and identifying feelings as they are being expressed by the members.

The practitioner can learn early on how uncomfortable or defensive a group is by sharing his or her own feelings of anxiety due to the group's newness and the ongoing demands of group life. Judging from the response of discomfort or spontaneity, the practitioner can learn about the group's ability to stay with feelings. When processes emerge that are leading to deflection or suppression of feelings, the practitioner assists the members by activating and valuing their emotional expressions.

The technique is also carried out by fine-tuning listening skills and attending to the verbal and nonverbal expression of affects. These expressions include manifest forms such as happy, uncomfortable, glad, disgusted, and the like. Nonverbal forms are evident in facial expressions and body language. Tones of expression are attended to as well. The emphasis is more on overt forms than on inferences a practitioner can make about covert feelings. Working on inferential feelings can overstep the members' abilities, causing more defensiveness and the risk of assumptions on the practitioner's part. Feelings are evident enough in the verbal and overt nonverbal processes in the group. By asking about feelings freely and acknowledging members' feelings, members are helped to develop and sustain an atmosphere of comfort, while learning about the values that accrue from leading with their emotions when interacting.

Illustration	**Mothers Mandated to Treatment for Child Abuse or Neglect**

A group of single mothers who have been mandated to group treatment for abusing or neglecting their children is meeting to focus on the difficulties of single parenthood without assistance from spouses, lovers, and families. The group has come a long way. They have set up a phone network with each other and have gotten support for this as an experimental part of their entitlement income. (They keep records of their calls and submit them monthly.) The practitioner, Gloria, is also the child protection worker, and many concerns about her role in the child protective services bureaucracy have been raised and dealt with in earlier meetings.

In this meeting, the members are talking about the experience of picking up the children from day care centers after work, training programs, or schools, and having to mother children. Annette says, "I'm just wiped out. I plop down on the couch, tell the boys to give me 30 minutes, close my eyes, and sometimes I have to plug them into the TV. But they are learning." Maxine adds, "Sara and David jump all over me—I'm exhausted." Sally blanches and says softly and with great intensity, "I slapped Joel, backhanded him with my knuckles, and his nose bled. I called Carol afterwards, but I had already done it." There is a stunned silence.

The practitioner, Gloria, says, "Oh-oh! I feel for you, Sally. It must have scared the hell out of you and frightened Joel. Wow!" Silence follows. The practitioner says to the group, "Say something to Sally." Others say they feel sorry. Annette says she feels scared for Sally and herself. Carol strokes Sally's hand. Margaret starts crying. The practitioner says, "Boy, this really gets to all of us." Then she says to Sally, "I don't want to tell you what you are feeling or to ask you what you are feeling, but I guess I would like to know where you are at emotionally." Sally says, "I'm horrified. I feel like a nasty bitch, like I did when I yelled at Freddie saying he was going to turn out just like his father, a fuckin' failure." Most of the women huddle around her, listening intently. There are tears, then silence. The practitioner remains quiet.

After a while, Gladys breathes a sigh of relief and smiles. Sally says to the practitioner, "Report me for abuse." Gloria says, "I feel that under the circumstances of who you are, what your pattern is, that this is an odd happening. You know that my colleagues and I deal with these judgments all the time. We are aware of the discomforts we feel in this role, and we are also aware of how you stay in touch with and on top of your feelings in the difficult situations you are in."

Discussion

It is evident that this group has been working on and through their issues of being single parents for some time. In this meeting, the group is in one of these states. Their effectiveness comes from their trust in one another and the group worker, which centers on the anticipation of acceptance of each other's feelings.

When Sally indicates that she hit Joel, the group does not expect retaliation from the members or the practitioner. In fact, this concern has already been dealt with. In this situation, the practitioner's relating to feelings through example and direction is a normative occurrence in the group. She clearly responds to the intensity of the moment with her exclamations of "Oh!" and "Wow!" This supports the group's ability to stay with feelings and validates the intensity of the experience for each of the members, as well as for Sally.

The practitioner then asks Sally directly to share what she is feeling. After Sally shares her reactions, the practitioner does not rush in with a response. Rather, through her silence, she allows the members time to experience their many feelings and to sort out their reactions. Breaking in with a sigh of relief, Gladys reflects the group's readiness to shift the mood and examine the event. Sally then begins to deal with her own judgment of herself by asking the practitioner to report her for abuse. Gloria tells her honestly that she does not think this is warranted. Her assessment is based on the intensity of the mutual aid in this group (as evidenced by their ability to accept and deal with each other's feelings), the telephone support network they have created, and the infrequency of the act of striking her child.

Silence

Silence is a technique that is used to convey respect and support for the struggles and capabilities of the members. It is used to help and encourage the members to be themselves despite the actual and perceived social pressures to conform to expectations. The practitioner's silence offers a way for members to reflect rather than to immediately react to internal (psychological) and external (social) stimuli. It may also be used to assess the group's relative autonomy from the group worker by noting the group's degree of comfort with the practitioner's silence and its capacity to work on its own in the face of it.

Silence is a technique that often can be misused by a practitioner to create a condition of anxiety in the group with the intent of spurring the members to work. Certainly this objective has its place, but only in a very technical and precise way as a type of confrontation; that is silence confrontation. However, it is by no means the main purpose of silence as defined for use in the humanistic model of social group work.

To enact this technique, the practitioner remains silent. The body language is relaxed; the look on the face is attentive, curious, and empathic. It is neither neutral nor distinctly emotional. When noting that the members are working productively in the process toward developing mutual aid and actualizing purpose, the practitioner may choose to remain silent because what he or she would say would not add anything to the members' processes. In fact, if the practitioner is questioned about his or her silence, a brief explanation of the silence and encouragement of the members to continue is warranted.

Illustration	*Couples Treatment Group*

A couple's group conducted at a community mental health clinic is meeting. Carl, a member, addresses the practitioner, "you've been quiet for so long today." "I'm listening to you," the practitioner says, "and taking in what you're all working on. Don't worry, when I feel I have something to contribute, I will." He then falls back into empathic and attentive silence.

The members continue interacting. Vince turns to Martin and Corinne and says, "You two have to stop blaming each other." He acknowledges his spouse and says "I feel almost contaminated by your battles when Maria and I leave here. I'm not blaming you. But it's like Sherrie said a few weeks ago, we carry each other home with us after group, don't we?" Others nod.

George and Terri turn to Martin and Corinne, saying they feel uncomfortable and worried for them. Martin and Corinne express positive feelings that the group is caring about them, but also show that they feel concerned and confused that the group is blaming them. George looks at the practitioner (who remains silent) and then continues talking to Martin and Corinne. The members appear to become more comfortable with Carl's silence, and as the meeting progresses no longer look in his direction for input or permission after members' seemingly charged reactions.

Discussion

This illustration represents the effective use of the technique of silence. When asked to intervene, the practitioner begs off, explaining to the members that he is listening and has nothing to contribute at that time. He does use a nonverbal directive for them to continue; they do so, with the practitioner listening attentively. When George looks in the practitioner's direction for participation, Carl continues his attentive silence. This gives the members the impetus to work on their collective issue—taking responsibility. It enables them to effectively work on this with the practitioner in the background, rather than the foreground, of their process.

Support

Support is used to reinforce forms and content of interpersonal expressions that affect the caring milieu of the democratic mutual aid system and working on purpose. To use support, the practitioner needs awareness of the ways in which people interact that permit open and undefensive transactions, which in turn foster give-and-take and the exploration of alternatives, as well as learning about choices and change.

The practitioner verbally and nonverbally directs positive cues and comments to encourage these types of interactions. This is done by pointing out to the group when and in what way members' intentions, activities, and processes are useful to the group's objectives. Support is an empathic statement by a practitioner highlighting a part of the process as helpful. Brief comments of affirmation and nods of agreement by the practitioner are also useful. There is an element of expertise in the use of support, since the practitioner highlights and underlines particular means as helpful alternatives for achieving certain conditions.

| Illustration | *Senior Citizens Naturally Occurring Retirement Community Group* |

Eleanor, Tom, Roberto, and Douglas, members of a naturally occurring retirement community (NORC) run through a community center, are discussing how to figure out their new prescription coverage. Some are also unclear about their medical plans. The other members, Nancy and Roseanne, are listening attentively. Douglas says he is concerned that he is spending too much out of his budget. Others talk about the high cost of doctors' visits. Douglas falls silent, shaking his head.

The practitioner, Betty, notes to herself that Douglas has retreated and says, "Douglas, you are on the right track. Isn't medical care expensive whichever way you cut it?" This revives Douglas, who says, "I picked a prescription plan. But then I read in the paper that some senior citizens have too much coverage. Maybe I have too much. But when I ask my caseworker, she says I have just the coverage I need. When I asked the union, they said the same thing." The practitioner says, "That's a good track to be on. Your funds are limited, and focusing on whether you have too much coverage is one good direction. Why spend unnecessarily?"

The group continues talking about how they will find out which prescription plan to select, and if they have too much coverage. Roberto says, "We need to talk to our doctors about our medical situations so we can pick prescription plans, since there is a deadline." The practitioner responds, "Talking to doctors and their staff, who often know more than they do, is a good idea." The group picks up on that. Roberto says, "Why don't we get a couple of people from the doctors' offices to come in and talk about prescriptions, medical plans, and then a union person to talk about those benefits." More affirmation and groans are heard from some of the members. Betty reflects, "I know, it is really such a pain, how you have to plow through all these details to figure it out." Members echo, "You've got that right!"

The practitioner says, "Douglas, didn't you say there was something in the paper about too much medical coverage? Wait a minute. I'll get my newspaper from my office."

Betty runs out to get the paper and returns. They all look at the article, which gives them further impetus to delineate their varied medical insurance plans to determine overlap and overspending. Roseanne and Douglas agree to work with Roberto to obtain information from their doctors, to see a union representative, and to arrange to have them come to a larger meeting of the NORC. Betty volunteers that she will go with them if they feel they need her. After some talk they decide to go without her, saying, "If we strike out this round, you can come to our rescue."

Discussion

The practitioner's intent in this excerpt is to be supportive of the members' efforts. She is aware that members are focusing on the realities of their situations with a system that has power over them. The practitioner supports their efforts, recognizing that it may be difficult to sustain these efforts toward clarifying with medical providers what kind of coverage is suitable. First, she shows support to Douglas by restating his perception and reaction. Second, she does not ask the group to share their feelings, for fear they will slip into their ambivalence. Rather, she is very direct in supporting the track they are on, one of trying to ascertain and clarify what is appropriate medical coverage.

Betty reinforces the feelings of frustration when bureaucratic regulations become too complicated for one individual to decipher. As the group begins to gather momentum toward finding a way to learn more details about their benefits, the practitioner spontaneously reintroduces the newspaper article on medical coverage to help further focus the members' efforts. Going to her office for her newspaper is also an act of support. She shows further support by stating her availability to go with them to medical providers.

Exploration

Exploration is a technique used to involve members in free-flowing expressions of feelings and perceptions about process and content issues. It is used to highlight the members' curiosities, and to enable the suspension of judgment for the sake of expanding awareness and understanding of emotional and ideational nuances. Exploration stimulates a process that surfaces and considers the pragmatic and emotional values of perceptions and feelings. Exploration also ties in with the norms that respect people's experiences and intellectual voices, as well as those that help them to determine their unique existence.

Through open-ended remarks or questions to members or the group as a whole, the practitioner stimulates the expression of perceptions and feelings. The practitioner shows curiosity regarding affects and ideas without projecting any sense of accusation, interrogation, or closure. When using this technique, the practitioner does not presume to have right answers. The practitioner directly asks the members to look at different perspectives concerning themselves, others, and situations as they are examining interactions. In effect, the practitioner shows that by being inquisitive with one another members can share and develop abilities as well as different approaches. Through exploration, the practitioner models how to be appropriately curious about others, how this helps to overcome feelings of intrusiveness.

Illustration	**Men With Chronic Disabilities**

Several men (mostly in their forties and fifties), who have been outpatients in a long-term hospital for persons with chronic and disabling diseases, have been involved in a socialization group for many months. Some live with their families, while others live alone or in nearby group residences provided by the hospital. Most are wheelchair-bound; some need special assistance in getting to these meetings.

The group has been a vital experience for these members. One of the issues has been the planning of a show at the hospital for the children's ward. Moe says, "It's hard for some of us to communicate with each other, and to plan events like this for the children without our aides helping us." Marilyn, the practitioner, says, "What do you mean, Moe?" He continues, "I guess I feel frustrated. We need other people to help us, and I want us to do this show, even though we need your help and our aides' too." Marilyn asks, "Anyone else got any thoughts on this?" Gabe says, "Yes, I feel frustrated too. But I'm getting a new cell phone that's easier to use. I will be able to call everyone more often. Listen, I have an idea for the show. I want to get my nephew's band to entertain. Do you think we could do a thing like that? The hospital would have to pay them, I couldn't ask them to come for free. I have a beautiful CD he gave me from weddings they play. He's also a magician, and I know they entertain at children's parties, too." Henry says, "I like it." The practitioner says, "Come on, let's hear more about this show."

More members start to talk about this. Xavier suggests they get some of the nurses and social workers to do a skit with the group for the children in the hospital: "Or, if that doesn't work, we could get a local comedian." The practitioner says, "These are all good ideas, can you go on?" Gabe then says, "Forget it. They won't come. And besides, I can't call to ask for a favor." He continues, "My brother, his father, hardly comes to see me—the bastard." Marilyn wonders, "What would it mean for you to call? Say more, Gabe." Gabe talks about not wanting favors from others. Marilyn wonders if others have similar feelings. Xavier and Willy acknowledge these feelings, with Willy adding that, "It's hard to be disabled and to feel you need people's help all the time." Willy then says to Gabe, "I've heard you play that CD of your nephew, and he is really good." Then he says to the practitioner, "Marilyn, does the hospital have a budget for this stuff?" Marilyn says that it does. Willy tells Gabe, "Then it wouldn't be a favor. He'd get paid. You would be doing him a favor. Come on, I'll call him for you if you want!"

After some thinking, Gabe says, "No, I'll call him. It has to be me. You're right. I have to work on my own feelings of pride. But maybe he'll be pleased. Besides, I've got my new phone." After some more enthusiastic talk, Gabe says to the group, "Hey, you guys, if my nephew says yes, you owe me for this one!"

Discussion

Several types of exploration are used by the practitioner in this illustration. She uses exploration with all the members to generate a clarification of feeling, again with all of them to generate a flow of ideas, and finally with one particular member to generate a flow of understanding.

At the start, the practitioner tries to help all of the members to examine the feelings of frustration they are having regarding their disabilities, especially as these feelings relate to their current objective of running a party for hospitalized children. Once Moe talks about his own frustration, the practitioner uses exploration by posing an open-ended question to the others; this allows more expressions of frustrated feelings by several members. Then the group spontaneously goes on to talk about the party rather than about their own frustrations. Gabe is so excited by the idea of asking his nephew to entertain that he bypasses his frustrations, focusing on his new phone and his new capability to communicate with others. The practitioner connects to members' desires to generate a flow of ideas and processes for the children's party, and further helps them bypass feelings of limitation and frustration.

"Come on, let's hear more on the show" is a further use of exploration. This use of exploration focuses on and stimulates members' capacities to generate creative ideas. One must note that the practitioner does not work with the group on the hows of lining up entertainers or of writing skits with the staff. To do so at this time would stymie a group whose members seem to need help in generating ideas more than they need to dwell on what they can or cannot do. Once possibilities are flowing, there is enough time to make plans.

In her use of exploration with one particular member, Gabe, the practitioner helps him to examine specific feelings. Her pointed but open-ended question, "What would it mean for you to call your nephew?" helps him look at his pride, as well as his angry feelings toward the brother who does not visit him often. Although Willy gives him the option not to call his nephew, Gabe's choice is to override his anger and pride to help in the group's efforts.

Identification

Identification is used to specify repetitive aspects of self-expression or process that are related to the group's purpose or norms. These may be patterns of behaviors that—once labeled and understood—can offer group members other viewpoints concerning events and their reactions to them. (Identification may be used as a precursor to the technique of confrontation by focusing on significant behavior.)

The practitioner specifies and characterizes directly specific patterns and expressions that are becoming evident in the group, asking the group and/or individual members to connect these behaviors to their current issues as these relate to process or purpose. The practitioner may also point out implications of currently labeled behavior to expand awareness of emotional expressions in the future.

| **Illustration** | **Single-Women's Socialization Group** |

The members in a young adult women's socialization group are talking about why they have been having difficulty dating interesting men recently. Tracy goes on and on, becoming more enamored with her own ideas than with hearing what others are saying. Members in the group begin to tune her out. Finally, Susan interrupts, expressing her own upset with the man she met last week (who turned out to be married and looking for a fling). "I never got the point until the end of the evening that he was just interested in fooling around, not in finding out about me." Jennifer jumps in, saying she had similar problems, and "I can't figure out how I pick them." Tracy begins to talk again about how she avoids these kinds of men by not going to the usual singles places. Gladys pipes in, "That's why you haven't been with anyone lately, you don't even try. Try Match.com." Jennifer impatiently says, "It was not at a bar where I met this guy. I met him when I did a consultation for my software company." Susan says, "You should see what happened to me! I met someone online, and it turned out after we communicated back and forth and I finally met him, he was very lively."

There is more talk; a lot of it seems to reflect impatience with each other, as well as some hostility. The women are having trouble hearing each other, and seem to be more intent on venting than listening. The practitioner, Inez, says, "Wait a minute. You're all doing something now that isn't helping you. You're all talking and no one is listening." There is silence. Then Jennifer says, "It's true, I was so stuck on telling my story that I don't remember a thing about what Susan said. I think it had something to do with meeting a live one online." Susan says, "Something like that." The practitioner states, "Maybe it would help to try to figure out what this means." The members begin to talk about how disappointed some of them are. This leads to more discussion about how angry some of them become when they are disappointed, and how much they want to hide the anger and disappointment by talking their way out of these feelings.

Later in the meeting, the topic of being able to listen clearly for cues from the men they are with begins to come up. The practitioner asks, "Isn't this connected to what was said earlier about listening to each other's cues in here?"

Discussion

The practitioner here identifies a pattern of behavior that is very close to the surface and pertains to all the members, giving them collectively the opportunity to note and to figure out the meaning of the behavior (not listening). There is much more to call their attention to. Identifying the absence of listening in the group points them in the direction of thinking about how this behavior is being enacted in their relationships with men and in other social situations. Through the surfacing of the issue of not listening, the members can move ahead and examine their current behaviors.

By asking the members later in the meeting how their issues of listening to cues from men relate to what was said earlier, the practitioner helps them to distinguish patterns in their forms of presentation from a variety of angles. At no time does the practitioner override the group's process. She gives the members ample opportunity to find out for themselves what the expressions of hostility are all about. She also gives them room to conduct their own feedback with one another. She does not interpret their behavior, but lets the interpretation emanate from them.

Focusing on "listening" rather than hostility, anger, and disappointment reflects the use of the technique of identification (whereas focusing on hostility and anger would represent the use of interpretation).

❖ SUMMARY

This chapter has discussed eight techniques the practitioner uses throughout the entirety of group life to achieve both of the dual objectives—developing the democratic mutual aid system and actualizing group purpose. These techniques are not merely specific to group work; they are generic to social work as well.

Demand for work is used to help the members remain on track in all aspects of achieving their objectives. Directing is used to move members into new situations, environments, or experiences that promise to help them to meet their objectives. Lending a vision provides expanded perspectives for the group and offers hope about future endeavors. Staying with feelings validates and emphasizes the fundamental significance of emotional interaction.

Silence is a technique used primarily to encourage the group's and individual members' reflections and autonomy; silence is not used to create debilitating anxiety. In using support, the practitioner reinforces the development of a caring milieu and fosters the members' efforts to meet their needs. Exploration uses curiosity and interest to help members look at the nuances of feelings and actions. The denotation of repetitive actions and feelings through identification is used by the practitioner to help members comprehend their meaning and importance.

In the next section, attention turns to viewing and assessing the significant feelings and patterns of the individual members within the changing phenomena of stage themes.

Techniques for Developing the Democratic Mutual Aid System and Actualizing Group Purpose		
Technique	**Intent—Used to:**	**Practitioner Behavior**
Demand for Work	Keep group to its dual objectives.	Point out "illusion of work." Point out tangential process when working on new venture. Remind group when more work is required.
Directing	Effect immediate change in group perception or action.	Verbally or physically ask the group or member(s) to change expression or action.
Lending a Vision	Offer hope, faith in process and purpose, and newer possibilities. Enable work to proceed.	State recognition of what is in group. Point out what can be.
Staying With Feelings	Relate from feeling rather than intellectualized perspective.	Help members express feelings as normative. Model feeling perspective. Redirect nonaffective expression and help member turn it into feeling.
Silence	Encourage group to be themselves. Foster growth of autonomy.	Noninvolvement, nonmovement, nonuse of verbal or facial expression.
Support	Foster behavior that sustains caring and purpose.	Verbally and nonverbally direct positive cues and comments to encourage behavior that sustains caring and fulfills purpose. Point out activity useful to caring and purpose; brief comments and nods of agreement.
Exploration	Enable flow of feeling that suspends judgment.	Use open-ended comments and questions. Show curiosity regarding nuances.
Identification	Foster recognition of experience not in group's full awareness.	Specify and characterize patterns of group expression. Ask group to connect behavior to current process and purpose.

PART III

Differential Application of the Humanistic Approach

9

Assessing the
Member in the Group

Assessment as a habit of mind is present from moment to moment as the group worker "listens" to make sure his or her interventions are attentive to client concerns.

—Germain & Gitterman, 1980

In developing assessments, the following must occur:

Social workers must make informed choices . . . including where and how to enter an individual's . . . or group's situation . . . which client messages to explore, and when to work on factual content or feelings. . . . Assessment relies on reasoned thought when making judgements at any moment during the session . . . and when constructing a formal assessment of person/environment exchanges following several sessions. (Germain & Gitterman, 1996, p. 42)

Assessment of the member in the group is based on the practitioner's perceptions and empathy—as well as knowledge and values—and is employed to guide the practitioner's use of techniques. The practitioner considers the meaning of unfolding events and interpersonal expressions, in order to empathize and interact with the member as he or she works on participation and purpose in the professionally guided social work group. The practitioner considers the stage themes of development of the group, along with salient group needs and member commonalities that enable the group's cohesiveness.

The practitioner reviews and reworks his or her developing observations in the process of helping the member take part in the group. The practitioner's stream of consciousness includes several steps: (1) naively perceiving the group phenomena, (2) suspending judgments in order to empathically understand the members' concerns, and (3) utilizing conceptual lenses to comprehend and intuit the meaning of members' interactions. As the last step in the assessment, the practitioner (4) tests out these perceptions and tentatively accepts or revises them.

❖ ASSESSMENT ACTIVITIES AND THE GROUP MEMBER

Stage theory has been used to understand the changing behaviors of different types of members—including children (Garland & West, 1983; Malekoff, 2006) and psychiatric patients (Garland & Frey, 1976; Miller & Mason, 2002)—during the group's evolution. The guiding assumption is that change in member behavior is in some ways shaped by the group's evolving stage themes, and that member behavior is not to be viewed apart from the stage context. Therefore, while in this chapter the individual member is examined, it cannot be emphasized enough that reverting back to theories about the individual that do not include the group context will offer insufficient data for arriving at an assessment. Theories that do not contextualize the member within the evolving group process and dynamic diminish understanding of the person's membership. The result is the negation of the complexity of the group context as a unique psychosocial arena for delving deeply into understanding of member behavior.

Furthermore, psychological and sociological constructs are necessary to provide the practitioner with conceptual lenses that may sharpen professional assessment. Sarri and Galinsky (1985) have delineated guidelines for assessing the group member. These include environmental and cultural factors, as well as personality dimensions that affect members' participation in the group's development as a helping milieu.

❖ ASSESSING THE MEMBER IN THE GROUP

This chapter presents ways of observing group member behavior that make use of stage themes in relation to psychosocial frames of reference. As the group moves through its stage themes, the members react to and contribute uniquely to the process. Stage themes reflect members' subjective reactions to their sense of the practitioner's authority and their own potency in the group experience. A member's stage theme reactions generally vary from slightly intense to more intense—the latter is governed by significant amounts of unreasonable reactions in comparison with the benign actualities of the process. Timing and pace in developing a mutual aid system and actualizing purpose are related to members' personal capacities of emotional and cognitive expression, their previous group experiences and skills, and the difficulties presented by the group's purpose.

The stage theme reactions of Stage Theme 1, "We're Not in Charge"; Stage Theme 2, "We Are in Charge"; Stage Theme 3, "We're Taking You On"; Stage Theme 4, Sanctuary; Stage Theme 5, "This Isn't Good Anymore"; Stage Theme 6, "We're Okay and Able"; and Stage Theme 7, "Just a Little Longer" can be tempered by the practitioner's use of technique. Throughout the process, the humanistic method lodges authority and leadership in the hands of the members along with the practitioner. Paradoxically, the accepting quality of the values and norms of this milieu can cause stage theme reactions to dominate a member's experience. The member in turn reacts further with anxiety or mistrust to the freedom of self-expression that is fundamental to the group. At the same time, these thematic subjective reactions interfere in the members' and the group's work; their manifestations also provide opportunities for members to change how they handle themselves. Stage theme reactions provide data about members in the process; both the practitioner and the member can consider how the member's participation is being affected by his or her external circumstances, as well as by the group experience itself.

❖ PSYCHOSOCIAL CRITERIA FOR ASSESSMENT

The approach in this chapter stresses psychological and sociological interpersonal criteria for assessment in the flow of the group process. When attention is drawn to interpersonal issues in the group, the practitioner can see how an emotionally fragile member will play out psychosocial limitations in the here-and-now interaction of the group. This helps to discern the difficulties the member is having in his or her actual experiences. Furthermore, the practitioner can note when an environmental constraint is the fundamental cause of difficulties in psychosocial expression in and out of the group.

The practitioner focuses on the following criteria, which provide lenses for assessing the member's behaviors:

- Capacity toward mutual aid and purpose
- Ego abilities and sense of self
- Social institutional environment
- Stereotypes and self-fulfilling prophecies
- Symbolic representations of the practitioner and group

These five psychosocial parameters for understanding the member are used throughout the process in varying degrees to help the practitioner develop empathic sensitivity to the member. These parameters differ in relation to how closely each of them keeps the practitioner connected to the member's immediate interactions in the group. Observations focused on a member's abilities to contribute to mutual aid, or on the member's symbolic representations of the practitioner and the group, are less apt to draw the practitioner's stream of consciousness into drifting away from the process during the meeting. These observations focus fully on the here and now, and data utilized are occurring in the present. On the other hand, focus on ego abilities and social institutional factors draws the practitioner's thinking to historical and political considerations away from the here and now as the practitioner attempts to complete a picture and integrate data. These data are used to complete the practitioner's perceptions of the member's presentation in the here and now.

To ensure that these criteria for assessing the individual member are connected to the evolving process of the humanistic group, each criterion will be considered within the context of the group's stage themes. For further clarification, see Table 9.1.

Capacity Toward Mutual Aid and Purpose

Garvin (1997) conceptualizes the following:

A classification of dimensions of group process . . . incorporates all of the sequences of events that might occur in the group. . . . These dimensions are the (1) goal-oriented activities of the group, and the (2) quality of the interactions among the members. The former largely corresponds to the goal attainment [actualization of purpose] and the latter to the group maintenance [developing a democratic mutual aid system] functions referred to in the small group literature. (p. 105)

Table 9.1   Criteria for Assessing the Member in the Context of Stage Themes of Group Development

Criteria for Assessing Member	Stage Themes of Group Development						
	Stage Theme 1: "We're Not in Charge"	*Stage Theme 2: "We Are in Charge"*	*Stage Theme 3: "We're Taking You On"*	*Stage Theme 4: Sanctuary*	*Stage Theme 5: "This Isn't Good Anymore"*	*Stage Theme 6: "We're Okay and Able"*	*Stage Theme 7: "Just a Little Longer"*
Capacity for Democratic Process and Actualizing Purpose	Democratic process: Extent of listening, communication; level of group skill; approach to difference.	Democratic process: Extent of inclusion or exclusion during leadership struggle; decision making, respecting others' rights.	Democratic process: Extent of joining others in taking on worker; ability to work out negative feelings.	Democratic process: Takes part freely in mutual aid. Purpose: Starts to work; sees own and others' abilities to grow.	Actualizing purpose: Sidetracked from task in face of difficulty.	Actualizing purpose: Ability to change versus sidetracked in the face of adversity.	Actualizing purpose: Can member take stock of growth and future goals?
Ego Abilities and Sense of Self	Clear versus diffuse level of self-worth; accuracy of self-perception.	Reactions to ambiguity and freedom; withdraw or rebel; anxiety level.	Ability to demystify practitioner; overidealize, or challenge and fear.	Challenged or fearful in intimacy; forward movement or hope or new crisis.	Extent of hopelessness, reluctance, fear; are these chronic or crises?	Hopeful or hopeless regarding change; able to take risks or fearing failure.	Temporary loss of mastery; level of denial or flight.

(Continued)

Table 9.1 (Continued)

Stage Themes of Group Development

Criteria for Assessing Member	Stage Theme 1: "We're Not in Charge"	Stage Theme 2: "We Are in Charge"	Stage Theme 3: "We're Taking You On"	Stage Theme 4: Sanctuary	Stage Theme 5: "This Isn't Good Anymore"	Stage Theme 6: "We're Okay and Able"	Stage Theme 7: "Just a Little Longer"
Social Institutional Environment	Extent of member's effective or ineffective environmental supports; level of testing of group.	Nonnurturing milieu may bring out anger, disappointment, powerlessness.	Member may fear co-optation.	Member may see group as second chance, or reinforcement of current supports.	Is loss of hope due to overwhelming environment? Consider member's prior strengths.	Does member see options for changing environment, supports, or economic factors?	Does member see broadened options at group's end?
Stereotypes and Self-Fulfilling Prophecy	Member vulnerability to being stereotyped; how member enters group; extent of stereotyping others.	Does stereotype pervade self-presentation; is member angry, frustrated, isolated?	Member may not take part in challenge.	What are member's latent or direct messages to air stereotypes?	Assess how stereotype feeds futility, avoidance of risk taking, or challenging the group.	Consider level of need to deal with obstacles of stereotype.	Fear of future stereotyping.

Stage Themes of Group Development

Criteria for Assessing Member	Stage Theme 1: "We're Not in Charge"	Stage Theme 2: "We Are in Charge"	Stage Theme 3: "We're Taking You On"	Stage Theme 4: Sanctuary	Stage Theme 5: "This Isn't Good Anymore"	Stage Theme 6: "We're Okay and Able"	Stage Theme 7: "Just a Little Longer"
Symbolic Representations of the Practitioner and Group	View of worker as standard bearer, as social control agent.	Extent of desire for worker to control; expecting to be disappointed by group and worker.	Now interaction with practitioner is salient.	Through what familial lens are practitioner and group being seen? What other lenses?	Ascertain member disappointments that prevent forward movement.	Meaning of practitioner to member: role model, teacher; meaning of members; how much does member take in?	Extent of reactions to abandonment; able to accept reality of relationship.

Examination of members' capacities to carry out the tasks called for in the social work group is a necessary part of the practitioner's skill. The abilities identified with mutual aid and democracy include caring, sharing, listening, decision making, and respecting differences. In this framework, the practitioner perceives how each member is joining with the others. He or she observes how the member learns about and appraises norms and values other participants bring to the experience, as well as how each member reacts to the practitioner's support of humanistic values and democratic standards. The practitioner discerns the extent to which the members express themselves in personally oriented or group-oriented ways, rather than blending both forms. For example, a member in a postprison support group who focuses on his problems securing a job, but does not ask other members about their experiences, is purely personally oriented. One who only looks at the plight of others in the group is group oriented. The extent to which the member's behaviors are process or purpose oriented is also considered, along with flexibility and expansiveness in role repertoire. The member's orientation toward power and efforts to control (rather than to influence) is viewed.

Abilities identified with achieving group purpose call for members taking risks toward changing dysfunctional interpersonal patterns as well as situational factors. Also called for is the member's expression of an increasingly broad range of feeling and a clearer communication style that reflects empathy and mutual respect. The practitioner considers how the member discusses and enacts his or her reasons for being in the group.

Stage Theme 1: "We're Not in Charge"

The practitioner assesses the member to support his or her functioning and to broaden the member's problem-solving and role-taking abilities. Some members will need more support for autonomous functioning than others.

At the start of group life, some members are silent and others take part cautiously. The practitioner considers the extent to which each member expresses process as the ability to build a group and connect to others in it, engages purpose through the ability to set and meet goals, or presents purely self-oriented behavior. The practitioner looks for preliminary enactments of listening, empathy, cooperativeness, and the ability to communicate clearly.

Showing empathy and appreciation for the mutual aid nature of the group experience, as well as tolerance for individual differences, are significant indicators of the member's ability to solve problems with others. The practitioner watches and experiences how each member reacts to his or her explicitness about humanistic values and democratic norms, and observes the member's skills in democratic participation. Members, because of age or institutional or subcultural experiences, may not be familiar with democratic modes and ethics, or they may be reluctant to apply them for fear of repercussions (for instance, as in the case of refugee groups; Glassman & Skolnik, 1984).

Considering the member's abilities to develop skills related to mutual aid and democratic process is more significant at the start than skills to work on purpose. The practitioner tests out the assessment by seeking to provide the member with alternate ways of interaction to see how rigid or flexible his or her self-expressions are in interactions with others. By offering a preliminary clarification of democratic process and mutual aid, the practitioner develops more clarity about the member's potential in this respect.

| Illustration | *Child Care Counselors Group* |

A group of child care counselors is holding its third session. Up to the halfway point in the meeting, most of the members are looking to the practitioner and imitating her comments, exhibiting Stage Theme 1, "We're Not in Charge," behaviors.

The practitioner notices that Rick has been silent and watching with a disturbed look on his face, fidgeting in his seat. She asks him, "Rick, you look disturbed by what's going on. What's happening for you?" Rick tactfully begs off; the practitioner empathically insists. Rick finally says, "I don't see things the same way you are putting them. I feel uncomfortable because the others seem to agree with you. Yet, I don't believe this group can belong to the members alone. They just look to you for advice now, so they are all very much looking for approval."

After Rick's presentation of his views, the practitioner says, "Rick, your differences with me and everyone else's differences with each other are what will make this group worthwhile and challenging. I do give my views, too. I consider them to be different, though not necessarily better than yours." Rick says, "Thanks. I really thought you'd be inflexible." The meeting continues with members now looking to Rick and one another more, and less to the practitioner.

Stage Theme 2: "We Are in Charge"

Faced with the prominence of the group's rebellion against the authority of the practitioner, some members actively take part in the power struggle while others withdraw, preferring not to take sides. For some members, affect is often intensified in the form of competitive feelings, while others try to hide such feelings by turning them into dependency or submission. The practitioner assesses the member's ability to offer nurturance, respect, and inclusion to the other members.

Some members may try to exclude others and show inflexibility with respect to tolerating differences. Some will attempt to preserve others' rights and foster inclusion by directly inviting their participation. However, cooperative modes usually are not responded to at this time; those efforts tend to be ignored. The practitioner has to tune in to and empathically address the disappointments or disillusionments of these members so that their input is not withheld from the group.

The roles the member takes give indications of how he or she reacts to the ambiguity of the normative crisis (Bennis & Shepard, 1962; Garland, Jones, & Kolodny, 1973). Some members try to avoid or deny the crisis by becoming rigidly task oriented. Some show interest in other people's feelings. Some seek power over others in order to maintain security and position.

The practitioner tests out his or her assessments by offering invitations to isolated and individualistic members that support their right to be different. The practitioner also interprets members' anxieties, power plays, and leadership attempts as manifestations of the search for group norms. The practitioner offers support to the member who becomes noticeably anxious in the throes of the group's ambiguity.

Stage Theme 3: "We're Taking You On"

The practitioner assesses members' abilities to join in directly expressing feelings about the practitioner. The practitioner assesses each member's ability to use feelings toward authority constructively within the group's democratic context.

The practitioner must discover the extent to which each member needs opportunities to deal openly with his or her feelings about authority in this group. Some members are motivated toward dominance and disapprove of the group's developing democratic power structure. The member's ability to acknowledge competitive and cooperative feelings with the practitioner helps work out stumbling blocks toward cooperation and cohesion. Members need to be assisted in handling their negative feelings in the interest of the group's forward movement.

The practitioner tests out members' abilities for sharing power by gauging to what extent each member is willing to engage cooperatively with others and the practitioner. An invitation to share power and position with the practitioner also helps the member who may be anticipating a strained relationship with authority figures.

Stage Theme 4: Sanctuary

The practitioner considers each member's ability to handle closeness. The practitioner notes when a member is experiencing pressure to conform to the high affect of this period, and he or she assists the member in recognizing that the price of belonging is not conformity.

The democratic mutual aid process is now becoming highlighted as the most useful means the group will have for achieving its purpose. The practitioner considers the extent to which members envision themselves as both helpers and receivers by looking at how actively or peripherally each member participates. The practitioner observes how supportive or guarded members' expressions of feelings are and notes the extent to which a member's mode of expression deviates from the dominant modes of expression in the group. Effort is focused on helping members develop role behaviors suitable for this stage. Note is taken of the degree to which members have given up their needs to control and the degree to which each member feels safety in the group.

The practitioner views how each member sees himself or herself in the helper-receiver roles. The practitioner supports the validity of skeptical members' feelings, which may relate to negative factors in the group.

Stage Theme 5: "This Isn't Good Anymore"

Some members' abilities for achieving purpose are not well developed. This type of member may give up when confronted with difficult and frustrating situations that result in threatening feelings. The practitioner notes the degree to which members lose their connections to the processes of mutual aid developed earlier. The practitioner weighs the effect of disenchanted members' feelings on others.

The practitioner reminds members of their commitments to work on the group's purpose with others and helps each member identify the emotional and situational roadblocks to involvement in this effort. The practitioner helps members reconnect to others, strengthens fragile bonds when necessary, and calls on the group's spirit of mutuality to solve problems.

Stage Theme 6: "We're Okay and Able"

The achievement of purpose is salient in this stage and is represented by members' capacity to work on effectiveness and change.

Consideration is given to each member's ability to develop a personal agenda for broadening self-expression in and out of the group. The practitioner's focus is also on the relative capability of each member to use the feedback process in the group and to deal with interpersonal and defensive barriers that sidetrack or inhibit change. Furthermore, the practitioner takes into account the member's ability and willingness to help other members achieve their purposes.

The practitioner observes how each member handles tension and difficulty in interpersonal relations, with interest in how openly members can change maladaptive communication patterns, try out varied role behaviors, and develop broader ranges of affective expression in the group. Consideration is given to how cognizant members are of risk and change processes, as well as to how connected or disconnected they are from fellow members and significant others.

Stage Theme 7: "Just a Little Longer"

The practitioner considers how each member may continue to grow after the experience. At the time of ending, members are often noted to have flattened or changeable affects.

Each member's ability to plan future agendas in the face of ending is crucial. An inability to do so may show a pattern of avoiding feelings of dependency and rejection that prevents members from moving on to their next steps. Finding supportive relationships that foster members' continued growth is important. A feeling that some members may have to "go it alone" is a clue that these members may feel mistrustful of other situations and supports that may be available.

The practitioner explores the importance of prior losses in relationship to the loss of the group experience as a place for support and accomplishment. Members are helped to consider how to continue work beyond the group through creating and pursuing necessary supports.

Ego Abilities and Sense of Self

One focus of assessment is on members' characterizations of self and abilities for self-expression. The assessment focuses on members' ego functioning in their interpersonal environments. Assessment of ego functions (Goldstein, 2001; Woods & Hollis, 2000) such as the ability to employ reality testing and judgment, the capacity to tolerate frustration and control impulses, the ability to develop and sustain object relations, and the use of defense mechanisms that inhibit or enable emotional expressions are used to observe members' presentations in the group process. The practitioner considers if each member's presentation aligns with his or her age and physically appropriate abilities or reflects impoverishment in the member's sense of self and the level of his or her ego functions.

The practitioner also considers the extent to which members present distinguishable or diffuse identities (Erikson, 1963), express self-worth or impoverished self-images, present feelings of mastery, demonstrate relative accuracy of self-evaluation, and manifest the ability to accurately discern their impact on others.

Since many groups have been formed of members with impaired ego functioning, it is all the more necessary for practitioners to take note of the impact of ego impairment on the group process, as well as to recognize the important role group practitioners play in facilitating the participation of members with fragile egos.

Stage Theme 1: "We're Not in Charge"

Ego functioning abilities are noted at the beginning, when each member is presenting himself or herself to the group. The extent to which members present clear, diffuse, or rigidly defined pictures of themselves may offer the practitioner a preliminary impression of how the group will unfold. The members' demonstrations of feelings of self-worth and mastery regarding prior and current situations, as well as abilities with respect to feelings of identity, integrity, and equilibrium are considered. Judgment, reality testing, memory, frustration tolerance, impulse control, and guardedness are taken into account. Though the accurateness of members' self-perceptions may not be clear to the practitioner at this stage, he or she gathers impressions by focusing on how the members hear and respond to each other's cues. A high level of resistance to efforts to curtail a monopolizing member's input may indicate a covering over of anxiety and lack of self-perception on the part of the member. A member's demonstration of intense anxiety during attempts by others to clarify the member's statements or feelings may be an indication of the member's identity confusion and fears about rejection and persecution.

A group made up of members with impaired ego functions, such as those with Alzheimer's disorder or developmental disability, requires the group worker to fill in the missing ego functions that facilitate and model connection and belonging among the members.

Stage Theme 2: "We Are in Charge"

The practitioner assesses each member's emotional equilibrium in and psychological perspective about the group process when there is conflict and anxiety about leadership. The practitioner also gauges the extent to which each member takes on leadership roles. He or she considers if members' presentations are consonant or in conflict with their ages and physical abilities. Prior hurts and anger with authority are apt to be expressed through passive or aggressive hostility toward members and the practitioner.

The practitioner offers acceptance to the anxious member and universalizes the feeling for all who are experiencing varying intensities of anxiety and social disorientation.

Stage Theme 3:"We're Taking You On"

In the context of challenges to authority, the practitioner considers each member's ability to view and react to the practitioner's authority realistically. The practitioner should be neither idealized nor denigrated. Inability to envision freedom from control, or anxiety about destroying or dethroning the authority figure, may underlie members' difficulties in challenging the authority figure, which enables coming to know about the practitioner's fallibility and humanness. The over-challenging and critical member may fear the practitioner's power. Distortions are often transferred from experiences with and perceptions of other significant figures.

The practitioner offers acceptance to the member who idealizes authority. When necessary, the practitioner does not challenge the idealization, because this issue will reappear later on and can be used by the group to help the member. The member who is afraid that a positive relationship with the practitioner will result in his or her loss of integrity through co-optation is helped through an affirmation of the boundaries and differences between the member and the practitioner. The overattacking member will need help in dealing with and rechanneling these misdirected feelings. By neutralizing their negative reactions, members can be enabled to join the group and maintain appropriate distance from the practitioner.

Stage Theme 4: Sanctuary

The practitioner considers the members' ego abilities and anticipatory anxieties in order to offer opportunities for corrective relationships through the group's resources. Each member is also given protection and permission to set an individualized pace, particularly if the group is moving too fast for the member into intimacy, causing him or her to feel identity confusion.

Some members may feel competent in intimate and interdependent situations; others may feel threatened and fear losing controls and boundaries. Intimacy should offer a renewed chance to develop and to feel self-worth, rather than stimulate emotional and identity crises that lead to avoidance of other members and the practitioner.

When noting that a member is fearful, the practitioner may respond directly by empathically reflecting these feelings or indirectly by universalizing the fearful feelings about intimacy experienced in varying degrees by all members. The practitioner tries to decrease intense levels of anxiety by ensuring the right of any one member to proceed at his or her own pace.

Stage Theme 5: "This Isn't Good Anymore"

By assessing members' ego abilities for dealing directly with inter-personal obstacles, the practitioner assists in attaining mastery and success rather than disturbing periods of difficulty and failure in rela-tionships. Attitudes of inferiority, incompetence, identity fragmentation, isolation, stagnation, and despair (among others) can draw members into anxieties and inabilities that were reflected in earlier struggles with the group worker, as well as with other members. Caught in negative atti-tudes and feelings, a member will have difficulty conquering defensive barriers in order to work on significant interpersonal issues.

Consideration is given to whether—and to what degree—hopeless and fragmented feelings are due to present stimuli, crises, or to chronic psychosocial conditions. The practitioner empathically points out hope-less attitudes and works with members to engender hope and involve-ment. Actions in new experiences and interactions counter negative feelings by developing feelings of pride through accomplishments.

Stage Theme 6: "We're Okay and Able"

As the members actively engage issues related to purpose in the group process, the worker attends to the members' presentations of attitudes, interests, wishes, motives, and plans. The normative age stage crises (Erikson, 1963; Greene, 1994) bring about periods of disequilibrium in each person's character, which are resolved with a predominance of synthesizing and comforting emotions through engaging experiences. When these age stage crises are not resolved, individuals experience ego dysfunction, problems in self-esteem, and identity distortions.

The practitioner assesses ego functions to support and accentuate change in interpersonal relationships. A member's positive or negative self-image influences how he or she is viewing the group's purpose. The chronic inability of a member to set personal agendas or follow through on them may indicate ego dysfunction and low self-esteem.

Some groups are comprised solely of members with impairment in ego functioning. Throughout, the protection necessarily provided by the practitioner in the form of filling in missing ego functions and providing safety in the process enhances goal attainment.

The practitioner gauges the extent to which members use their own ego abilities to undertake new experiences without the need for sustainment (Woods & Hollis, 2000) by the practitioner. The group worker also considers how aware members are of their own shifts in patterns of self-expressions in interpersonal relations. Active awareness is a sign that a member is able to use the group as a helpful medium of change. When this is the case, conscious ego functioning that includes the ability to interact and to present feelings of self-awareness and identity is manifest.

Stage Theme 7: "Just a Little Longer"

As the group comes to a close, the practitioner is interested in how aware members are of their regressions in social and emotional interactions. A member who discerns this pattern recognizes the necessity for the regression and does not become lost in it or overanxious because of it. The practitioner also assesses how capable members are of refocusing attention on identifying the external supportive frames of reference and situations each is in and will join. The practitioner attends to the members' effective uses of judgment, reality testing, and memory as means of gauging the value of new environments and relationships.

The practitioner also considers the real and fictionalized references each member makes about the practitioner's image. The more fictionalized, the less the member is owning his or her experience in the group; the less fictionalized, the better able the member is in handling fear of the unknown.

Prior traumatic losses are rekindled as the group comes to an end. The practitioner takes into consideration that recall of prior losses may interfere with ego functioning to the extent that members lose confidence in their gains in the group.

Illustration	***Adult Relationship-Building Group***

In an adult relationship-building group, Maurice is recounting his experiences on a date a few nights earlier. Earlier, during Stage Theme 5, "This Isn't Good Anymore," Maurice experienced great difficulty moving forward. The group is now in Stage Theme 6, "We're Okay and Able," and the members are confronting him. He is acting attentive and connected, but Victor, the practitioner, sees Maurice swallowing and looking angry. Victor questions, "What's up Maurice?

You have an angry and defensive attitude." Maurice's Adam's apple moves again; he fidgets and starts to sweat. The practitioner alters the course of the process by saying to the group, "Let's give Maurice room to breathe, to get his bearings. None of us moves at the same pace."

Later, as the group is coming to a close during Stage Theme 7, "Just a Little Longer," Maurice, looking distraught and anxious, is encouraged by members to speak up. He tells the group about how difficult it is for him to leave because he still becomes upset when he remembers how abandoned he felt when his mother was hospitalized for a long-term mental illness when he was 7 years old. The practitioner helps him to express his feelings of abandonment and loss and to consider the ways he can manage his feelings about leaving the group, as this brings up reflections of the past. The members offer support and some share similar feelings. Throughout this process Maurice is becoming more comfortable, his anxiety dissipating through the discussion.

Social Institutional Environment

The member's connection to the social institutional environment has several dimensions. One is that of primary and secondary socializations (Berger & Luckmann, 1967). These stem from family sources (of primary socialization) and institutional sources (of secondary socialization). Other dimensions are the sociocultural and political ones of social class, race, ethnicity, and religion (Devore & Schlesinger, 1995). Other dimensions that will influence the member's view of the group and his or her membership in it include educational level and access to upward mobility, both historical and current. Each of these dimensions will affect the member's values and interactions.

Furthermore, the degree of environmental support that members experience from family, friends, networks, workplace, and community institutions such as schools, religious groups, and social agencies will shape their involvements in the group. The kinds of resources and opportunities for mobility that members have in the community will affect how they need and use the group.

Stage Theme 1: "We're Not in Charge"

The practitioner assesses with an eye toward assisting members in altering their social and political environments, as well as their perceptions of them.

Manifested in the members' early behaviors in the group is the degree to which they are part of supportive or unsupportive external environments. A member with effective environmental supports, or a member seeking a change in environmental affiliations, may demonstrate fuller connections toward the group experience and practitioner while testing less. On the other hand, anger and unbridled expressions of frustration may be indicative of ineffective environmental supports and limited access to social mobility.

The practitioner validates members' judgments of and experiences with their impoverished and rejecting environments. The practitioner is careful not to blame members by denying the power of deprivations, further reinforcing their feelings of victimization and hostile aggression or self-denigration.

Stage Theme 2: "We Are in Charge"

A member who has experienced a long history in nonnurturing milieus may react with cynicism, anger, and frustration toward the practitioner. Lack of confidence in the environment can carry over into the group. The barriers to social mobility and the desire to overcome powerlessness are more keenly experienced at this stage by members who have been denied access to environmental resources. Therefore members' frustration, hopelessness, and anger are heightened. The degree to which other members and the practitioner can act with sensitivity toward such members, whether or not they themselves have had effective environmental experiences, is crucial.

The practitioner validates members' anger, frustration, and feelings of powerlessness with the aim of directing the energy from disappointment into the will for problem solving. All members benefit from this, learning the truth about the relationship between social and political deprivation and personal survival in the sociopolitical environment.

Stage Theme 3: "We're Taking You On"

The practitioner assesses the extent to which being deprived of rights and entitlements leads members to see the group as a depriving environment. A member experiencing deprivation will value actions much more than words, despite the fact that a concerted use of both is necessary. The member may be suspicious of the other members' dialogue with authority for fear that the members are being co-opted by the "power structure" through its words, without concomitant acts and deeds.

The member who is necessarily suspicious of words is useful in the group's process. The practitioner affirms this suspiciousness and brings its critique into play so that its perspectives become part of the group's effort to affect authenticity. Through this type of affirmation, the member—having real reason to be suspicious—is helped to develop the means to deal with those who have power and control over his or her circumstances through the uses of strategies that include self-awareness, empathy, reality testing, social coalitions, and political compromise.

Stage Theme 4: Sanctuary

Where a member's external environmental supports have been ineffective, the safety of the group may provide an opportunity for the member to experience the group as a secure, effective, and valuable social and political milieu. The group may also provide the member support in gaining necessities from his or her social environment. For a member who is in effective social milieus, closeness in the group may gird his or her feelings of caring and communion through adding to the member's abilities to be and become with others.

The practitioner affirms the member for whom the group represents an effective and nurturing milieu in contrast with his or her current sociopolitical environments.

Illustration   *Sobriety Group*

In the early life of a sobriety group, Joe is quiet, keeping a distance even when members are gathering their strength during Stage Theme 2, "We Are in Charge." The practitioner is cognizant that this member has virtually no other sustaining networks and is using the group as his sole source of support. The dominant concern of the practitioner is whether the members will help Joe belong. Furthermore, by focusing on social institutional factors, the practitioner becomes aware that Joe's lower educational level (in relation to the other members)—as well as his distinct status as the lone blue-collar worker in the group—might be making it more difficult for Joe to become a part of the group. At the same time, the practitioner notices that several of the members have driven Joe home to his modest rooming house after the past two meetings, despite his objections.

During Stage Theme 4, Sanctuary, the members, as if realizing the special importance of this group to Joe in meeting his need for environmental resources, form a supportive net for him by driving him to the sessions and meeting him for refreshments. This marks the beginning of Joe's ability to share his pressing concerns with the members at future meetings.

Stage Theme 5: "This Isn't Good Anymore"

The practitioner now considers whether any member's loss of hope and fear of failure are due to factors outside the group. Consideration is given to whether members are struggling with environmental factors such as poverty, homelessness, joblessness, racism, or family illnesses that cause overwhelming obstacles that suppress hopefulness and will. Members' prior abilities to deal with environmental stressors are taken into account as well.

The practitioner helps members to develop their feelings of assertiveness and will in relation to the actual realities that are causing feelings of futility. The practitioner validates futile feelings and supports assertive acts in order to stimulate movement toward alternatives.

Stage Theme 6: "We're Okay and Able"

The practitioner is interested in helping members to develop personal approaches and political attitudes that will enhance their effectiveness in dealing with environmental obstacles.

Consideration is given to the approaches that members develop for confronting their current circumstances and to the ways in which members deal with cultural, racial, and economic dynamics. Each member's abilities to behave in different ways in these circumstances is noted in relation to the counterforces of hurt, anger, and frustration, as well as others' attempts to suppress the member's actions. The practitioner also identifies and helps members to secure opportunities and concrete resources.

Stage Theme 7: "Just a Little Longer"

The practitioner considers how the members are carrying out specific actions in their social environments. Separating from the group's nurturing milieu is especially disappointing for members whose immediate environments are unsupportive and dangerous. Such members will have to take the initiative in creating new options, including opportunities for their own social mobility and securing of concrete resources.

The practitioner explores members' anxieties and concerns about surviving in their current circumstances without the group's support. Alternative helpful situations are considered to replace unsupportive ones. Before the group's end, the practitioner takes special steps to ensure that each member has become connected to supportive situations provided by agency and community institutions.

Stereotypes and Self-Fulfilling Prophecies

Stereotyping and self-fulfilling prophecies in the members' presentations—centered on race, class, gender roles, ethnicity, sexual orientation, religion, physical condition, or psychological state—provide the practitioner with another lens for assessing significant aspects of interpersonal relations in the group's process. The social psychological factors of stereotyping and self-fulfilling prophecies interact with members' intrapsychic factors to bring about impoverished social relationships, identity confusions, restricted ego functioning, and experiences of dominance and submission in social relationships.

Stereotyping and self-fulfilling prophecies interfere with members' experiences of self and others in the group. However, with effort, the toxic effects of these dynamics can be neutralized. The humanistic group fosters a process that is inhospitable to character assaults and discrimination. The injuries sustained through stigmatization create pain and anticipation of rejection, which—along with the group's acceptance—may paradoxically increase a member's testing of the safety of the group.

The practitioner remains attentive to the effects of stereotyping. The practitioner considers how stereotypes and stigmas affect members' sense of belonging and acceptance in the group. The practitioner looks to the circumstances of stereotypes to provide grist for the mill for changes of self and other in the process.

Stage Theme 1: "We're Not in Charge"

Since stereotyping is likely to occur during periods of first impressions, the practitioner considers how each member is characterized by and characterizes others. This is done to safeguard members' initial entries into the group and to prevent judgments or stereotypical perceptions of one another.

The practitioner uses his or her awareness of a member's class, ethnic, cultural, religious, and racial affiliations as sources of potential negative stereotypes. He or she takes note of the conflict-free or negative, self-fulfilling, stereotypical image the member may bring to the group. He or she looks for ways the group members perceive the individual and how the member reacts to the group's stereotypical and nonstereotypical expectations. People who anticipate being the brunt of stereotypes approach groups wanting to know if they will be accepted. The practitioner responds to these cues, opening up the issue of acceptance and expectations, empathizing with issues related to self-fulfilling prophecies as well as racial, ethnic, and gender stereotypes.

Stage Theme 2: "We Are in Charge"

Some members may view the practitioner and peers as people who dominate others. These fears are aroused as the members grapple with using democratic norms and humanistic values that run counter to those in their actual life situations.

A member's conscious awareness about his or her possible stereotypes, and others' reactions to these, will assist the member in functioning in the group. These stereotypes may pervade members' presentations of self in the form of self-fulfilling prophecies. A member bearing a stigma may pose an indirect challenge to the others to react by displaying negative attitudes about the group's activities or by sulking.

As cliques vie for leadership, the practitioner is alert to any member's use of stereotyping to dominate or exclude others. This guards against the development of covert undemocratic norms that undermine humanistic values. The practitioner paves the way for everyone to look at stereotypes, stigmatizations, and behavior that may create self-fulfilling prophecies in order to develop the group norm of inclusion of members who are different.

Stage Theme 3: "We're Taking You On"

A member who has been stereotyped by other members, but does not feel stereotyped by the practitioner, may not become involved with the other members in challenging the practitioner. This member will need help and support from the practitioner to challenge the members who are doing the stereotyping.

The practitioner is not immune from stereotyping members. Accepting this, the practitioner looks for evidence of his or her acts of overt and covert stereotyping. Owning one's part requires a direct question: "Am I misperceiving you?" Furthermore, the practitioner should give an authentic response to the member's answer. He or she may have to ask, "Am I in any way offending you?" The practitioner affirms and supports the member's feelings, acknowledging and apologizing for any distortions. The practitioner may also ask the other members what they have perceived about the practitioner's behavior, eliciting their reactions to his or her actions.

Stage Theme 4: Sanctuary

During this time of safety and closeness in the group, values and norms that promise humanism and democracy result in a feeling of safety and relaxation. This may be more pronounced for the member who is treated as an object of derision and discrimination in the external environment. On the other hand, a negative reaction to the atmosphere of the "sanctuary" that tests its reliability is also not unusual. In some instances, members can band together, assuming superior attitudes toward others and stereotyping and rejecting others in and out of the group.

The practitioner considers how to help members change the negative anticipations that have developed in prior social experiences. Effort is also turned to raising the group's collective awareness about the toxic effects of stereotyping so that the quality of sanctuary can serve as a safe haven in which to develop individual and group efforts to confront stereotyping and discrimination.

Some members may send out signals that they wish to discuss stereotypes in order to test the group's willingness to accept them. The practitioner should attentively develop this theme because it offers a chance for deepening acceptance among all the members. All members will be helped to broaden their social skills and connections by dealing with stereotyping.

Stage Theme 5: "This Isn't Good Anymore"

The practitioner considers how to help members deal with their feelings of futility in reaction to others' inabilities to inhibit stereotyping. The member who is losing faith in the group's capacity to view him or her as a real person, rather than in the frame of a stereotype, needs to be brought back into the interaction to confront the stereotypes and to appraise the kind of interactions he or she is having in the group. The member who moves away from group life because of concerns about stereotyping challenges the group to prove itself once again as a milieu that can transcend acts of discrimination and stereotyping that are prevalent in the external environment.

Stage Theme 6: "We're Okay and Able"

At this time, members are motivated to work on the real-life issues that brought them into the group. The practitioner assesses the emotional impact of stereotyping, causing interpersonal barriers. The practitioner evaluates the degree to which members retreat from social and political interests and involvements for fear of rejection and suppression. Consciousness of the ubiquity of "isms"—ethnocentrism, racism, sexism, ageism—is brought to the fore to help members work on these issues through comprehension and action.

The practitioner attends to how members, by means of innuendo or direct name calling, distort others' personalities and actions. Members

are assisted in engaging specific individuals to develop constructive ways of challenging and overcoming the use of stereotypes and
discrimination.

Illustration   *Pregnant Women in a Prison Group*

A group is composed of pregnant prisoners in an urban prison with a large majority of nonwhite prisoners. At the first meeting, the practitioner has just finished
introducing the group experience as "a place for mutual support and survival for
pregnant prisoners, your babies, and your families while in and out of prison."
A member asks in Spanish if the practitioner can speak Spanish. The practitioner,
a white male, is about to say "no" when an African American member emphatically says, "We don't want no people who can't speak English in this group."
An Arab member looks visibly pained. The group worker responds, "In this group,
people who speak any language or have any religion have membership. And if
some of you aren't bilingual, or don't wish to translate, I will find a way of keeping it going." Two people move forward and begin translating.

Later on, during Stage Theme 2, "We Are in Charge," the African Americans
and Latinas begin to challenge the worker's way of observing their interactions.
As the challenge continues they become more and more fearful, because whites
are dominant in the prison power structure; this mirrors the political and economic situations in their communities. Out of this fear the members start raising
their hands to speak, like school children asking the teacher for permission. They
will not respond to the practitioner's questioning this; he lets it go and recedes
into the background, hoping they will be less fearful. Still they raise their hands.
Eventually, the practitioner pulls his chair visibly outside of the circle, and avoids
eye contact. This helps the members' face-to-face interactions. One African
American member takes note that the guards are more prejudiced against the
Arab woman. She notes gratitude that they actually noticed that. "Oh, we have
nothing against you. I know it's been bad for Muslims after 9/11. The guards are
worse to you because of that."

They talk further about how to interact in the group and how to share strategies
for survival in prison. Eunice instructs the practitioner to "join in, and give your opinions, too," adding as an aside to the others, "He's okay." Others nod in agreement.

Moving into Stage Theme 4, Sanctuary, the members talk about how well-off
they are compared with other prisoners who don't have the group. Attitudes of
superiority and racial epithets about other women prisoners that reflect the
power structure in the setting are heard. The practitioner wonders, "How will you
handle this special view of yourselves back in the cell block? You are putting
yourselves on pedestals." This brings about further discussion about being victimized by the system.

During their work together at Stage Theme 6, "We're Okay and Able," the women move into talking deeply about the stigmas of racism and sexism they face and will face, along with overcoming obstacles from having been in prison. The creation of opportunities in the context of discrimination is considered.

Stage Theme 7: "Just a Little Longer"

Separating from the group may rekindle fears of being stigmatized. This may be expressed by denials of the group's value and loss of the sense of mastery gained in the group as the members reestablish interpersonal defenses to survive in rejecting and denigrating environments.

The practitioner explores the members' denials of the group's significance to determine if these denials are related to fear of being seen and dealt with stereotypically in future social interactions. The practitioner considers to what degree the members' own effective approaches and attitudes to defend themselves and to seek support from others in situations are characterized by values and norms that are shaped by stereotyping and discrimination.

Symbolic Representations of the Practitioner and Group

Assessing the reactions of members to the evolving process is done by considering how frequently and with what intensity members attach symbolic significance to the role of the practitioner. Reactions to the practitioner will depend on each member's prior issues and history (Garland et al., 1973) with regard to authority figures and the meaning of group life. The practitioner and members may be seen as harsh or benevolent authority figures, familial parental or sibling figures, or as representatives of social institutional control. Members may attach parent and child symbols to themselves or to the practitioner, because the small group in its development will adopt a "familial frame of reference" (Garland et al., 1973, p. 50) wherein members exhibit behaviors and expectations that represent prior familial interactions. These perceptions, if not age appropriate, distort the realities of the relationships and the potential for productive accomplishments in the group. The practitioner will have to consider the relative fluidity and rigidity of these frames of reference, and how these affect each member's participation in a productive process.

Stage Theme 1: "We're Not in Charge"

The practitioner formulates a tentative assessment of the members' perceptions of him or her, enabling members to deal with distortions

that interfere with the trust necessary for involvement in a full interpersonal process.

Members perceive the practitioner's reactions and the group's
affiliation processes in relation to other helpers and groups they have
experienced (Shulman, 2006). This will be expressed to a greater or
lesser extent depending on their anxiety about membership in the
group and the type of authority the group worker will use. Some
members may perceive the practitioner in the capacity of standard-
bearer of the group, or some may view the practitioner's image of the
humanistic group with skepticism.

The practitioner considers the extent of members' willingness and
abilities to engage with him or her directly. The practitioner may be
responded to with trust or mistrust, as an enabling expert or a depriving agent of social control. The members' symbolic views of the practitioner also skew and shape their perceptions of other members.

The practitioner can test out his or her assessments by inactivity,
seeking to note changes, or confirmation. Then the practitioner may
engage symbolic distortions to alter the member's perceptions by
restating the practitioner's role or the group's purpose. If clarification
of these factors becomes difficult, then the subject has to be dropped
until later on in the process to avoid stubborn attitudes that may bol-
ster further symbolic reactions. The practitioner hopes that the member's experiences in process will be corrective without confrontation.

Stage Theme 2: "We Are in Charge"

The practitioner assesses each member's perceptions of the power
of the authority role to help in clarifying distortions and expectations
attendant to it. This enables members' fuller ownership of and responsibility for the group process.

Members who are feeling powerless may express desires for the
practitioner to assert control so as "to provide security for the immature organism" (Bion, 1961, p. 74) and preserve the group. Members
may cloak the worker in the garb of a "group deity" (p. 148) who has
"a reputation for knowing a lot about groups" (p. 30). Others may
question the practitioner's ability to meet their needs or view him or
her as an obstacle to the process and "simply ignore his or her presence" (p. 34). At this juncture in the process, the practitioner may be
symbolized as an agent of depriving and repressive social institutional
structures. This may be expressed by expectations of disappointment
about the worker and the group ever being helpful.

The practitioner tests out the assessment of the members' realistic
and unrealistic expectations by creating opportunities for dialogues so

that actual interactions can pave the way for truer images of the practitioner.

Stage Theme 3: "We're Taking You On"

The practitioner here is interested in helping the members experience him or her as an actual human being with a specific role and expertise in the group.

When taking on the practitioner, each member is attempting to clarify his or her perceptions and feelings about the practitioner as an authority figure, while asking for reactions from and dialogue with the practitioner in return. Interactional realities are the salient material to engage around, rather than those that are historical or intellectualized. This juncture in the process is the practitioner's opportunity to reach the member who is most distant, angry, or disappointed to begin the process of forming a relationship that is based on current interactions and changes in behavior rather than on projections from the past. The practitioner invites the member's feedback, responding in a way that helps the member develop a direct and meaningful relationship with him or her.

Stage Theme 4: Sanctuary

At this stage, the practitioner and group are usually symbolized through a familial lens (Garland et al., 1973). Given this, much data may emerge about what interferes with members' age-appropriate abilities to interact. The practitioner can be cast into the image of an all-knowing parent who can develop the best group, or as an ignorant failure of a parent who is incompetent and will not experience good feelings. He or she also runs the risk of being perceived as a political collaborator who should join this special group as a sibling against parental figures, or as someone who can never join in because his or her lifestyle is "so different." These parental and politicized symbolizations may cause the member to defensively seek the protective comfort of the group's sanctuary.

The practitioner works on engaging distortions of these sorts by acknowledging the members' feelings and working with them to clarify perceptions of the practitioner's behavior. Some transferential material can be left unexplored by the practitioner if this material has a positive effect on shaping the member's role in the group.

Stage Theme 5: "This Isn't Good Anymore"

When the group is feeling down on itself, the practitioner deals with the members who express this viewpoint most often. He or she openly explores the reasons that members feel unable to move forward and focuses on the members' particular disappointments in the methods of the practitioner, other members, and the group as a whole.

The practitioner recognizes that he or she is called on to offer corrective experiences, as an authority figure that differs from those in authority with whom the members have had negative experiences. He or she actively helps the members examine their pessimism deriving from the expectations that someone in authority will be a source of frustration rather than a source of support for meeting needs.

Stage Theme 6: "We're Okay and Able"

The practitioner considers how he or she uses the worker role to create bonds with the members that enhance their abilities to work on change while minimally encumbered by distorted views of the group worker that hamper growth. When a member wittingly juxtaposes and alternates distorted and realistic perceptions of the practitioner and the group, he or she shows signs of knowing the symbols for what they are—masks that interfere with relationships. Members actively engage in the process, identifying symbolic distortions as obstacles to their work in the group.

In the change process, members may utilize the practitioner as facilitator, role model, or teacher. Members borrow abilities and take recommendations from the practitioner more often as they accept the practitioner as a separate individual. The practitioner considers the amount of direction each member is able to take, and the degree of connection each member has to him or her. When not symbolically distorting, the member connects to the practitioner as an authoritative enabler.

Illustration	Teen Parent Group

At the 10th meeting of a teen parent group, Jessica asks Heleena, the practitioner, "What makes you so special that you can help me out?" Heleena responds, "Jessica, I have my training to help me and my desire to help all you young women and men try to rear your children, and to enjoy yourselves with others." John says, "It's so hard to come home, get the kid from day care, and feel connected. Forget it! And on Saturday night, when I know all my friends are out, and I have r-e-s-p-o-n-s-i-b-i-l-i-t-y!" John turns to Heleena and asks, "You were a teen once, how did you handle the desire to be with your friends?" Francie cuts in, "Don't tell yet, Heleena, because you're not the teacher. Just write it down." Heleena says, "Okay, let's all write down how we handle responsibility. Then we'll all go around and read what we wrote." The members agree. "Don't cheat,

Heleena," is heard from Francie. They laugh. Heleena says, "This is good stuff for role playing. By the way, let's not forget the picnic in a couple of weeks for the children and grandparents. This is another responsibility to plan and to enjoy."

After the discussion of responsibility, Jessica comments, "Heleena, you make us feel good. You are nicer to us than anyone else." Heleena feels misunderstood and suffocated by the "good parent" label of this perception. She is aware that Jessica and the others are fickle; 20 minutes earlier, Jessica had tested her ability, a phenomenon that happens regularly in this group.

At later meetings, after a year of work together, during Stage Theme 6, "We're Okay and Able," the group is talking about how they feel so old and so young at the same time. They are alternately caught between trying to meet their responsibilities and resenting them as well. After talking about wanting her mother to help her with her daughter, Jessica says to Heleena, "I wish that I could go back to school." Heleena, aware of Jessica's special need for support and her sensitivity when she experiences rejection, chooses to respond directly before eliciting the group's response: "That sounds like a fine idea. What did you have in mind?" Jessica gathers up her strength and talks about becoming a nurse. Heleena supports her and universalizes her experience for the group: "Alice and Inez, when you went back to school, it seems to me you felt good." This gives the cue to Inez who responds directly to Jessica, "It's true, Jessica, I like it. It's hard, but I like it. Why don't you come down to the school and I'll show you around. We'll get some booklets and you can spend the evening, if your mom will babysit." Jessica says, "Oh, for school, my mom will babysit," and looks at Heleena. Heleena responds with a smile of approval.

Stage Theme 7: "Just a Little Longer"

When the group moves toward ending its process, a member's perceptions of the practitioner can shift from experiencing the practitioner as realistic and enabling to perceiving him or her as all-comforting or all-rejecting. This will be evident by attitudes and activities wherein the member moves back to earlier ways of depending on or challenging the group worker.

Members in this stage experience feelings of comfort or abandonment by other members, as well. Each member needs to view the practitioner and group experience through significant frames of reference that serve as realistic models for future relationships. The practitioner assesses how intensely each member remains lodged in the midst of perceptual distortions. This is done to gauge what type of emotional and social issues may be obstacles for the members in future situations, and how able the members are in working through these feelings as they move on. The practitioner identifies the extent to which these are stage specific or fundamental to the character, pattern, and personality of each member. If the latter is evident, confronting these distortions at the end will be counterproductive for the member, stimulating regressive attitudes and activities.

❖ SUMMARY

This chapter focused on psychosocial criteria and perspectives for assessing the member in the group. The habit of assessment helps the practitioner empathize with and observe the member as a distinct person in the process. The following dimensions of members' behavior were considered: (1) ability to take part in processes that develop democratic mutual aid and that actualize purpose, (2) ego abilities and sense of self, (3) the social institutional environment, (4) stereotypes and self-fulfilling prophecies, and (5) symbolic representations of the practitioner and the group.

To shed light on the changing nature of member behavior during the group's development, these dimensions were delineated in the context of each of the seven stage themes. Each criterion casts a different light on the perceptions the practitioner experiences when observing and assessing members. The task of the practitioner is to shift from one type of lens to another and to be aware of the effect these lenses have on his or her perceptions, empathy, judgments, and acts of engagement with each member.

10

Fields of Practice and Humanistic Group Work

T his chapter considers humanistic values and democratic norms as they are differentially applied to group work in three fields of practice. These major fields of practice—mental health, substance and alcohol addictions treatment, and health care—were chosen for special consideration. Providing benchmarks for these practice fields for the enactment of group work's ethical dimensions and guidelines for the practitioner will strengthen their application and guide agency practice with groups in these domains.

Group treatment approaches have been increasingly used in mental health, especially in programs for persons with serious mental illness (Miller & Mason, 2002; K. Zuckerman, personal communication, 2001). Another developing area is substance and alcohol addictions treatment (Cicchetti, 2008; Cicchetti & Goldberg, 1996; Glassman, 2001), wherein a blending of social work values with addictions reha-bilitation values in group treatment has occurred. In the health field, social group work is being practiced in oncology, chronic illness, and

HIV-AIDS (Glassman, 1991; Hayes, McConnell, Nardozzi, & Mullican, 1998; Heckman et al., 1999; Northen, 1983).

Several of the democratic norms discussed in Chapters 1 and 2 will be examined as these pose particular ethical dilemmas for practitioners in the fields of mental health, addictions, and health. The following are among these norms:

- The norm for protecting the rights of every member to contribute to and receive resources
- The norm for the participation of all
- The norm for caring versus exploitive relationships
- The norm for developing open decision-making processes
- The norm fostering diversity rather than conformity
- The norm for directly expressing reactions to the practitioner

❖ MENTAL HEALTH GROUPS

Many treatment and support groups in the field of mental health are conducted within the milieu therapy designs of continuing day treatment (CDT) and intensive psychiatric rehabilitation treatment (IPRT) settings. These programs are associated with hospitals or outpatient mental health clinics. The groups conducted in these environments service people suffering from a range of psychiatric disabilities and serious mental illnesses who also use psychotropic medications. Milieu treatment programs use a range of therapy and activities groups as their major modality, with supplemental support provided by individual therapy. These programs use group and community membership as a vehicle for enhancing the self-esteem and psychosocial functioning of persons with serious mental illness. By providing a framework for structuring and organizing a fragmented ego, the therapeutic milieu gives hope to the member and a vision of future activity that is not completely driven by the mental illness.

The clinical therapy groups found in outpatient mental health clinics, or family service agencies, where treatment is primarily individual weekly psychotherapy, tend to be used as a secondary not primary intervention. Direction for working with these groups is provided throughout this volume and will not be addressed specifically here.

It has become increasingly evident in treating persons with serious mental illness that mutual aid and membership in a therapeutic community support clinical social work services and psychiatric interventions. The development of a wide range of treatment groups as a legitimate therapeutic intervention demonstrates that the effort at cost containment by managed care companies through the replacement of individual treatment with group treatment turned out not to have been detrimental to clients (Harris, 2004). Mental health treatment goals are met through the interpersonal bonds that are developed in a therapeutic community, which, despite the limitations of mental illness, are built on the right to participate in a socially and emotionally supportive environment and the norm fostering the participation of all members as important ingredients of treatment.

The humanistic values underpinning the therapeutic community are the members' rights to belong, to be heard, to take part, to be included, to be different, to have an accountable worker, to have freedom of speech, and to make decisions that affect their lives.

The therapeutic community participants' easy access to a variety of groups as a place for self-expression enables the operationalization of the humanistic value, the right to freedom of speech and expression. This value is reflected through the democratic norm for maintaining an open communication system, which helps members to focus on their interpersonal issues and concerns.

Another development has been the growth of self-help programs such as Fountain House (http://www.fountainhouse.org), a club house model that uses a range of activities, including a governmental structure, to further the independent functioning of persons recovering from mental illness. The National Alliance for the Mentally Ill (NAMI) (http://www.nami.org) provides support and strengthens family members' skills in fostering the independent functioning of a person with mental illness. These programs lend more credence to group work's ethical base as the underpinning for guiding and directing rehabilitation and support programs. In these programs where members assume major responsibility for the workings and activities of the program, the humanistic values of the inherent worth of the individual and the right to freedom of choice are strengthened through the democratic norms for protecting the rights of every member, fostering an equal distribution of power, and developing open decision-making processes.

Practitioner Role

In the context of a therapeutic community such as a CDT or IPRT, the practitioner's role has several key elements. The practitioner must attend to the development of a democratic mutual aid system rather than making assumptions that the members are "too sick" to generate their own interpersonal structures. The practitioner also has to ensure that members take responsibility for asking each other how they are doing. This fosters social connection among members who might have been experiencing social isolation that results from mental illness. Through the use of encouragement skills, the practitioner endeavors to teach members that their concern for one another and observations of each other have utility in the mutual helping process. Workers can also help all group members present their observations of and concerns about each other. By strengthening social and observational skills in the group and community meetings, these interventions maximize members' chances for increased independent functioning outside of the program.

Along with knowledge and skill in group work, practitioners in therapeutic community groups must have knowledge of mental illness and its debilitating factors, *DSM-IV* diagnoses, and therapeutic intervention, as well as a working understanding of how medications assist in the treatment process. Group practitioners should use theories about individual dynamics, including understanding the members behaviors within the context of stage themes of group development (see Chapter 9), psychosocial and medical histories, and family dynamics as they are currently affecting the group members.

Illustration	**Therapeutic Community Treatment Groups on 9/11**

Nothing attests more to the strength of a therapeutic community and its treatment groups than the way in which group members and staff at a downtown New York agency 10 blocks from the World Trade Center disaster reacted on the morning of 9/11. Karen Zuckerman, the educational coordinator responsible for 200 interns at FEGS, described how the agency helped clients on that day and subsequently (K. Zuckerman, personal communication, 2001).

Staff providing services to clients with serious mental illness met with their groups that morning, using the group process to help clients ground their fears and express their horror and grief over the disaster. The fact that the group meetings were an expectation by clients that day, rather than a unique occurrence, allowed the easy expression of feelings by many, which contributed to their sense of being cared for during the evolving painful and stressing drama. In the process of being helped by staff and each other, clients learned their emotional state was shared by staff, which normalized their reactions and strengthened their cohesion that day.

During the morning, agency executives visited the group meeting areas, talking informally with clients and staff to provide further support; this continued well beyond September 11. The most important and immediate concrete service provided that day was that every single client was given safe transportation and escorted home. In the days to come, every client had a place to go for support and connection as they were quickly transferred to agency CDTs in other parts of the city. They were picked up and returned home safely until the downtown site reopened the following week. Staff members were also transferred to other boroughs, which enabled clients to engage with staff and their treatment community during the reassignment. Through these efforts, Zuckerman relates that clients knew "the agency was behind them."

As a testament to the power of group work, the community that had been created earlier through the intensive group work program helped clients, staff, and social work interns support each other through this very difficult period. Zuckerman describes the "healthy loss of boundaries," an unusual fluidity in practitioner and member roles that reflected an emotional flexibility that was believed to have helped everyone to feel support in the situation. In addition, all of New York City's more than 3,000 graduate social work students had started field work the day before, only to find themselves in a new place with new people, not knowing what to do. The students were given a great deal of support by the staff of the program until they could move into the more traditional part of their student role that began occurring in the weeks to come.

Discussion

The humanistic value that members have responsibility for one another through everyone's involvement in collective treatment endeavors was clearly demonstrated and heightened that day. Members of the therapeutic community who were attending daily were supported in a range of groups on that day. Practitioners helped members express their mutuality and the norm for caring and mutual aid versus exploitive relationships, which provided a base of acceptance and growth through poetry, art, support, and other groups. The "belonging" system created through democratic group norms was harnessed that day, and in the weeks to come, to assist members in maintaining their mental health and well-being despite the tragedy.

Furthermore, intrinsic in this therapeutic community is the value that people are inherently worthy. Members experience this value daily through activities related to the norm of protecting the rights of every member, which had special meaning for this stigmatized population on that day. Members were able to discuss their fears and issues in an open and empathic environment, and this was fostered by the practitioner in the group and furthered by the presence of the agency executives. There was enough trust in the process to express a range of feelings, and this shows that the humanistic value of difference is enriching, and the norm of fostering the expression of difference rather than a push for conformity were operational, despite the many serious mental health issues of this population.

Illustration	*Poetry Writing Group in a Day Treatment Program*

Margie, a 45-year-old member of a poetry writing group in a day treatment program, has expressed the sadness she feels about her sister's cancer and imminent death. Two of the nine members seem unresponsive and somewhat avoidant of this theme. Another member, Drew, advises Margie that "they're just scared of sad topics." Several agree that Drew is right. When Margie says she wants to read her poem, one member says she will come back after Margie is finished. Other members ask her to read it. Margie thanks everyone and goes on to read her poem. When she is finished, the practitioner, Erika, asks, "How are you, Margie, and everyone doing?" Margie cries, noting upset and fear about losing her sister. Drew shares that when he lost his mother he was very frightened as well. The practitioner asks, "Drew, how did you deal with your loss?" He says, "I put myself in the hospital, with the help of my social worker and psychiatrist. I didn't want to go at first, but they made me realize that things could be worse if I didn't."

Erika asks Margie how she is reacting to what Drew said. Margie notes, "I don't want to think about going to the hospital but I want to be with my sister. I am afraid." Helen adamantly states that everyone is different, advising Margie not to take what Drew said to mean that she should go to the hospital. The practitioner points out that it is "normal for someone who anticipates a loss to be sad and depressed. I would be more concerned if you didn't feel this way, Margie." Margie goes on to talk about how helpful her sister has been to her as they have gotten older and that her sister is all she has.

Discussion

The practitioner's ease in accepting the member's decision not to listen to the poem indicated to the group the affirmation of the humanistic value that difference is enriching and the democratic norm fostering members' diversity rather than a push for conformity. Further, this approach by the practitioner demonstrates a recognition of the members' ability to tolerate others' problems and an understanding that a range of behaviors is acceptable in groups for persons with psychiatric issues. The practitioner role centers on dealing with the charged affect, obviously showing confidence in the group members' acceptance of each others' differences. The patient who can go to the hospital with the help of the worker and psychiatrist reflects behavior that is an acceptance of realistic norms about the interdependence of the client-worker-psychiatric system.

❖ HEALTH CARE GROUPS

Many different kinds of groups in health care exist (Glassman, 1991; Northen, 1983) in cancer (Euster, 1990; Seitz, 1985; Trachtenberg, 1972), neonatology (Bocat, 1988; Quinn & Feehan, 2007), pediatric oncology (Foreman, Willis, & Goodenough, 2005), and HIV-AIDS (Kaslyn, 1999; Pinto, 2000; Sarracco & Cicchetti, 1996). Some health care groups use a short-term structure, designed to deal with an immediate crisis, while others are longer term groups developed for people and families facing chronic health issues. Several unique group formats have been at the forefront, such as telephone groups for the homebound (Heckman et al., 1999; Kaslyn, 1999), various breast cancer support groups (Adelphi, 2008; Galinsky, 1985), and groups for persons infected by and affected by HIV-AIDS (Pomeroy, Kiam, & Green, 2000; Sarracco, 1997).

There has been in health care a long and steady history of social group work practice. Despite the drive to cost containment, some groups dealing with health issues continue to flourish within the medical setting, while others have been developed outside the medical system altogether (Adelphi, 2008). One example has been the long running groups at Gay Men's Health Crisis (http://www.gmhc.org/about.html). Though present research is inconclusive regarding the impact of breast cancer support groups on prolonging life, recent studies show that support groups "enhance mood and reduce perceived pain severity" (Goodwin, 2004, p. 4244). Group work has been done for parents of children with cancer (Foreman, Willis, & Goodenough, 2005), for fathers of children with spina bifida (Nicholas, McNeill, Montgomery, Stapleford, & McClure, 2003), and in treating children with questionable genital identification (Nielson, personal communication, 2007).

A central issue in health care groups is the potential violation of humanistic values and democratic norms (Glassman, 1991; Northen, 1983) due to the vulnerability of group members in relation to illness as well as to the health care system itself. An ill person faces many issues (Northen, 1983), which include social isolation, stigmatization, loss of sense of self, and passivity in response to a medical bureaucracy or insurance providers. A major healing factor of the social work group in health care is the group's potential to enable an ill person or family member to improve adaptation, reduce isolation and despair, and redirect stress in order to cope with factors that undermine adaptation.

Practitioner Role

The working knowledge and understanding of group work's humanistic values and democratic norms need to be applied within the context of a health crisis and weakened emotional state of the members and their families (Glassman, 1991) to facilitate their empowerment within the health care system and in their lives.

Since many health care groups are conducted in interdisciplinary settings, prior discussion by coleaders is required about the conceptual underpinnings of the group, group goals, and the differentiation of roles. This is because professionals from different disciplines may be more apt to have different goals and objectives. For example, social workers may be running groups with nursing or nutrition department members, and clarity of group purpose and role expectations enhances the development of the group's process.

Many of the groups in health care require flexibility in structure, particularly in developing alternatives to the traditional long-term group. Short-term crisis intervention groups that enable the expression of current pressing issues also afford members the benefit of maintaining a sense of empowerment beyond the group's termination. In long-term groups, accepting and encouraging flexibility in attendance patterns is an adaptation that accommodates the downswings of an illness or a transportation problem.

Humanistic values germane to the health care group are people's responsibility for one another, the right to belong and to be included, the right to freedom of choice and to determine one's destiny, and the right to question and challenge those who have an authority role in the members' lives. The democratic norm fostering caring and mutual aid counters isolation, fear, and despair during illness. The norm permitting everyone's participation maintains the flow of inclusion so that all members may respond to one another, thereby enhancing self-worth and maximizing social connection for the ill person. The norm fostering transparent decision making helps members consider how medical decisions are being made, and by providing opportunities for shared control, enhances the dignity and self-worth of people who are not readily in control of their own destinies.

Conducting groups in health care requires the practitioner to have understanding of the biopsychosocial dynamics of the health issues and diseases the group members are dealing with. The practitioner should have knowledge of the physiological effect of these health issues, the psychosocial factors, and how these influence group participation and membership. Moreover, the practitioner requires responsiveness to the recurring crises of illnesses as these crises affect the patient, the family, and the other group members.

| Illustration | Group for Parents With HIV-AIDS |

In this HIV-AIDS parents group, members are dealing with their illness, the issue of when to tell their children, and how to make plans for their children's care when they die. Lisa starts this meeting by sharing that she is feeling afraid she will be unable to work. Billy asks her if she has had a recent physical setback. "No, I am trying to plan ahead." Billy says that he doesn't like to plan ahead. Dottie tells him that she has to think about it because she doesn't want to leave her 8-year-old with no options. Stacy says that she and Ken keep trying to talk about options for their daughter but they can't stay on the topic. Ken agrees. The group worker, Rene, says, "Some of you seem to be having difficulty focusing on the future and planning for the kids." Silence. She goes on, "Why is that so hard?"

Billy says he is having a hard time because his mother wants his kids, and he is worried that she is too old to do the job. He believes she is jealous of his late wife's mother, who also wants them; she is younger and more capable. He hopes his mother doesn't fight him in court. Frederica says with confidence, "My ex's mother is less 'mental' than my mother—so I want her to have my daughter." Everyone laughs. "I already told that to my mother." Talk continues about their family members and the need to proceed legally.

The practitioner asks, "What goes into deciding who you want to have your kids?" Dottie says, "We should ask the kids." Billy says, "How can we ask the kids if they don't know we're sick?" Dottie says she thinks they know anyway. She says, "I think we want to be in denial, and most of the time it's easier not to talk about it—why mommy goes to the doctors all the time, why I take all these pills."

Gloria says, "There are so many different opinions on when you tell kids." The practitioner asks, "Does that confuse you? All those opinions?" Gloria says, "Yes." The practitioner asks, "What about the others here?" Ken says that it's hard to incorporate all those ideas. Dottie says, "We didn't all answer Rene's question." Billy says, "You mean about why it's so hard to plan for the kids?" "Yes," she says, "that question." Billy replies, "That's because we don't want to look at the future and to consider the future without ourselves in it—to see them grow up."

The group worker, Rene, says, "You've all been so strong, and each of you has your own unique issues regarding making plans. This is a hard one. There are family issues, there are legal issues. How do you want to approach the planning process?" Ken says, "I think we have to try to talk about our issues in here, because alone we can't do it. In here, together, and with Rene, maybe we can go ahead and do this." Rene asks how people feel about going ahead and planning for the children. There is a lot of agreement, "Yes, we have to. We can't be selfish." Then she suggests the group start by airing some of the individual issues, like family pressures, and their own relationships with potential caretakers.

Discussion

The major issue in this meeting centers on the members' feelings regarding their illness and their conflict about taking control of the difficult and painful decision of planning for their children's future upon their deaths. The value that people have a right to determine their own destinies is difficult for these members to operationalize due to their sadness about themselves and their children, and the complexity of managing family members' feelings and dynamics. Yet, positive forces among the members propel them to begin making decisions about their children, thereby enacting the norm fostering transparent decision-making processes. The practitioner's role is to assist members in engaging their decision-making processes to face their difficulties in determining what is best for each member's child, despite intimidating family issues, and to facilitate their effective empowerment within the legal system.

The value people are responsible for and to one another is presented in Ken's articulation of the norm for mutual aid and caring as vital in helping the members meet the challenge of planning for their children's futures.

A major issue for the practitioner is knowing when the group is ready to face their own mortality and its impact on their children's well-being. The group worker takes a risk by asking why it is so hard for them to deal with this issue, in that they could have continued to avoid the necessary work. Through this intervention, she helps members begin to grapple with their own decision-making potential.

The worker is at first met with silence and then a response by Billy about family issues that paves the way toward problem solving and planning. The recognition is expressed that planning for their children's destinies involves understanding of complex family dynamics, the ongoing vicissitudes of members' family interactions, and the development of skills to address these directly. Furthermore, group members openly recognize the importance to their successful resolution of the task ahead of their compliance to the norm for mutual aid and caring as they face this emerging challenge.

That these clients are in a vulnerable state is without question. However, by reinforcing a beginning review of legal considerations, the group worker is able to introduce the possibility of future discussion of the impact on their lives of the many bureaucratic structures outside of themselves that come with this illness—in this case legal as well as medical structures.

❖ SUBSTANCE AND ALCOHOL ADDICTIONS GROUPS

Many groups in substance abuse treatment are long term and often open ended in structure, taking place in the context of residential or day treatment programs. The phases of the open-ended groups usually follow Galinsky and Schopler's (1987) fourth group type, infrequent change for a few members (see Chapter 11), wherein cohesion and the cycle of work are similar to that found in long-term closed groups. The trend in addictions treatment is for groups to be co-led, often by more than two persons, representing the full spectrum of professional and nonprofessional standards for their roles in the group. The requirement of verbal participation for all group members is strong, and a frequent problem revolves around the misinterpretations of meanings ascribed to some member behaviors by the group's nonprofessional leaders.

Though substance and alcohol addictions is a field of practice in which traditionally numerous groups have been used, many have had a history of being based on norms that are in direct opposition to group work's democratic norms. Humanistic values commonly at risk are the right to belong and to be included, the right to freedom of speech and freedom of expression, the right to question and challenge those in authority who have a role in their lives, and the right to be different. Democratic norms often transgressed or frequently not developed in the group have been the norm for maintaining an open communication system without reliance on a narrow ideology, the norm guiding the use of inclusion versus exclusion as a healing tool, the norm fostering dealing directly with feelings about the practitioner's role, and the norm fostering members' diversity rather than a push for conformity.

Value conflicts about group and therapeutic community norms, as well as the role of helpers, were made more visible in substance abuse treatment by the introduction of professional social workers into groups to function alongside peer helpers, many of whom were in recovery themselves.

Numerous conflicts continue to arise between the professionals and nonprofessionals about the role of the practitioner, particularly around broader social work ethical constraints related to boundaries, self-disclosure, and management of clinical issues. Nonprofessionals may misinterpret or denigrate members' presentations and behaviors, or permit boundary breaches in the group that would be unacceptable in the professional realm. Professional social work supervision should correct and redirect these interventions in the group, thereby preventing them from having damaging effects on members. Incorrectly imposing their own issues and identifications on group members may neutralize the potential effectiveness of peer helpers' interventions. When peer helpers lack fundamental understanding of the right to belong, the right to freedom of expression and the norm fostering difference versus conformity, they may critically judge or not accept a member's form of participation. Peer helpers with a solid foundation in humanistic values and democratic norms are more likely to provide positive input and perspective for the practitioner and group.

However, professional social workers and other mental health providers in substance abuse treatment programs will have prominence as the mental health arm of the program, which clearly affords them numerous opportunities to introduce and operationalize social group work values into the evolving process.

Some group types with a self-help framework, such as AA, do not function with a professional social worker in them. In these groups, members are usually not permitted to react to each others' presentations, which increases members' protection from potential distortions and overreactions. Peers, who themselves have demonstrated long-term involvement in their own rehabilitation, mentor others' efforts to maintain sobriety.

Practitioner Role

Group practitioners should understand the conceptual underpinnings that underlie the formation and practice of rehabilitation in their program, as well as group work theory and its value base. This permits the development of group treatment designs and interventions that more effectively integrate social work values with necessary substance abuse treatment approaches.

The practitioner role is to sustain group work's humanistic values and democratic norms, to bring them out into the open to the group, and to point out transgressions and unprofessional behavior when it is occurring. The professional is required to guide, direct, and bring to bear his or her expertise to support the facilitative intentions of other helpers even if they have less training.

Practitioners in addictions treatment groups should have knowledge of the physiological effects of drug and alcohol addiction and the physiological consequences of the recovery process, as well as an understanding of the commonly used medications for redressing physical and psychological impacts of addictions. Knowledge and understanding of mental health issues and how substances are used to mask emotional factors is essential. Further knowledge of family systems and communication theories commonly reflected in addictive families and individuals should guide the group practitioner in this area.

Illustration	Maintaining Sobriety Group

Joe has been quiet in the group this session. The substance abuse counselor, Matt, asks Joe why he has been holding out on the group, why he hasn't been forthcoming. Joe says he has "nothing to say" and that he was listening. Lawrence quips, "Joe just doesn't want to say, that one always has something to say." He adds that from Joe's body language he knows Joe doesn't want to say what's on his mind. Felicia says, "Others are not talking, why are you picking on Joe?" Matt continues to push Joe, raising his voice at him: "Hey, you're just being lazy."

The social worker, Nora, cuts in, "Joe is not ready or available now. So let's try to see if someone else has something to tell us today. Maybe later Joe will want to talk to us. You don't have to talk if you don't want to." Julio says that he is pissed at Matt for pushing Joe like that. Matt says, "I don't like cop-outs." Julio says, "No one likes cop-outs, but who made you boss and judge?"

Nora then notes that this kind of fighting isn't going to get them anywhere, and she asks for others to talk about how they've been doing lately. Helen says her boyfriend sent a message to her in the rehab program, so she wants to break curfew and sneak out to see him. She goes on to protest the "no sex" rule and says she wants to go see him. Lois says the sexual prohibition is to keep everyone focused on self-understanding rather than on being high. "Yes, but my boyfriend is gonna hang out with that little bitch if I don't have sex with him and heaven knows . . . " Darryl says, "forget him if that's how he's gonna be. He doesn't understand the seriousness of your situation if he's begging you for sex or if you think he'll cheat with someone else." They start to make comments among themselves about sex and being sex deprived, and then they laugh.

Discussion

A major issue in the group revolves around the value that the members have the right to question and challenge those with whom they have an authority relationship in their lives. One must examine the extent to which members are permitted to challenge the worker(s) in this session with regard to their behaviors in the group and the impact of these behaviors on the members. The norm for expressing directly their feelings toward the practitioner is only tenuously established, in that although one member, Julio, does challenge the worker, there is no further discussion by other members of Matt, as an authority figure to whom the critique was directed. The social work practitioner redirects the group away from fighting toward a different theme. This incident requires discussion outside of the meeting by the coleaders as well as group work training, which includes emphasis on values and norms as the underpinning for practice. The extent of the resolution most likely will be determined by the place of the social work profession in this setting and the way in which professional values are imparted to paraprofessional staff. The worker has to continuously assert this value in the group.

The other major issue centers on the value that difference is enriching and the degree to which it is operationalized by the group through the norm fostering the expression of difference. One member shows anger at Matt for pushing Joe, indicating that Matt usurped his authority and power in the group. The practitioner clearly affirms Joe's right to speak, or not to, without engaging Matt in a conflict. By redirecting this issue away from a "fight" as she describes it, she moves the group toward a different problem area that is not directly related to this norm. The conflict about issues of conformity and difference will require further attention.

Wrapped around the value that people have the right to freedom of choice is the norm governing how member behavior outside of the group is shaped by standards guiding behavior in the group. Sex is prohibited in this treatment community. Many powerful norms in therapeutic communities govern how members conduct their lives outside of the group. Despite knowing these rules before they agree to membership, clients in their in vivo encounter with these rules often raise their doubts and highlight their feelings about having to yield to the control the program has over their lives. While this group challenges the prohibition, it is not to the degree that they rebel against it and leave the program. The discussion about relationships is a latent discussion about intimacy, positive and negative relationships, along with a covert expression of feelings about their compliance to the authority of the program, and the discreet reaction to one worker's use of his authority.

The professional social worker in this session should help members discuss and formulate a clearer understanding of their issues with the authority and power of the workers, as well as the thorny issue related to the authority of the program over their conduct in their lives. It will occur more readily when Nora and Matt are on the same page regarding dealing with member participation.

Social workers in substance abuse treatment agencies need to engage in dialogue with colleagues about the enactment of group work values and norms and the value conflicts their enactment heightens.

❖ SUMMARY

The humanistic values and democratic norms of social group work have always been a work in progress. Some contemporary definitions of practice in certain fields have been altered in fundamental ways. Mental health has changed due to the effective and once unimaginable use of psychotropic medications to improve people's lives, which has led to the new group work that is widely institutionalized in milieu treatment programs serving these clients. Health care has been changed through the development of medical treatments and self-empowerment approaches that allow people to manage many diseases more effectively over longer time frames. Substance abuse treatment, with its multifaceted complex of group meetings, has evolved into a major technology so cogently developed that it is being exported by the social work profession to the global community.

Practitioners with groups have adapted to the current evolving practice context by applying understanding of group work practice and theory derived not only from the lens of group work's history, but through the acumen a studied analysis of the present contributes.

PART IV

Practice Variations and Contingencies

11

Short-Term, Single-Session, Open-Ended, and Structured Groups

Social work agencies conduct many groups that depart from the traditional long-term closed-group model. While these groups may be built on social work values and practice principles, their limitations of time, agenda constraints, and/or fluidity of membership pose particular practice dilemmas for the group worker. For example, the constraints of time affect the practitioner's ability to guide the development of a belonging system built on relationship, mutual aid, and democratic process. A fluctuating membership during the life span of the group poses difficulties in the development of group cohesion. The practice issues that require attention by practitioners with short-term, single-session, structured, and open-ended group designs are considered in this chapter.

❖ SHORT-TERM GROUPS

Short-term groups are those that meet from three to eight sessions. A short-term group usually will be developed by an agency around a particular theme or to deal with a special issue. Many short-term groups are education- or growth-oriented rather than for support or remediation purposes. Groups for parent effectiveness training, psychoeducation, and discharge planning are frequently formed within a short-term model. In developing and defining a technology of practice for these groups, the assumption is made that the short-term nature of the group's professionally guided life is a function of a thoughtful discussion and planning process.

Of major importance is that the limitation of time in short-term groups will not permit a detailed working on and working through of complex needs. Some objectives, processes, and techniques of the humanistic method are curtailed, while others are magnified within the confines of time (Alissi & Casper, 1985). The shortening of time has the advantage of permitting the telescoping of particular needs and can be used to highlight a single or specific issue.

The practitioner in the short-term group is required to partialize areas of concern to predetermine which purpose-related needs to address, which goals might prove functional for the members, and which issues to avoid because they require more work than the time limits permit. Movement toward accomplishing humanistic group work's *dual objectives—developing the democratic mutual aid system* and *actualizing group purpose*—is accelerated through the efforts of the practitioner. The group worker will collapse the process of meeting each of the objectives by either directly providing for them or bypassing certain processes altogether. While the development of programs and other opportunities for role rehearsal may be heightened in the short-term group, dealing directly with multiple aspects of the practitioner's authority and the surfacing of most conflicts are avoided.

The authority issues that are a necessary part of the group's development, member growth, and attainment of the group as a sanctuary are also dealt with in an abbreviated manner in a short-term group. The practitioner points out to members that while he or she has set agendas prior to the first meeting to enhance productivity within the constraints of time, the group members have the option of modifying the group's design and agenda. This often allows members to reflect on the time constraints and consider together the need for their effective use of time.

During the first meeting of the short-term group, it is necessary for the practitioner to define the stated purpose of the group, to pose to the group the necessity for members to consider at least one goal each person would like to reach or one issue each would like to have dealt with by the group's end, and to state clearly the number of sessions the group will have to achieve these goals. This helps members stay focused on the work. Hand in hand with sustaining the group's stated purpose, the practitioner has the additional and essential task of helping the group grasp from the outset how their work will be managed. The practitioner tells the group about the primacy of mutual aid and relationship among the members as the tool for help, as well as demonstrates through the use of technique how he or she will not be the main source of help; the goal is for them to hear and learn from each other's varied perspectives and feelings. The practitioner also has to be mindful of the latent content being presented in the group and how to manage potential conflicts that may or may not be productive for the group in helping it to move forward to meet goals.

Another latent theme in a short-term group is the necessity for the members to accept that they may be taking part in meetings with people they do not necessarily like or whose actions are unappealing or distasteful to them. By and large, reality about the short-term group enterprise serves to facilitate members' recognition that interpersonal conflicts generally will not be aired. Members accept everyone's right to take part and are encouraged to suspend their personal reactions for the sake of their own and others' participation in the group.

Honed and focused assessment by the practitioner is necessary in the short-term group context. Assessment requires practitioners to rely on knowledge of stage theme behaviors and issues to shed light on the group's movement, and to center their attention on when it will be necessary to collapse or by-pass processes and telescope them for the group's review and understanding.

An additional framework for assessing social work groups that are not fully formed group entities has been developed by Lang (1986). Lacking in certain properties of the social work group, yet formed within the framework of social group work values and practice, the short-term social work group may be defined as a type of "collectivity." The variables Lang uses to assess short-term groups include (1) frequency and duration of meetings; (2) context and setting; (3) differences and traits of individual members; (4) characteristics of the group entity itself such as the fit of members, their interactional skills, and the stability of attendance; and (5) professional variables centering around the practitioner's practice framework and skill.

The frequency and duration of meetings in a short-term group (Lang, 1986) mitigate against the group's ability to work in depth on many issues. Thus, those few issues selected for work should be the most consonant with members' needs. In making these selections, the practitioner is called on to stimulate the group's efforts by explicitly lending a vision concerning how the issues will be worked on in the group and away from it. During pregroup contacts and the first session, the practitioner may present the group's goals within the confines of instruction, rather than lengthier time-consuming discussions, to focus in so that work can begin. Throughout the group's short existence, the practitioner will need knowledge of the fit of members, their interactional skills, and their stability of attendance, especially with regard to the members' interpersonal processes of mutual aid. The practitioner also will need to know about the members' individual variables—life-cycle factors and limitations as these interact with group issues.

The technical skills for guiding members' work on process and purpose in an abbreviated structure are required. Therefore, another factor is evident regarding the degree and level of practitioner activity. In short-term group work, time leaves the practitioner in a circumstance where he or she must be more active than in a fully formed long-term group (Lang, 1986). The practitioner uses more interactive, experiential, and didactic activity in the short-term group. Visual and aural aids are used. In addition, the techniques of role rehearsal and programming with significant others are of great value in a short-term group.

In the long-term group's process, more of an interplay between experiential and reflective modes occurs. In the shorter process, the members need interactions that help acquaint them with themselves and their activities in their roles. From this point of view, the group worker quickly partializes the phenomena in the first session and selects and presents to the group a focus on those aspects of interaction that will help the members carry out actions. The practitioner may develop role rehearsal opportunities to help in immediate interpersonal expressions.

Illustration	Neonatology Group for Parents of Newborns in Intensive Care

This is the first meeting of a neonatology group for parents of newborns in the intensive care nursery of a large urban children's hospital. The mothers have just given birth to these babies, and have been here from 1 to 3 days; the infants will remain for several weeks after the women are discharged. The intent is for this group to continue meeting two times a week for a total of eight sessions while the mothers and fathers are returning to the hospital to visit and care for the infant (Bocat, 1988; Quinn & Feehan, 2007). Four women and two men are present at this first meeting; the practitioner has also asked a nurse to take part.

As they gather, the women begin to talk about how difficult it is for them to see their babies looking so frail, with tubes attached to them. One man shares feelings as well. The practitioner suggests that this is a difficult time and that "we wanted to bring you together so you can talk about your feelings and get support." Mala says, "Sometimes it's so hard to watch them poking around at my baby. I have to walk out." The practitioner responds, "I know it can be hard to see all the activity some times." The nurse nods. The practitioner asks, "Does anyone else react that way?" Felicia, who gave birth to triplets, tells the group how hard it is for her to go in when they are poking and bothering her babies, and how she doesn't understand it all. Rafael, Felicia's husband, says, "I have to trust they know what they are doing," Diane tells how awful she will feel about going home tomorrow "empty handed." Felicia agrees that she will feel the same way. Her husband tells her, "Let's try to be patient and hope they can get the babies' lungs working on their own."

After 25 minutes, the practitioner notices that Anna and her husband Kenny have not spoken yet. She directs her attention to them saying, "You've been so quiet. What are your reactions?" Anna, with much hesitation, softly talks about her sister having given birth to a stillborn a few years ago and how terrified she was of losing this baby. Kenny looks so choked up he can't talk. The rest of the group falls silent. The practitioner says, "I guess this hits home, doesn't it." All agree. Felicia says that she sometimes has a hard time being with the babies, because she is so afraid of losing one of them that she is afraid of loving them too much. The practitioner says, "This is not unusual. Many parents in your situation feel this way. That's a reason for having this group, so you can talk about these feelings." Anna admits she has a hard time even going to see the baby and how awful and guilty she feels.

Felicia talks about her own difficulty seeing the babies and tries to reassure Anna. Anna reaches for Kenny's hand. She says, "I get so upset because we don't know what the outcome will be." Kenny says, "I don't know what to tell Darryl at home about his baby sister. And Darryl hasn't even seen her yet." The practitioner asks the group, "What do you think Kenny can say?" Antoinette says, "I think you have to bring Darryl to see the baby." Felicia says, "You can tell Darryl that the doctors and nurses are taking care of the baby so she can get strong enough to come home." More discussion ensues. Questions are asked about how to help siblings at home cope with multiples. After some talking, the group is of the opinion that the children at home should be talked with but not frightened, "even though we feel scared." Kenny says, "I feel better just knowing how to approach Darryl, and thinking about how to bring him in to see the baby." The practitioner says, "Boy we've said and done a lot today."

Vivian, the nurse, says, "I just want to tell you that the infants start out looking so weak and vulnerable. But we've seen them thrive in intensive care and they are tough little guys. They respond to you. So if you want to know what to do, just holding them can help, and talking to them and making contact with them."

As the group is winding down, the nurse and practitioner suggest they all go to the ICU together to look at the babies. This is met with much enthusiasm. As they are walking over, the practitioner tells the group about the 10-year reunion they had recently of the ICU babies and how wonderful it was to see them now. The members "ooh" and "aah," and the practitioner asks if they can meet in two days. Most of the women will have been discharged by then. "But we'll be spending a lot of time here," says Anna. "Any time you say, we can meet," Felicia chimes in. The nurse and practitioner set the time and everyone agrees.

As they walk down the hall, the practitioner and nurse remain available to answer questions. Talk continues. The practitioner asks Mala if her husband can come next time and if Dina's boyfriend is available too.

Discussion

This illustration demonstrates the partializing, focusing, and programmatic interventions the practitioner uses. Because at the start the members spontaneously talk to one another, the practitioner does not intervene to talk about group purpose or structure. She answers a question directly and undefensively, and she acknowledges the frustration and anxiety they must be feeling so as to provide a further catalyst for talk on a feeling level. Once the group has gotten off the ground and talk about the babies' apparent frailty surfaces, the practitioner supports their expression of feeling.

This is a short-term group of people in a crisis situation. There is no time to wait for the group members to draw out the quiet members. After giving it 25 minutes, the practitioner asks Anna and Kenny directly how they are feeling. This surfaces their concern about a prior loss of a newborn, which presents extra difficulties for them. Talk about this fear of losing their baby brings to the surface another very hard issue for the parents—making the commitment to the babies. The practitioner is quick to universalize the ambivalent feelings. This enables others to talk about their fear and ambivalence. In two instances she weaves the group's purpose ("to get support") into the content presented.

When Kenny asks what to say to the child at home, the group shifts into its next level of process and problem solving. Together, the group decides that the child at home should not be alarmed. The father is an important figure because he is at home while the mother is in the hospital. He has to prepare the older child for the delayed arrival home of the new baby and plan the older child's visit to the hospital.

The nurse is an important member of the team, and she uses herself prudently through the vantage point of her expertise. Her presence communicates the need for medical understanding, and her support and caring for the women comes through. The meeting closes with a group activity, visiting with the babies. As they spend this time together, the parents will have a chance to raise questions and think about new things to talk about. Talking about the reunion of the ICU babies is calculated to lend a vision and give hope to the parents.

The men become increasingly involved, and by the end Kenny is responding to someone other than his wife. This poses good potential for including the men at future meetings. The practitioner informally sets up inclusion of two missing men at the end of the session.

Short-term groups like this one need focus and clearly conceived issues to deal with; this one has them. The past is not deal dealt with, only the present situation. People are permitted to be with each other in whatever way is comfortable. One man is permitted to use his wife as the main connect to the group for the time being; this is acceptable.

❖ SINGLE-SESSION GROUPS

Single-session groups are usually formed to handle a crisis or to present a particular topic to a group for their understanding, review, and support.

The group requires the focused efforts of a practitioner to bring to the group's attention a particular issue, and at the same time ensuring that every single member has been able to react and to present to the group his or her most prevalent concern regarding the issue or theme.

Therefore, had the neonatology group illustrated above been a single session, it would have been even more important for the practitioner to ensure the participation of every single member around the most pressing issues in a neonatology unit—parent-child attachment and the ability of parents to bond with their babies. In this kind of single session, the practitioner would have to help members voice their fear and ambivalence, while lending them a vision for the future that further strengthens potential bonding capacities. In addition, the group worker would have to assess the high-risk parents through a variety of observations. The structured ending enabling the parents in the group to visit their babies would give the practitioner in a single-session group further opportunity to support vulnerable parent-child relationships and bonding. If time permitted, dealing with sibling-related issues would have been given opportunity for airing as well.

❖ OPEN-ENDED GROUPS

In agency practice, some situations and programs develop in which people congregate in subgroups and collectivities with fluid boundaries. The open-ended group gives people the opportunity to take part in group life while entering and exiting at their own pace. Membership in open-ended type groups changes over various time periods, usually with some definable nucleus maintaining the group's continuity and history. The open-ended format offers a group the opportunity to meet needs and solve problems without members required to make a commitment to attend all the time. This is useful for people whose life demands require more flexibility, who may feel over committed, and who cannot commit to more than several meetings. Examples of these groups include a single-parents group at a community center, a hearing-impaired group at a nursing home, and a teen-discussion group at the child guidance center.

The unique phenomena and practices of open-ended groups have been identified, discussed, and researched by Galinsky and Schopler (1985, 1987), who have been in the forefront of creating understanding of these groups. Research findings indicate (Galinsky & Schopler, 1985) that virtually all open-ended groups have developed entry and exit rituals, with the nucleus or core members usually assuming the responsibility for orienting new members and helping members who are leaving to finish their work before they exit. In some instances, groups experience a pattern, with one or two members leaving and coming every week. This format poses the most difficulty for the practitioner (as well as for the members) because of the amount of time and tediousness of the effort spent in endless orientations and departures.

On the other extreme are the groups whose members leave only at infrequent intervals, with new ones also entering at infrequent intervals (Galinsky & Schopler, 1987). In such situations the group and the practitioner will have to orient the new member to the group's culture, while being aware of culture-related group phenomena the new member will not understand or will misinterpret when they appear. Advance warning will have to be given to new members to ask for explanation of processes they do not understand. However, responsibility for this ongoing orientation remains with the practitioner and the group's nucleus, not in the hands of the new member. For instance, a member who is puzzled by an apparent shortcut in a decision does not know that one month prior the group spent time on this issue. Having to be sensitive to these processes places pressure on the practitioner—who most often is the carrier of group history—to interpret and translate.

Some open-ended groups have been found that experience long periods of stability during which there is no change, followed by periods of great flux during which many members leave and new ones come in a cluster (Galinsky & Schopler, 1987). This structure is most helpful to the practitioner and members, because the period of stability permits them to experience the group as a well-structured and strongly cohesive entity. Many of the practices used in long-term groups apply during this time; work that is done has continuity for members and it is possible to carry the work from meeting to meeting.

In working with open-ended groups, the practitioner's effort is toward applying the fullest range of group work technique with all the members, trying to motivate each member's potential and capability. Sometimes the nucleus will carry responsibility for conducting programs and events that others will participate in who will not be involved in preparation for them. When using the technique of programming the practitioner will work with the nucleus, poll everyone who is there for input, and help them include as many others as possible in the delegation of tasks. At times, as with the short-term group, the practitioner will have to compress the process or telescope issues in order to build a beginning, middle, and end to the meeting.

An aspect of the practitioner's role is also to reach outside the boundaries of the current core members—to those members who come and go—in order to expand and recruit others into the core of the group. Working with the core members to recruit others for the group is another typical process in the open-ended group situation.

The dysfunctional form of the open-ended group is one wherein professionals and agents with formal power to sanction group experiences will not allow a full membership group to exist for fear that power will be taken away from them. At the same time they will impose sanctions against specifying, requiring, or taking steps to identify new people who will benefit from the experience and attend regularly. This comes about as a result of personal discomfort with power, projections, and fear of danger in the group. The practitioner in such situations is at risk of being seduced into maintaining the illusion of an open-ended structure and a "pseudo-open" group. Skill is required in recognizing the phenomena, working with the group, modifying its structure, and enabling the inclusion of members within the framework of a closed-ended humanistic group method.

| Illustration | *Women's Support Group in Prison* |

Each week at the same time, Carrie, the practitioner, goes into the women's cell block to work up a list of group members for that evening's meeting of the women's support group. Several factors influence the open-ended nature of this group; women come and go, depending on their sentences; women are in different moods from day to day; and who comes very often depends on whose attendance the prison officials encourage and enable. Carrie wishes the culture of the group experience to disseminate into the culture of the cell block. She calculates that over time she will get to work with many of the women and the cell block culture.

Once again, 15 women sign up to march past the guard a half hour later, get a pass, and meet Carrie a few hundred feet (and four gated checkpoints) away in the group meeting room. Six of the women on the list are the regulars—the nucleus that is "always" in attendance, although over a 6-week period the nucleus changes. The remaining nine are either new or women who came to some sessions and then skipped several meetings.

By 7 p.m., nine of the women who signed up arrive—five of the nucleus, and four of the new members and "rotators." Carrie welcomes them warmly, invites them to sit, and politely waits for the process to start. This night Mona, a new member, says to Carrie, "What's this group for?" Carrie responds, "It's a place to talk about issues people have here." Elvira, of the nucleus says, "It's a talk group. We give each other advice on how to survive in here." Silence. Paula, also a newer member, says to Carrie, "So you're like a teacher, teach us." Carrie says, "Not exactly. I join you all in raising issues that bother you so we can see how you can help yourselves and each other."

Brenda plunges in, saying that she isn't sure she wants her kids visiting her in prison. "They frisk the baby's diaper!" Anger and frustration is expressed. Then the women talk more about their feelings and the pros and cons of their children and families visiting them. Carlotta says that her cousin is in another cell block "right in this place, and I can't get to see her." The practitioner validates how difficult this must be for her. The women discuss several approaches Carlotta can take with the guards. Carrie volunteers, "If you want, I'll see what I can find out about policies they have about this, without rocking the boat for any of you in here." Carlotta asks her to wait another week. Carrie continues by asking, "What are some of the other troubles the rest of you have with visiting or in other ways?" Vera, new to the cell block, asks about how someone finds out about visiting. Several members explain to her.

The session continues with the women talking about how others in the cell block are curious about what goes on in the group. Several members say that it is not just curiosity; it's also a feeling that some of the group members have a clique that the others are not a part of. Carrie interjects, "Sometimes it helps if you let them know they can come." Many of the women are trying to talk at once; Carrie is conscious of encouraging the interweaving of process between the members in the nucleus and the new members, and helping those in the nucleus direct the process so others don't monopolize it. (The women are so in need of attention, and lonely, that they will talk on and on.)

At the good and welfare at the end of the meeting, Carrie is the last to speak. She expresses her reactions and says she hopes "to see all of you, and others, next week—pass the word about the group." The practitioner accompanies the women to the first checkpoint, consciously and actively interacting with the core and the new members, continuing to encourage their participation. She assures them they will see her next week at 6:30 "scaring up names for the list."

Discussion

Several contextual factors are important dimensions for this group. One is the informal structure of the guards who help decide when and which women will attend the group meetings. The other aspect of the informal structure revolves around the culture of the women's cell block, and how participation in this group affects participation there. The practitioner is very conscious of the group's place in the system; by consistently reminding members to invite others to attend, she ensures that women in the cell block do not feel closed out of the process. This could create feelings of jealousy or anger if women did not feel the group was available for all of them. Carrie exhibits her understanding of this dimension when she volunteers cautiously to find out about the policy governing visitations of family members within the prison itself, if the member wants her to.

The practitioner expects to be challenged by new members, who are prone to wonder why this practitioner would want to come to a prison to help these women survive. Though this concern is not expressed directly to Carrie, a challenge is almost immediate from one new member. The practitioner, with the help of the members, can put the new participants at ease so that work can begin.

The process is accelerated by Carrie's intervention, which moves the group beyond her but does not avoid her centrality, either. She helps all members participate in airing their concerns about visiting, especially with regard to children. She also invites collective participation, which is aimed at helping the women talk to each other within the group and in the cell block.

Members turn to talking about how they are affecting the cell block by attending this group. The practitioner encourages them to invite others to attend; this reminds members that they didn't close out others by participating. The opportunity is clearly available for all.

Before they leave, the practitioner uses the good and welfare at the end of the meeting to help provide closure for the evening. This is especially important in a group that may feel fragmented and in which members may not return the following week.

As they leave the room, the practitioner escorts them to the first checkpoint. She interacts with all of them, and she again asks them to invite others. She promises to return, firming up the usual time and place, as they walk away talking together.

❖ STRUCTURED GROUPS

A major challenge to social work with groups is the use of a variety of structured and curriculumized group designs whose very structure places focus on the practitioner and may minimize the ability and potential of the members to develop an interactional process centered on support and mutual aid.

Social work agencies are using these groups for a variety of reasons. The first is the potential for attaining successful outcomes, especially because of the belief by agency administrators that structure will compensate for lack of group work training opportunities for staff. A further reason to rely on curriculumized and structured groups has to do with the constraints of funding sources that mandate that certain topics must be addressed at each weekly meeting, and provide curricula and accountability measures to further ensure that these goals are attained. On a positive note, some practitioners suggest this group design may incur desired outcomes and behavior changes.

Social workers with structured groups have to approach their practice by understanding that the curriculum represents nothing more than the group's purpose and that it merely provides a framework and elaboration of the content having to do with those issues members most likely will focus on in a group formed to meet the goals of this theme. For example, a structured parenting group for biological parents whose children are in foster care will identify significant topics that necessarily require attention in order to enhance parenting skills for these high-risk members with vulnerable parent-child relationships. A knowledgeable and skilled practitioner with groups should have as an initial goal in the structured group the development of a mutual aid system and should view the curriculum as central to actualizing purpose. In the democratic mutual aid system, the interaction and support of the members is used to enhance their parenting, to strengthen their confidence in their roles with their children, and to help them to deal with the pitfalls from their past that brought about their problems with their children. The group practitioner with a structured group develops the traditional processes of a group and recognizes that social work values, norms, and skills override the strict adherence to a curriculum and agenda. The practitioner has to ascertain how to use the structure or agenda to meet members' needs and develop a cohesive group built on the humanistic values and democratic norms of the social work group.

❖ SUMMARY

The four group types that depart from the closed group—the short-term group from three to eight sessions, the single-session group, the various open-ended group forms, and the structured group—require the practitioner to have an understanding of the dynamics of group development in a long-term closed group while at the same time adapting to the unique requirements of each of these group types. In the short-term group, the group worker has to focus on a specific issue and at the same time catalyze or by-pass certain group development processes. The single-session group requires telescoping one issue and ensuring that every member can meet a goal within that issue. In the open-ended group, the practitioner has to focus on inclusion of members who are not as active as the inner core, utilizing entry and exit rituals, while also providing status and empowerment for the inner core. In the structured group, the worker has to attend to developing a democratic mutual aid system and flexibly adapting curricula so that members rather than the worker develop centrality and ownership in the process.

12

Contingencies

For groups to meet and to function effectively, several issues have to be addressed. Practitioners have to devote considerable energy to planning and initiating a group. Since group workers will be called on to talk with members outside of the group, it is necessary for them to have knowledge of practice guidelines for both informal and formal between-session meetings. Issues in copractice with groups need to be highlighted. And lastly, postmeeting concerns require consideration. This chapter addresses the details related to these concerns.

❖ SETTING UP THE GROUP MEETING

A group meeting environment is the physical space that the practitioner and group members use for their meetings. This environment is important because it is composed of physical spaces and objects that have logistical as well as symbolic significance. Logistically, it has to be accessible to the members. The route used for getting to the meeting area has to be easy to map out or if not straightforward, mapped out in advance so members can navigate their way to it. Members with physical difficulties have considerations that will have to be accounted for when they are given directions on how to get to the meeting and the room. Once in the environment, chairs, tables, sufficient lighting, ventilation, and space for movement should be considered as significant factors to be attended to by the practitioner.

The meeting environment also has symbolic significance. Its condition, implements and objects, location, and where it is in relation to its surroundings may affect the members' and practitioner's views of themselves. A neatly furnished lounge communicates a different message than a room with cast-off furniture that is not well kept.

The practitioner at the outset has primary responsibility for being involved in the selection, logistics, and symbolic dimensions of the group's meeting environment (Kurland, 1978). This may be done before the first meeting or later on, with or without the group's input. The practitioner must become familiar with both the symbolic and logistical aspects of the environment in order to be prepared to assist the members with their reactions.

In selecting the environment, the practitioner may also choose to reorganize it. Tables can be moved to the side to better accommodate a circle that invites people to look around at one another, to move around, and to use the floor. It is very difficult to set up role plays when people are seated around tables; this kind of arrangement mitigates against the creative energy that can flow from groups. It is also difficult to see and relate to people sitting along the sides of rectangular tables.

Children's groups may require a large room with tables to one side and floor space on the other, suggesting a range of possibilities for experiences, programming, and interpersonal relationships. By way of contrast, a room with a one-way mirror suggests a particular view of the nature of the relationship between the members and the practitioner— an "us-and-them" framework that should immediately be explored in the group. A refreshment table suggests that some provisions will be made to accommodate members who might need some sustenance after a long day at school or work. Large name cards (that can be read across the room) used at every one of the early meetings may help people tune into one another and the practitioner, avoiding the embarrassments related to not remembering names that can occur in group situations.

❖ PREPARING FOR THE INITIAL MEETING

In preparing for the initial meeting, the practitioner might have, by design or chance, formal or informal pregroup contact with prospective members. The formality of pregroup meetings will vary with the agency's function, the group's purpose, and the amount of time the person will be asked to wait before the first meeting.

As the agency representative, the practitioner is expected to respond directly to questions asked by prospective members, offering a view of the group's purpose as well. The practitioner elicits the member's view of how his or her needs might be met within the context of this group, and lends a vision about how the group might work. Some members will have questions about how group work technically functions. Others will have ambivalence about taking part; this, too, will call for a direct but uncomplicated response. Providing an orientation to the nature of group participation by describing and discussing the give and take of group life, the processes of mutual aid, and the democratic modes to be used helps allay people's fears by giving a framework within which to understand and experience the means to be used.

The practitioner's response to questions and discussion of group purpose, followed by encouragement to try a meeting and see how the experience feels, usually facilitates initial entry. Sometimes a prospective member may not be certain that group participation will be useful in meeting his or her needs. In this case, more time spent with the person in examining the group's possibilities in light of the person's unique needs may prove to be helpful. Stressing that the opportunity to hear perspectives we cannot know also helps people ascertain the rich potential a group offers.

Some agencies conduct complex intake interviews for all new clients, whether they are interested in joining a group or participating in individual counseling. How this format is used to create a group is often determined by agency purpose. Formal intake is not a necessary prerequisite for group participation. However, a formal intake procedure does not necessarily have to be detrimental to group membership. There is no reason why a psychosocial intake process that is a routine aspect of agency practice cannot be used constructively to facilitate entry into a group. The practitioner is called on to design the contact in a way that helps prospective members gain a clearer understanding of the group experience and the value of belonging to a mutual aid system. The practitioner talks about how group method helps people help themselves and one another through the membership role with its tasks and responsibilities. The practitioner also seeks to find out about the potential members' previous group experiences and what they anticipate.

In formally meeting with each prospective member, the practitioner is tuning in to the members' interpersonal abilities, considering what their entries into the first sessions will be like, and what their capabilities and problems in membership might be. The general aim is to find ways of assisting each of the different people to fit into the beginning process. Also considered is whether there is good reason to dissuade a person from group membership because the individual will not be a good fit, or already has a command of the issues to be addressed by the group, or because he or she will be unable to make effective use of it at the present time due to individual factors and constraints. In these situations, the practitioner helps the person find other more suitable resources.

Illustration	**Preparing for the "Black Men on the Rise" Meeting**

In trying to set up an initial meeting for the Black Men on the Rise program, the practitioner has been on the phone a good number of times with prospective members in the past 3 weeks. He has also received calls from potential members who have questions and doubts. As he gathered information from different men, he was able to talk in general to them about the various issues black men face—career, single parenthood, maintaining marriages and relationships, and overcoming drugs and jail.

One conversation with Len quickly moved into the prospective member's talking about the details of his issues with his former girlfriend, who he says does not want a reconciliation, even though he feels it would be best for the children. The practitioner interrupts, "Boy, Len, that is a difficult spot. And it's not uncommon for people to have these feelings. In fact, one of the men interested in joining the group mentioned how guilty he was feeling about the children because his wife wanted to reconcile with him. Others have talked about what it's been like to be a single father, and to maintain involvement when you're not the person the child lives with." The practitioner also notes that one prospective member shared that he is in a new marriage and has young children with his second wife and older children from a prior relationship, and he is dealing with complex issues around these two marriages. Len tells the practitioner that he has a friend with that same problem.

During the start of the first meeting, the practitioner opens by saying, "I've had opportunity to talk with each of you in the past few weeks by phone and e-mail, and I have gotten a sense of why you have come. Why don't you start by going around, giving your names, and also stating what brings you here to the group, or anything else you want us to know about you." After they spend 15 minutes on the introduction, the practitioner points out hearing both commonalities and differences in their issues. He says, "I hear a similar desire to get to know yourselves a little better, to deal with issues related to being black men in the society. Then related to that are issues in your own families, how to deal with your own families, and to develop skill in dealing with a range of issues related to jobs, bosses, and expectations. This gives us a start, doesn't it? What do you think? What would you like to get out of this?" Members now begin to talk more about what they want out of the group.

Discussion

This illustrates a clear-cut example of group practice without formal pregroup interviewing. The practitioner uses the pregroup information he received on the phone to prepare himself for the group, to develop a sense of the members' issues, and to gauge their reactions. Pregroup contacts of any type are aimed to motivate actual participation in the first session. They are designed to stay away from working on issues in the one-to-one mode. Thus, the practitioner does not probe Len's feelings about his ex-girlfriend, nor does he relate to the possibility that Len might also be having difficulty accepting the breakup. Rather, he universalizes Len's concerns and redirects his effort toward thinking about membership in the group. The practitioner lends a vision for the group at this very early premeeting stage and connects himself to Len in an effort to motivate his interest in the first meeting.

At the meeting itself, having already discussed their goals and interests in the individual phone or e-mail contacts with the practitioner, the members are prepared to enter into a beginning process of searching for commonality and examining the potential of mutual aid processes.

❖ INFORMAL BETWEEN-SESSION
    CONTACTS WITH PRACTITIONER

Once the group is underway, meeting with the practitioner between sessions may be a positive continuation of the group's work efforts. This is especially true when programs are being planned, tasks are being completed, roles are being rehearsed, and decisions made in the group are being followed through by the members. In such instances, the members may call on the practitioner to help gain access to agency resources and personnel. Contacts with the practitioner represent a continuation of the type of between-session interactions members are having with one another.

In some situations, contact occurs when members frequent the agency setting for more than the group meeting—either for leisure-time activities, therapeutic communities, or residence. Whether the practitioner is approached for advice or supportive intervention, the principle of humanistic group method is to shape the contact so that the member can bring relevant concerns to the group members at the forthcoming meeting. If many members try to talk to the group worker outside of sessions about issues directly related to the group, this suggests that the group as a whole may be having difficulty dealing with some issues. The practitioner redirects the issues back to the group without becoming overly involved in out-of-meeting problem solving.

While it is generally recommended that members use the group as their central arena for work related to group purpose, from time to time members will require opportunities to meet with the practitioner in between group meeting times. Members may have particular crises or needs that depart from group purpose. Some purpose-related problems cannot wait to the next meeting or will not get enough attention unless the group meets more than once a week. Scheduling an extra group meeting is optimal, though not always possible. Therefore, seeing members between sessions to deal with the realities and anxieties of particular problems and to direct the members back to the group for more work can be an imperative. Though the hope is that members have enough supportive networks among themselves to speak to one another between sessions, there may be situations and times when this is not possible.

Illustration | **Meeting With Member From Cancer Support Group**

The practitioner, Herb, in a cancer support group hears that Ethan, a group member, has left a message that he hopes the practitioner can see him that day. Herb calls him back, saying, "Hi, Ethan, I got your message. What's the matter?" Ethan answers, "There was a spot on my lungs. I don't know what to do. It's too much to handle." Herb responds, "I'm sorry, Ethan, really sorry." Ethan says, "Damn it, I have been hoping for the best, and anticipating the worst. I have to go back to treatments. We are trying to cope." The practitioner asks, "Who knows?" Ethan says that only his wife knows, and that he is too uptight to even think about it.

The practitioner says, "It sure is a low blow. I'm here and I am listening. I have another 5 minutes right now, but we can talk later." Ethan thanks Herb and the practitioner continues, "Go on with what you were saying." "Of course my wife knows, but I cannot deal with telling anyone else." "Does that mean the group, too?" asks the practitioner. Ethan answers, "Yes, for now. I wanted to talk to you first, to get my head together. I don't want to upset them either. They're all going along, hoping they won't get it back. I can't tell them this." Herb says, "What about one person in the group for now, since we don't meet again until next week?" Ethan says, "Not yet." The practitioner responds, "Okay, whatever you want. I have half an hour this afternoon or an hour tomorrow when I can see you. What's your preference?" Ethan decides to wait until tomorrow.

When Ethan sees the practitioner the next day, they talk about his illness and his anxieties about his job, treatments, dying, and how to tell his sister and brother-in-law. The practitioner listens, is supportive, and points out how hard it is for Ethan to bring bad news to people. The practitioner is also aware how difficult it is for Ethan to ask for help, but he appropriately chooses to let that issue surface in the group. They talk again about telling the group, and Ethan decides he will call his friends in the group, Tony and Lenore, with whom he talks frequently.

Discussion

The member has had some devastating news. First, the practitioner offers clear-cut support and affirmation, as well as his own reaction of upset to Ethan's bad news. Certainly this news is completely within the purpose of the group and will have to be expressed there. At this time, however, Ethan needs the opportunity to talk with the practitioner. This is in part because he is experiencing some difficulty reaching out to the group members, but also because he is in crisis.

The practitioner tests to see whether a gentle nudge will help Ethan make a call to a group member; he finds out that Ethan is not ready. This message confirms the need for the meeting with the practitioner, who quickly offers it. Seeing that Ethan is willing to wait one day shows that the brief phone work may have already offered some support. The practitioner does not probe for feelings beyond those that are manifest.

When seeing Ethan the next day, the practitioner permits him the opportunity to share his concerns and fears about the recurrence of the cancer. What becomes evident is that Ethan is also having difficulty telling his sister and brother-in-law. The practitioner helps him make the connection to being afraid to tell the group. This gives Ethan the impetus to tell two trusted friends in the group before the next meeting. The practitioner is careful not to diffuse Ethan's future work in the group by dealing with the latent issues concerning his reluctance about asking for help that goes along with telling the group. This, being a very difficult time for Ethan, would be an inappropriate time to work on changing behavioral patterns.

❖ FORMAL BETWEEN-SESSION CONTACTS WITH PRACTITIONER

These types of contacts occur when a practitioner works individually, in family or marital sessions, or in a community organization committee with group members. Each method has somewhat different objectives and processes, and clients, patients, or members also have different qualities whose boundaries and parameters need to be respected. The mutual agreement of the practitioner and member is called for regarding how the member can integrate the group meetings with the other sessions. This will open up opportunities for the practitioner and member to make relevant comments in the group about the issues without violating the boundaries of each experience.

| *Illustration* | *Group Therapy Meeting* |

Rivka is in a clinical individual-therapy relationship with the practitioner, David, as well as in the group. During the group meeting, Rivka says, looking directly at the practitioner, "This issue between Celine and me is just what I was talking with you about in our sessions." The practitioner says, "This crossed my mind, too. Looks like you are about to bring it up. So go ahead." After Rivka presents some of the issues she has been working on individually with him, David asks Rivka to look at ways this issue is playing itself out in the group. Members begin to look at the pattern in the group from different angles.

Later in the session, Bonita says, "David, can I be in individual therapy with you, too?" David says, "It's possible for any of you to be in individual, if you and I explore our views on its value for you. Also, we all have to be careful to look at the many aspects of this possibility. For instance, one issue to consider is if it is really good for you. Another question to ask is if you want it because another group member has it and you might be feeling you are missing something. What are you thinking and feeling?"

Discussion

This illustrates a not-so-rare occurrence that places the practitioner in the situation of having information about a member that is not in the group's domain. In addition, the practitioner runs the risk of being the subject of group competition, and the member runs the risk of group envy. In this meeting, raising the issue of feeling one member has something the other one does not have helps all the members examine their needs and irrational feelings that come about when they think one member may be getting something special in the relationship with the practitioner.

❖ POSTGROUP RESPONSIBILITIES

Much necessary work will occur prior to and during the very last session of the group. However, following the last session, the practitioner may remain involved with group members in effecting referrals, entitlements, and communications about their situations. Particularly in settings where daily contacts occur, there will be interactions with group members. Some extra time may be needed to end the contact with the practitioner.

If ongoing professional contact continues after the group's ending, there may well be opportunity for references and allusions to the group experience. These allusions should not be allowed to break the boundaries of propriety by violating the person's and others' confidentiality. It may come about that the former member needs guidance and counsel that properly fits with the professional's role. If this is the case, time should be set aside for help or referral, but not to open up or explore issues that were manifest or latent in the person's group experience.

Some persons may need further opportunity for contact with the practitioner after the last session. Appraising what the person is asking for, and the group worker considering how to assist, is useful. This stance acknowledges differences among members in approaches to handling endings. The practitioner may have to indicate that it is not possible to be as deeply and frequently involved with the former member, pointing the person toward other sources of assistance.

What professionals tend to call "loose ends" at the group's conclusion is really part of the process. The practitioner needs to ensure that referrals have been effected, and that the former group members know how and when to move on to other resources. The practitioner is available to colleagues to help them contact and understand the needs of former group members. Finally, the practitioner finishes off the process by updating professional records and statistics.

❖ COPRACTICE

Copractice (Papell & Rothman, 1980b) is the situation in which two persons assume equal responsibility for work with a group. This model of professional involvement can lend itself effectively to the objectives processes, techniques, values, and norms of the humanistic method. Copractice has the potential of adding an ingredient to the group process that is not present when there is one practitioner. This ingredient gives the members a chance to take part with two practitioners who interact with one another and who may have different styles in the group.

The practitioners in this arrangement are not ranked (Levine, 1979). Asking a line worker or student intern to work with a senior practitioner in the group to enhance learning is not copractice because of the unequal distribution of power and authority (Herzog, 1980). While this format may enhance some aspects of learning, the added person is never allowed the position of experiencing himself or herself in the group with the full responsibilities, obligations, and sanctions of the professional. What usually happens is that the junior partner takes an inordinately long time to become effective in the process and to take risks that are group oriented. The junior partner tends to talk to members one at a time, rarely focusing on or raising those group process issues that are in the domain and authority of the group practitioner. Also because they feel like they are being watched by a supervisor, these practitioners have great difficulty relaxing and getting into the situation. Practice is thus stilted and narrow, rather than expansive and creative.

The decision to copractice, thereby, is usually a practical one based on what benefits members might derive from two practitioners. Sometimes a mix of gender is helpful to a group, either for role modeling or to serve as a symbolic parental pair. This can be true in a teen group, a residential treatment group, or a children's group. Sometimes a racial or ethnic mix is useful as a symbolic way of connecting oppressed minorities with the mainstream (by enabling trust from the members via the modeling of trust between the pair). Also, in some settings in which the connection to a professional is central to the change process, two practitioners are likely to provide more emotional choices for members whose interpersonal connections are weak. In some settings, especially institutional ones, copractitioners from different disciplines may enrich the treatment process, such as a nurse or psychologist practicing with a social worker. Very often, social workers will focus on the group process, nurses may concentrate on medical content, and psychologists may deal with clinical or learning issues depending on their training. At other times, the group's work itself might be too draining for a single practitioner—as in some cancer support or HIV-AIDS groups, where certain feelings of the practitioner have to be siphoned off outside the group in order to help the members. In some community or work groups, the copractitioners provide more opportunities for members to make connections to necessary tasks.

The decision to copractice with a group also should be based on whether these colleagues can carry out the activities and emotions necessary to the undertaking. Two practitioners cannot go into a group unprepared, from session to session, to develop the method and its processes. First, they need to have a prior history and relationship with one another that is not conflictive. Two people with differing styles and approaches to a group cannot be put together for the sole purpose of creating a balanced experience for the members. Copractice is not a question of balance created by parallel play. Actions of practitioners need coordination, which requires added time and effort. Time is needed each week for the copractitioners to debrief after the group. It is necessary as well for the copractitioners to conduct a premeeting session that better focuses their joint efforts.

Presession meetings aid the practitioners in sharing their perceptions and feelings about one another and examining the nature and characteristics of their relationship with the group. The process they will use together will be a reflection of what they expect to happen in a group. Focusing on the group's stage themes (see Chapter 3) and sharing their personal reactions to the members and to each other with regard to these themes is a helpful approach to framing the copractice issues. They both have to consider the extent to which each practitioner is feeling invested in the group during Stage Theme 1, "We're Not in Charge." During Stage Theme 2, "We Are in Charge," the process centers primarily on the members, not the practitioners. A copractice model here might adversely affect group autonomy if the practitioners collude to maintain their power by preventing the group from directly taking on the workers, as in Stage Theme 3, "We're Taking You On." The members may view two people presenting a united front as capable of controlling the group; they are hard to beat. In this model, two people—not one person—will be in authority, and both will have to be dealt with by the members, which interferes with independence and autonomy. As the members move toward the stage of "We're Taking You On," the practitioners are called on to present their interaction for scrutiny and engagement to assist the group in becoming a democratic mutual aid system. The members may attempt to divide them into "one of us" and "not one of us," perhaps to diffuse their power; one practitioner may move to protect the other from the confrontation. These concerns and issues require honest exploration between the practitioners in the interest of strengthening the members' autonomy and development in the democratic process. Upon some resolution of authority issues, the copractitioners may be more favorably viewed as the group accepts the positive aspect of copractice—having two professionals helping them.

During Stage Theme 4, Sanctuary, the pair should display closeness with each other in the group, rather than being afraid to let the group see their professional bond. Showing the group their relationship opens up opportunities for the members to explore group fantasies about their relationships as friends, lovers, or "mom and pop" (Garland, Jones, & Kolodny, 1973). These views need not be dealt with directly at the time; they may be useful to explore later on. As the group turns its effort toward actualizing purpose—with its ups and downs—the roadblocks of Stage Theme 5, "This Isn't Good Anymore," may create feelings of responsibility in the practitioners for the group's limitations. In addition, copractitioners may blame each other for the group's inability to deal with its issues. When the group feels the effects of Stage Theme 6, "We're Okay and Able," the practitioners should provide each other with latitude and support to interact in their creatively unique ways with any of the members.

Copractitioners also will share their reactions to each other's use of techniques throughout the group. In addition to examining their own relationship, they need to share their observations and reactions to members in order to consider the helpful or dysfunctional effects their collaborative effort is having on the members. Copractitioners must examine the roles they play and their communication patterns in terms of what techniques they are using and who speaks primarily to whom and for what reason. They also might consider who has better access to particular members and which of them becomes particularly responsive to certain members. The techniques of the method serve as a guidepost for examining their own propensities to use certain interventions and omit others, thereby providing helpful self-awareness for both practitioners.

How the practitioners intervene in the group process will affect how the members perceive their professional power and authority. Certain acts of initiative and confrontation are perceived as having more potency. When members look at the two practitioners, one may be seen as a taskmaster while the other may be viewed as a confronter or as the peacemaker. Copractitioners must consider what stimulates these perceptions.

Differences of race, ethnicity, and gender between the practitioners will be viewed differentially by members (Davis, 1984; Garvin & Glover-Reed, 1983). Often, women and members of minority groups will be seen as less potent "junior partners," regardless of prior training and skill. The group members perceive occurrences through lenses that may be distorted by stereotypes. Dealing with the phenomenon of stereotyping explicitly in the group enhances the humanistic values and democratic norms of the method and utilizes the method to enhance members' social functioning with different types of people in authority roles. However, the issue of stereotyping must be aired regularly between the pair.

Finally, the copractitioners may be called on to handle interpersonal conflict between themselves. One practitioner may take issue with an approach the other uses in a meeting, or the two of them may find themselves going off in different directions. A conflict may be reflective of stage issues. The type of honesty and forthrightness required to copractice will tax and strengthen the practitioners' personalities, knowledge, and skill. The professional rewards from these efforts center around receiving the validation, feedback, and critique that group practitioners rarely have the opportunity to get unless they are supervised using videotapes.

Illustration	***Copractice in Adolescent In-Patient Psychiatric Hospital Group***

Ted and Doris are copracticing with the socialization group in an adolescent in-patient psychiatric hospital program. The group has met daily for seven sessions. This meeting continues on the theme of members being spontaneous with each other in informal encounters during the day. Ted and Doris are sitting away from each other, a decision they made from the start to avoid being focused on as a "powerful force," and so they can interact with members in small talk before the meeting starts.

Cindy says, "Hey, Jacko, I like coming over to talk and joke with you. I'm a social butterfly and I like it." She is wearing a butterfly T-shirt. Jack says, "Yeah, it's nice" and notices that Ted and Doris also talk. "When you two see each other, you acknowledge each other—and us, too." Doris says, "I like to do that, even though I get so busy and single-minded sometimes."

As this goes on, Matt is scowling more and more. He mutters to himself frequently, finally lurching forward in his chair and exploding at Ted, "You are watching the group and taking notes for Dr. Carmichael!" Everyone, including Ted, registers surprise. Ted says, "Matt, these are just my papers for my doctoral work that I carry around." He passes the papers around through the members to Matt, who just holds them limply. Doris says, "Ted, go over and show him the papers." Ted follows her direction and crouching in front of Matt, shuffles through the papers, reading parts to him. He shows them to others across the room as well. Doris and several others get up and walk over to chat with Matt. "Come on buddy, don't freak out," Cindy says, now sitting next to him. Echoes of "Ted's not playing with you, honest," can be heard from the others. Matt mumbles slowly as he handles the papers, then calms down and gets in a better mood. In the shifting around, people have changed seats with Ted on one side of Matt and Cindy—the most gregarious of them all—staying on the other side.

After the session, the copractitioners leave the day room. In a private office they begin to debrief. They talk about what was satisfying and effective. Ted says, "I'm glad you told me to go over to Matt, that was great. Once you said it, a light-bulb popped up. I thought, that's his way of asking for interaction. It worked out." "And that Cindy," Doris says, "she said she was a social butterfly. She gets them out of themselves when she's like that." "We did a good job, eh?" Ted says. Doris agrees, noting, "It's so important that we have not been sitting next to each other. I think it's easier for them to connect to each of us that way."

Discussion

What is crucial here is how the practitioners follow each others' instructions. This comes from their pre- and postsession meetings, in which they have discussed what they see people doing and how they themselves are interacting. Following directions in this way comes from their abilities to hear and listen to each other without being defensive. It is obvious that their interaction is not stilted; if it were, Doris could not take the risk to ask Ted to move over toward Matt. And even if Ted did follow Doris's direction, it might be less likely to be effective because of the power struggle he would be having with Doris. These copractitioners have sufficiently discussed and worked on their different perceptions of the group so that when their own conflict-laden issues are present, they are not acted out before the group. Ted is able to trust Doris's lead. Neither of them is afraid to fail in the other's eyes. Enough flexibility is available so that they will work to find a different route for reconnecting to members who need them.

Another important feature is that Doris and Ted sit apart. This nonverbally communicates to the members that they will not use their dyad to protect themselves in uncomfortable situations.

❖ SUMMARY

This chapter has presented some special considerations for practitioners. The time frame and physical location of the group will affect its process. The types of formal and informal contact with members the practitioner has between sessions will be determined by agency structure and member need; these will affect the group. Meeting with some members after the group has terminated may be required to ensure effective referral processes.

Copractice as an approach is recommended only for professionals with equal status and the ability to develop forthrightness and mutuality with each other. In this way, they can model cooperative behavior following each other's lead and sharing openly in the group. Copractice can have negative consequences for the group when the practitioners have minimal rapport. Without cohesion in the copractice relationship, the group members cannot work on their authority issues for fear of taking sides in a pair that has covert conflicts.

References

Adelphi. (2008). *Support groups.* Retrieved May 28, 2008, from http://www .adelphi.edu/nysbreastcancer/support.html

Alissi, A., & Casper, M. (Eds.). (1985). *Time as a factor in group work.* New York: Haworth.

Asch, S. (1965). Effects of group pressure upon the modification and distortion of judgments. In H. Proshansky & B. Seidenberg (Eds.), *Basic studies in social psychology* (pp. 393–401). New York: Holt, Rinehart & Winston.

Bennis, W. (1964). Patterns and vicissitudes of t-group development. In L. Bradford, J. Gibb, & K. D. Benne (Eds.), *T-group theory and laboratory learning* (pp. 248–278). New York: Wiley.

Bennis, W., & Shepard, H. (1962). A theory of group development. In W. G. Bennis, K. Benne, & R. Chin (Eds.), *The planning of change* (pp. 321–340). New York: Holt, Rinehart & Winston.

Berger, P., & Luckmann, T. (1967). *The social construction of reality.* Garden City, NY: Doubleday.

Bernstein, S. (1973). Conflict and group work. In S. Bernstein (Ed.), *Explorations in group work* (pp. 72–106). Boston: Milford House.

Bion, W. R. (1961). *Experiences in groups.* London: Tavistock.

Bocat, M. (1988, October). *Groups in neonatology.* Paper presented at Group Work Conference, Akron, OH.

Boyd, N. (1971). A definition with a methodological note. In P. Simon (Ed.), *Play and game theory in group work: A collection of papers by Neva Boyd* (pp. 141–148). Chicago: Jane Addams School of Social Work.

Bradford, L., Gibb, J., & Benne, K. (Eds.). (1964). *T-group theory and laboratory learning.* New York: Wiley.

Ciardiello, S. (2003). *Activities in group work with school age children.* Warminster, PA: Marco Products.

Cicchetti, A. (2008). Group work with people with problematic substance use. In A. Gitterman & R. Salmon (Eds.), *The encyclopedia of social work with groups* (pp. 218–221). New York: Routledge.

Cicchetti, A., & Goldberg, E. (1996, October). *Application of social group work to chemical dependency treatment.* Paper presented at Association for the Advancement of Social Work With Groups Conference, Ann Arbor, MI.

Coleman, P., & Deutsch, M. (2006). Some guidelines for developing a creative approach to conflict. In M. Deutsch, P. Coleman, & E. Marcus (Eds.), *The handbook of conflict resolution: Theory and practice* (2nd ed., pp. 402–413). San Francisco: Jossey-Bass.

Coyle, G. (1948). *Group work with American youth.* Reprinted by *Journal of Sociology and Social Welfare, 1978.*

Davis, L. (Ed.). (1984). *Ethnicity in social group work practice.* New York: Haworth.

Deutsch, M. (1968). The effects of cooperation and competition upon group process. In D. Cartwright & A. Zander (Eds.). *Group dynamics* (pp. 461–484). New York: Harper & Row.

Deutsch, M., Coleman, P., & Marcus, E. (Eds.). (2006). *The handbook of conflict resolution: Theory and practice* (2nd ed.). San Francisco: Jossey-Bass.

Devore,W., & Schlesinger, E. (1995). *Ethnic sensitive social work practice.* Boston: Allyn & Bacon.

Erikson, E. (1963). *Childhood and society* (2nd ed.). New York: Norton.

Euster, S. (1990). Rehabilitation after mastectomy: The group process. In K. Davidson & S. Clarke (Eds.), *Social work in health care: A handbook for practice* (pp. 495–510). Binghamton, NY: Haworth.

Falck, H. (1988). *Social work: The membership perspective.* New York: Springer.

Foreman, T., Willis, L., & Goodenough, B. (2005). Hospital based support groups for parents of seriously challenged children: An example from pediatric oncology in Australia. *Social Work With Groups, 28*(2), 3–21.

Galinsky, M. J. (1985). Groups for cancer patients and their families: Purposes and group conditions. In M. Sundel, P. Glasser, R. Sarri, & R. Vinter (Eds.), *Individual change through small groups* (2nd ed., pp. 515–532). New York: Free Press.

Galinsky, M. J., & Schopler, J. W. (1985). The patterns of entry and exit in open-ended groups. *Social Work With Groups, 8*(2) 67–80.

Galinsky, M. J., & Schopler, J. W. (1987, October). *Group development in open-ended groups.* Paper presented at the Group Work Symposium, Boston.

Garland, J., & Frey, L. (1976). Application of the stages of group development to groups in psychiatric settings. In S. Bernstein (Ed.), *Further explorations in group work* (pp. 1–33). Boston: Charles River.

Garland, J., Jones, H., & Kolodny, R. (1973). A model for stages of development in social work groups. In S. Bernstein (Ed.), *Explorations in group work* (pp. 17–71). Boston: Milford House.

Garland, J., & West, J. (1983). Differential assessment of school age children: Three group approaches. In N. Lang & C. Marshall (Eds.), *Proceedings, 1982 Symposium, CASWG, Toronto* (pp. 130–148). Toronto: Committee for the Advancement of Social Work With Groups.

Garvin, C. (1997). *Contemporary group work* (3rd ed.). Needham Heights, MA: Allyn & Bacon.

Garvin, C., & Glover-Reed, B. (Eds.). (1983). *Groupwork with women—groupwork with men.* New York: Haworth.

Germain, C., & Gitterman, A. (1980). *The life model of social work practice.* New York: Columbia University Press.

Germain, C., & Gitterman, A. (1996). *The life model of social work practice* (2nd ed.). New York: Columbia University Press.

Gitterman, A., & Shulman, L. (Eds.). (2005). *Mutual aid groups, vulnerable and resilient populations, and the life cycle.* New York: Columbia University Press.

Glassman, U. (1991). The social work group and its distinct healing qualities in the health care setting. *Health and Social Work, 16*(3), 203–213.

Glassman, U. (2001, October). *Translating group work's humanistic values and democratic norms across fields of practice.* Paper presented at Group Work Symposium, Cleveland/Akron, OH.

Glassman, U., & Kates, L. (1983). Authority themes and worker group transactions. *Social Work With Groups, 6*(2), 33–52.

Glassman, U., & Kates, L. (1986a). Developing the democratic humanistic norms of the social work group. In M. Parnes (Ed.), *Innovations in group work* (pp. 149–172). New York: Haworth.

Glassman, U., & Kates, L. (1986b). Techniques of social group work. *Social Work With Groups, 9*(1), 9–38.

Glassman, U., & Skolnik, L. (1984). The role of social group work in refugee resettlement. *Social Work With Groups, 7*(1), 45–62.

Goldstein, E. (1995). *Ego psychology and social work practice* (2nd ed.). New York: Free Press.

Goldstein, E. (2001). *Object relations theory and self-psychology in social work practice.* New York: Free Press.

Goodwin, P. J. (2004). Support groups in breast cancer: When a negative result is positive. *Journal of Clinical Oncology, 22*(21), 4244–4246.

Greene, R. (1994). *Human behavior theory: A diversity framework.* New York: Transaction.

Gruber, H. (2006). Creativity and conflict resolution: The role of point of view. In M. Deutsch, P. Coleman, & E. Marcus (Eds.), *The handbook of conflict resolution* (2nd ed., pp. 391–401). San Francisco: Jossey-Bass.

Harris, E. (2004, October). *Groups in mental health treatment.* Panel presentation, Glassman, U., Chair, at Group Work Symposium, Brooklyn, NY.

Hayes, M. A., McConnell, S. C., Nardozzi, J. A., & Mullican, R. J. (1998). Family and friends of people with HIV/AIDS support group. *Social Work With Groups, 21*(1/2), 35–47.

Heckman, T., Kalichman, S., Roffman, R., Sikkema, K., Beckman, B., Somlai, A. & Walker, J. (1999). Telephone-delivered coping improvement intervention for persons living with HIV/AIDS in rural areas. *Social Work With Groups, 21*(4), 49–61.

Herrold, K. (1965). [The first group laboratory program in 1948 of the National Training Laboratory at Bethel, Maine, which spawned the first T-group]. Unpublished raw data, as described in detail by participant Professor Kenneth Herrold of Columbia University Teachers College in his classes.

Herzog, J. (1980). Communication between co-leaders: Fact or myth. *Social Work With Groups, 3*(4), 19–30.

Homans, G. C. (1950). *The human group.* New York: Harcourt College Publishers.

House Plan Association. (1965). *A group work program for college students.* New York: City College, City University of New York.

Jewish Community Relations Council. (2008). *Commission on intergroup relations and community concerns: Youth bridge program.* New York: Author

Kaslyn, M. (1999). Telephone group work: Challenges for practice. *Social Work With Groups, 21*(1), 63–77.

Klein, A. (1953). *Society, democracy and the group.* New York: Women's Press & William Morrow.

Konopka, G. (1978). The significance of group work based on ethical values. *Social Work With Groups, 1*(2), 123–132.

Konopka, G. (1983). *Social group work: A helping process* (3rd ed.). Englewood Cliffs, NJ: Prentice Hall.

Kurland, R. (1978). Planning: A neglected component in group work. *Social Work With Groups, 1*(2), 173–178.

Lang, N. (1972). A broad range model of practice in social work with groups. *Social Service Review, 46*(1), 76–89.

Lang, N. C. (1981). Some defining characteristics of the social work group: Unique social form. In S. L. Abels & P. Abels (Eds.), *Social work with groups: Proceedings 1979 symposium* (pp. 18–50). Hebron, CT: Practitioners Press.

Lang, N. C. (1986). Social work practice in small social forms: Identifying collectivity. In N. C. Lang & J. Sulman (Eds.), *Collectivity in social group work.* New York: Haworth.

Levine, B. (1979). *Group psychotherapy, practice and development.* Englewood Cliffs, NJ: Prentice Hall.

Levine, B. (1991). *Group psychotherapy, practice and development.* Prospect Park, IL: Waveland Press.

Lindeman, E. (1980). Group work and democratic values. In H. Trecker (Ed.), *Group work: Foundations and frontiers* (Rev. ed., pp. 13–25). Hebron, CT: Practitioner's Press.

Lowy, L. (1973.) Decision making and group work. In S. Bernstein (Ed.), *Explorations in group work* (pp. 107–134). Boston: Milford House.

Malekoff, A. (2006). *Group work with adolescents: Principles and practice.* New York: Guilford.

Masanek, I. (2001, October). *The democratic group.* Keynote address, Group Work Symposium, Akron, OH.

Middleman, R. (Ed.). (1981). *The nonverbal method in working with groups.* Hebron, CT: Practitioner's Press. (Original work published 1968)

Middleman, R. (Ed.). (1983). *Activities and actions in groups work.* New York: Haworth.

Milgram, S. (1963). Behavioral study of obedience. *Journal of Abnormal and Social Psychology, 67,* 371–378.

Miller, R., & Mason, S. (2002). *Diagnosis: Schizophrenia*. New York: Columbia University Press.

Nafisi, A. (2003). *Reading Lolita in Tehran: A memoir in books*. New York: Random House.

National Training Laboratory. (1966–1967). *Manual for participants*. Washington, DC: Author.

Nicholas, T. B., McNeill, T., Montgomery, G., Stapleford, C., & McClure, M. (2003). Communication features of an online group of fathers of children with spina bifida: Considerations for group development among men. *Social Work With Groups, 26*(2), 65–80.

Northen, H. (1983). Social work groups in health settings: Promises and problems. *Social Work in Health Care, 8*(3), 107–121.

Olmstead, M. (1959). *The small group*. New York: Random House.

Papell, C., & Rothman, B. (Eds.). (1980a). Co-leadership [Special issue]. *Social Work With Groups, 3*(4).

Papell, C., & Rothman, B. (1980b). Relating the mainstream model of social work with groups to group psychotherapy and the structured group approach. *Social Work With Groups, 3*(2), 5–22.

Pinto, R. (2000). HIV Prevention for adolescent groups: A six-step approach. *Social Work With Groups, 23*(3), 91–99.

Pomeroy, E. C., Kiam, R., & Green, D. L. (2000). Reducing depression, anxiety, and trauma of male inmates: An HIV/AIDS psychoeductional group intervention. *Social Work Research, 24*(3), 165–169.

Quinn, K., & Feehan, R. (2007, June). *Successful groups in large institutions: The neonatal intensive care experience*. Paper presented at Group Work Conference, Jersey City, NJ.

Sarracco, M. (1997, March). *Group work in HIV/AIDS: Responding to the unique challenges of a multi-faceted community*. Paper presented at American Ortho Psychiatric Association, Toronto.

Sarracco, M., & Cicchetti, A. (1996, July). *Creating effective support groups for PWAs*. Paper presented at National AIDS/HIV Forum, Seattle, WA.

Sarri, R., & Galinsky, M. (1985). A conceptual framework for group development. In M. Sundel, P. Glasser, R. Sarri, & R. Vinter (Eds.), *Individual change through small groups* (2nd ed., pp. 70–86). New York: Free Press.

Schwartz, W. (1961). The social worker in the group. In R. Pernell & B. Saunders (Eds.), *New perspectives on services to groups: Theory, organization, practice* (pp. 17–34). New York: National Association of Social Workers.

Schwartz, W. (1976). Between client and system: The mediating function. In R. W. Roberts & H. Northen (Eds.), *Theories of social work with groups* (pp. 171–197). New York: Columbia University Press.

Schwartz, W., & Zalba, S. (Eds.). (1971). *The practice of group work*. New York: Columbia University Press.

Seitz, M. (1985). A group's history: From mutual aid to helping others. *Social Work With Groups, 8*(1), 41–54.

Sherif, M. (1965a). Formation of social norms: The experimental paradigm. In H. Proshansky & B. Seidenberg (Eds.), *Basic studies in social psychology* (pp. 461–470). New York: Holt, Rinehart & Winston.

Sherif, M. (1965b). Superordinate goals in the reduction of intergroup conflict. In H. Proshansky & B. Seidenberg (Eds.), *Basic studies in social psychology* (pp. 694–701). New York: Holt, Rinehart & Winston.

Shulman, L. (2006). *Skills of helping individuals, families, groups, communities* (5th ed.). Belmont, CA: Thompson Brooks Cole.

Theodorakis, M. (1973*). Journal of resistance.* (G. Webb, Trans.). New York: Coward, McCann & Geohegan.

Timerman, J. (1981). *Prisoner without a name, cell without a number.* New York: Knopf.

Toseland, R., & Rivas, R. (2004). *An introduction to group work practice.* New York: Allyn & Bacon.

Trachtenberg, J. (1972). Team involvement and the problems incurred. In M. D. Anderson Hospital (Ed.), *Rehabilitation of the cancer patient* (pp. 181–189). Chicago: Yearbook Medical.

Trecker, H. (1972). *Social group work.* New York: Association Press.

Vinter, R. (1985). Program activities: An analysis of their effects on participant behavior. In M. Sundel, P. Glasser, R. Sarri, & R. Vinter (Eds.), *Individual change through small groups* (2nd ed., pp. 233–246). New York: Free Press.

White, R., & Lippitt, R. (1968). Leader behavior and member reaction in three social climates. In D. Cartwright & A. Zander (Eds.), *Group dynamics* (pp. 318–335). New York: Harper & Row.

Whittaker, J. K. (1985). Program activities: Their selection and use in a therapeutic milieu. In M. Sundel, P. Glasser, R. Sarri, & R. Vinter (Eds.), *Individual change through small groups* (2nd ed.). New York: Free Press.

Woods, M., & Hollis, F. (2000). *Casework: A psychosocial therapy* (5th ed.). New York: McGraw-Hill.

Yalom, I. D. (2005). *The theory and practice of group psychotherapy* (5th ed.). New York: Basic Books.

Index

About the Author

Urania Glassman, MA, MSW, DSW, LCSW, has been Director of Field Instruction at Wurzweiler School of Social Work of Yeshiva University since 1993. She has authored many articles on group work and field education, and she has been presenting on these topics at national and international conferences for three decades. She has been involved with the Association for the Advancement of Social Work With Groups (AASWG) since it convened its first Group Work Symposium in Cleveland in 1979, and was cofounder of the NY Red Apple Chapter of AASWG. She consults to agencies on group work, field education, and staff supervision. She cochaired the School's 3-day 50th Anniversary Conference in 2007. Dr. Glassman's entry on group work's humanistic values and democratic norms is included in the forthcoming *Encyclopedia of Group Work.*

Her role in field education includes developing and cochairing the Field Symposium at the Council on Social Work Education (CSWE) and the North American Network of Field Educators and Directors (NAN-FED). She sits on the CSWE Commission on Curriculum and Educational Innovation (COCEI). Her most recent paper is "Field Education as the Signature Pedagogy of Social Work."

Dr. Glassman was on the Adelphi University School of Social Work faculty as Director of Field Instruction. She chaired the group work and foundation practice sequences and taught group work, foundation practice, casework, and the seminar in field instruction.

Her 13-year staff role at the House Plan Association of the City College of New York included its directorship. This unique multifaceted group work student activities program revolved around small friendship groups developed by student leaders and supervised by professionals. A group dynamics design included human relations training programs to enhance student development.

Dr. Glassman has her MA from Columbia University Teachers College and her MSW and DSW from Adelphi University SSW. Her private practice is with individuals, groups, and families.